OVERSIZE

P9-ELH-316

THE COUNCIL
AND THE FUTURE

Ut unum sint: That they may be one

THE COUNCIL
AND THE FUTURE

TEXT BY MARIO VON GALLI   PHOTOGRAPHS BY BERNHARD MOOSBRUGGER

McGRAW-HILL BOOK COMPANY   NEW YORK   TORONTO   LONDON   SYDNEY

This book is the result of an intensive, four-year collaboration between the two authors and is the product of their personal involvement in the events of the Council. Mario von Galli wrote the text and selected the Council documents and speeches included here. The photographs are the work of Bernard Moosbrugger who was also responsible for over-all design and layout. The drawings, done in Rome during the Council, are the work of artist Fritz Weigner.

The pictures on pages 216/217 and 228/229 by permission of UPI, Len Sirman Press und NASA.

The cover stamping is a reproduction of a commemorative coin given by Pope Paul VI to all non-Catholic observers of the various Christian Churches at the end of the third session of the Council. On the front, Christ is surrounded by Churches of various Christian confessions, with the inscription: *Ut unum sint* ('That they may be one'). On the back cover (the reverse side of the coin) is depicted the gospel-scene: Peter, in fear of drowning, seizes the saving hand of Christ.

IMPRIMATUR
TURICI 15 APRILIS 1966
F. X. WALKER PRAET. VIC. PROV. HELV. SOC. JESU

Table of Contents

1374214

Introduction   8
Pope John XXIII unfolds the Plan of the Council   12
Arrival of the Bishops   16

Chronicle of the Second Vatican Council   31
The Death of Pope John – The Election of Pope Paul   36

Three Trends of the Council   63
The Bishops   84
How did the Bishops live in Rome?   100
Message of the Council Fathers to all Mankind   109
Selections from the Constitution on the Church   110

Inner Renewal   113
Aggiornamento or Inner Renewal   124
The Role of the Theologians   130
Selections from the Constitutions on Sacred Liturgy and
   on Divine Revelation   137

Ecumenism and Religious Liberty   141
The Community of non-Catholic Christians   152
Have Expectations been Fulfilled? (A response by
   Oscar Cullmann)   165

Structures of the Church   169
Structural Reform in Externals   180
Selected Addresses   193

Church, Laity and World: Schema 13   197
Auditors and Journalists   208
The Council and the World   214
Pope Paul's Message to the UN   231

Council Speeches   235
I *A New Spirit*
The Vernacular in the Liturgy   Maximos   235
The Church's Mission in the World   Rugambwa   236
Papal Infallibility   Descuffi   237
Eastern Church Bishops' Conferences   Zoghby   238
Collegiality Means What it Implies   Jacquier   238

Cooperation of Bishop and Priests   Hurley   239
Charismatic Gifts in the Church   Suenens   240
Bishops' Use of the Double Standard   Carli   241

II *Dialogue within the Church and with non-Catholics*
The Ecumenical Dialogue   De Smedt   245
Ecumenism and Salvation History   Pangrazio   247
Ecumenism Means no Oversimplification   Gouyon   248
Ecumenical Mission Projects   Rakotomalada   248
Painful Points in the Ecumenical Dialogue   Frings   249
Mixed Marriage and Catholic Education of
   Children   Heenan   250
The Declaration on the Jews   Lercaro   255
Responsibility of Christians for Atheists'
   View of God   Seper   257
The Roots of Atheism   König   258

III *Signs of the Times*
The Church's Debt to the Modern World   Schmitt   261
On Evangelical and Subhuman Poverty   Silva   262
Marriage as Community of Life and Love   Léger   263
Cultural Reform in the Spirit of Evangelical
   Poverty   Lercaro   264
The Church and Contemporary Culture   Elchinger   266
War as a Question of Conscience   Boillon   271
The Times Are Urgent – Much Must be
   Changed   Arrupe   272

IV *The Church on the Move*
Respect for the Opinions of Mankind   Cushing   275
Suppression of Liberty and Confession of
   Guilt   Beran   276
A Cautious Spaniard on Religious Liberty   Bueno Y Monreal   279
Tradition and Sacred Scripture   Meyer   280
Freedom for Scriptural Research   Butler   280
Disappointment in the Schema on Priestly
   Life and Ministry   Döpfner   281
Married Part-time Priests   Koop   282

Final Address of Pope Paul   287

The 16 Documents and their Consequences   296

The prophets of doom always talk as though the present, in comparison to the past, is becoming worse and worse. But I see mankind as entering upon a new order, and perceive in this a divine plan.

(John XXIII)

Introduction

Never was a council so variously judged as the Second Vatican Council. Some speak of a turn toward the secular; others express a boundless disappointment. These are the two extremes, and between them there is a many-runged ladder of every gradation of black and white. The darkest judgments are, interestingly enough, found primarily among well-educated Roman Catholics. More exciting is the fact that the most positive opinions come most frequently from non-Catholic Christians rather than from Roman Catholics— if one ignores the paid praise-singers and writers, as the *Osservatore Romano* describes them.

The positive thinkers point out that this Council evoked worldwide interest, unequalled by any other religious event in many a year, an interest which spread far beyond Catholic circles. Even atheists and communists could not overlook it. There was no newspaper, radio or TV station that did not several times give Council reports. And of course when, for four years in a row, highly placed and intelligent men from all over the world, 2,500 bishops from all continents, meet together for three-month periods to openly and seriously discuss spiritual problems—well, in times like ours, of which it is constantly said that they are drowning in technical problems, economic disagreements, and questions of political power, such a reaction to a non-secular event is surely sensational.

Another way of approaching an assessment is to start off by saying that the convocation of the Council was a great deed of Pope John XXIII's; it was further enhanced by the high goals he set for this assembly. Whereas almost all previous councils were meant to separate the sheep from the goats, in order to condemn an opinion or a man, this time there were to be no excommunications. All energy was to be con-centrated on a positive reformation of teaching and of practice. To achieve this, Pope John XXIII headed the Council toward the ecumenical way, toward the opening of the Roman Catholic Church to other Christians; and he emphasized this goal through the establishment of a Secretariat for Christian Unity, and by inviting non-Catholic Christians.

His concern for freedom of expression was boundless. This was most surprising since this was a 'Vatican' council, held at the Vatican where the pope lives. One knows what battles were fought in the past over the meeting place of councils—'the closer to Rome the less freedom of speech' seemed to be the rule. At the Council of Trent, moreover, there was a protracted tug of war between the emperor and the pope, till finally the much-too-small and uncomfortable little town on the Etsch was chosen—only because it was located almost precisely halfway between the power of the Emperor (Charles V) and that of the pope.

The first Vatican Council—that of 1869–1870—confirmed such considerations. No one can quarrel with the statement that there the bishops' freedom was severely curtailed through indirect methods. Besides, after the definition of the primate and the infallibility of the pope, any council held in Rome, the pope's 'home', had to appear beclouded from the start. This was precisely what attracted Pope John. He wanted to achieve positive proof that, in spite of the definition and without rebellion, complete freedom of expression was possible. And that is exactly what he achieved.

The non-Catholic Christian observers were no less astonished than the bishops. And what the fathers said about the College of Bishops (at the pope's side and together with him) and what they instructively formulated was really only a theological superstructure or, more accurately, the theological foundation of that which this Council—in contrast to quite a few earlier ones—had already experienced. All of this was conceded by the 'others', the disappointed ones. They can do no other since the facts are so close at hand. They are disappointed nevertheless. But why? They ask what actually *happened*. A few tangible changes became apparent in the liturgy. Still many agree with the Spaniard, José Luis Aranguren, who opined in a radio speech that reform in the liturgy gives the community of the faithful the good and soothing feeling of 'being modern' without at all changing the fact that one remained 'conservative through and through'.

A lot was heard at the Council of the reform of orders and of seminaries, of the upgrading of the laity, of the dignity of individual man, of the necessary dialogue between laity and hierarchy, of the autonomy of the secular domains of culture, sciences, social and economic life. *But what really happened?* Everything seems to be going along in the good old way.

On the other hand the Index of Forbidden Books was allowed to die a natural death. And there will be a condensation of the 2,414 paragraphs of the Church's law book [legal code] to one quarter of its present length. Only framework laws are to be kept, and the close details of execution will be worked out by several bishops' conferences.

Besides the above, bishops conferences will now be instituted on a national basis everywhere. This was certainly not an established practice before. As a matter of fact it was at the Council that, for the first time in history, a united Italian bishops' conference was born. These assemblies must meet on a regular basis and have firm statutes and a permanent secretariat. Here all common churchly questions will be discussed, and when necessary, decisions of a binding nature for all may be reached.

Above and beyond the national conferences, continental ones are to be set up. In Africa and South America this has already happened; in Europe people are busy making it happen now. And below the bishops' conferences every individual bishop is to institute a council on the care of souls. He is to set up a kind of parliament, made up of noteworthy pastors and lay people—both men and women. Even though this parliament has but an advisory capacity, the bishop cannot in general effectively oppose the will of the majority. Again, over the bishops' conferences the pope (at the request of the Council) instituted synods, over which the pope himself presides. There will be a universal Church, one that encompasses the whole world, and the greater number of whose members will be elected by bishops' conferences; plus regional councils and synods for specific fields of knowledge which will be set up in a similar way. And yet again, under the jurisdiction of the bishop's conferences, every pastor (as far as possible) should set up a committee for the laity of his congregation for the care of souls, which will support him in caring for and directing his parish.

There is no doubt that this considerably loosens the till-now strongly centralized and hierarchic structure of the Church. Through this the Church has become more adaptable and more flexible. Our times demand it—conditions vary so much from continent to continent, from land to land; one only has to contrast North and South America, Spain and France. Of such things one must admit that they are after all only organizational procedures. And even these were left remarkably undefined by the Council, often expressed merely as advice or as a wish.

The Council actually promulgated few decrees of a binding nature. The whole reform consists of theological—though indeed unusual—reflections and declarations, characterized by an astounding recognition of indebtedness to a remarkable number of practical stimuli. But almost nothing is compulsory. Even the explanation of religious liberty—which raised so much dust—contains several small, mild, auxiliary sentences which, for instance, make it possible for the Spanish government to make only trifling changes in its laws on religious questions to satisfy the letter of the Council explanation, although it would totally contradict the spirit which the declaration breathes. So it went in other matters. What happens then if, now that the Council is over, the bishops execute only what the letter requires?

I have heard that a well-known theologian refers to the Council as a 'Dionysian Saturnalia'. Was it really only a 'festive noise', during which all basic differences of viewpoint were forgotten, engendered by a romanticism under the spell of which one dreams of a Church in which hard reality did not and could not exist? In this form the question reminds one of the biblical account of the events of Pentecost. There also were people who—seeing the Apostles filled by the Holy Ghost, speaking in all tongues—spoke of a 'festive noise' and meant: 'they are drunk on sweet wine.' The question: Was it the Holy Ghost or the sweet wine? could only be answered by history.

Astonishingly enough, before the Council John XXIII, laughing happily, awaited a 'renewal of the Whitsun events'. A lot of theologians laughed mockingly at the time and said: 'A Council is a gathering of the highest churchly authorities, the bishops, who are designated to lead the Church. From such a committee one may expect decisions about the true and the false, and ordinances of a practical nature, for such is their sphere of authority. The presence of the Holy Ghost is promised insofar as they will not blunder. But it is not the place for charismatic new perspectives on the future of the Church, for theological opinions or practical initiatives. The Council only has to assemble, examine what is already available, and express its authoritarian opinion about it.' The laughter of the theologians and that of Pope John were opposed to each other. And then something happened which looked astoundingly like the Whitsun event. Whether it was a 'Dionysian Saturnalia' or really a Whitsunlike manifestation, history will have to determine here too. But if history has expressed itself in favor of the Holy Ghost and against the sweet wine in the matter of the broadcasting of Christianity, then—if Pope John was right—a long period may lie before us in which, slowly but surely despite handicaps and setbacks, the spirit of the Council will fight its way through.

And that is the aim of this book: It does not intend to be a history of the Council—one can learn that in a concentrated way by reading the chronicle with which this book begins. It also is not meant as a detailed survey of the sixteen Council documents which are presented here as the tangible result of the Council. Instead it highlights the more important documents, of which there are four—the Council constitutions. They relate to the liturgy, revelation, the Church, and the stance of the Church *vis-à-vis* the world. The heavyweight document is the one on the Church; on it the Council worked longest and most painstakingly. And it is to this Council as the trunk is to a tree. From it branches grow, often divided into twigs. These twigs are the decrees and explanations of the Council. The four *constitutions* represent the declarations of the Council that mattered most to the fathers; the *decrees* point the way to the methods by which they can be realized in everyday life. So from the introspection of the Church gathered together goes forth the decree on missions, as well as the most noteworthy announcements on ecumenism, the Jews, non-Christian religions, the Eastern Churches, and religious freedom. From the debate on the hierarchic structure of the Church grew decrees about bishops, priests, and education for the priesthood. The separate testimonies about the apostolate of the laity, media of communications, and Christian education represent branches of the chapter on the laity. From the debate on evangelical councils comes one branch, the decree on the renewal of the life of the religious orders.

But it is not to explain these that this book is written but to proclaim the new orientation which, in spite of its differences with the old, is yet not a break from the tradition of the Church. Even here certain basic tendencies can be discerned, sometimes obviously and sometimes only in tiny details; they appear in certain formulations and even in certain omissions, and they permeate the whole. What we shall focus on here are the peculiarities of the Council—the newness of it, its surprises and its hopes and opened doors. Who would have thought that the almost 2000-year-old Church suddenly would begin to sing a new song which would undermine the walls of Jericho, whose sounds would loosen the hinges of long rusty bridges and send them crashing down to span deep moats which had irremediably separated this Church from other Christian churches and from the modern world?

A last suggestion for the reader: This is a volume of pictures and text. The *and* indicates neither an unrelated association, nor the emphasis of the one above the other. These are not two books—a picture book and a textbook—which have been intermingled more or less tastefully, and could have been published just as well, and possibly better, as separate volumes. Essential statements which are necessary to a real understanding of the Council, and which one cannot find in the declarations nor in the speeches, are found in the pictures. The pictures are not mere illustrations completely subordinated to the text. And the text is certainly not an extended caption to the pictures. What we have done here is arrange a kind of marriage of picture and text; both have become as 'one flesh'. Though partners, each yet remains an individual. But since neither pictures nor text nor even both of them together can totally recapture the spirit of the Council and its atmosphere, every main section of the book begins with a drawing which tries to round out the real picture of the Council through an artist's intuitive approach. The drawings at the end of each section correspond to the short documents from the Council texts, the papal addresses and the like.

In this manner we have sought the many-layered truth about this happening and tried to recreate it. Only after the reader has absorbed the whole thing—not piecemeal, but as a harmonious whole—only then will he grasp and understand what consequences will come from it, far beyond what was said and written at the Council.

Pope John XXIII
Unfolds the Plan of the Council

Venerable Brothers,

Mother Church rejoices that, by the singular gift of Divine Providence, the long-awaited day has finally dawned. Here at St. Peter's tomb, under the auspices of the Virgin Mother of God, whose maternal dignity is commemorated on this feast, the Second Vatican Ecumenical Council is solemnly opened.

The Ecumenical Councils of the Church

All councils —the twenty ecumenical ones, as well as countless important provincial and regional councils —that have been held through the centuries, clearly testify to the vigor of the Catholic Church and are happily recorded in her annals. . . .
They steadfastly proclaim the glory of that divine and human institution, the Church of Christ, which takes its name, grace and its power from Jesus himself.
Yet beside these reasons for spiritual joy, we cannot deny the sorrows and bitterness which have for 1900 years, in long succession, darkened this history.
Every time ecumenical councils meet, there are solemn celebrations representing the union of Christ and his Church, and spreading the light of the truth; they guide individual man as well as families and society along the right path. They awaken and strengthen spiritual forces, and ever direct hearts toward true and everlasting goodness.

(Continued on page 25)

Pope John was less than enthusiastic about the business of the grand entrance called for at the opening of the Council. In private conversation afterward he described it as 'baroque and little suited to the present day'. What he disliked primarily were the palm branches, the canopy, and the sedan chair with all its trimmings and ornaments. He had at first intended to enter on foot behind the long column of bishops. But his entourage, which he later called his 'crown of thorns', argued that the people wanted to see him, and that this would be possible only if he used the sedan chair. Then he gave up resisting. Later more and more of the baroque features vanished. Pope Paul VI consistently pursued the same course—to the horror of the guardians of ceremonial etiquette.

19

For three and a half years all of St. Peter's was offered up in sacrifice to the Council. A hundred years ago the right transept alone had been spacious enough to accommodate the fathers of Vatican I. Now even the very skillful seating arrangement, using the entire nave, was not always adequate. It was designed to seat 2200 persons but more than 2500 appeared for the opening. So at the time of peak attendance some had to sit on stairs; this impeded the speakers' access to the microphone installed in front of each section. This twenty-first council was the first really 'ecumenical' council; it actually encompassed the whole of the inhabited world. That meant not only large numbers, but also the meeting of very different worlds; here for the first time there were native bishops from Asia, Africa, and all the missionary regions.

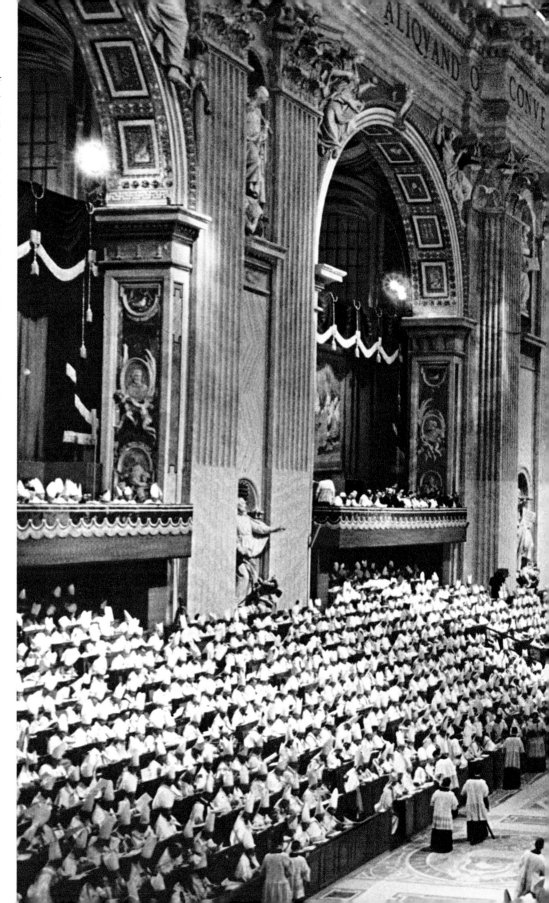

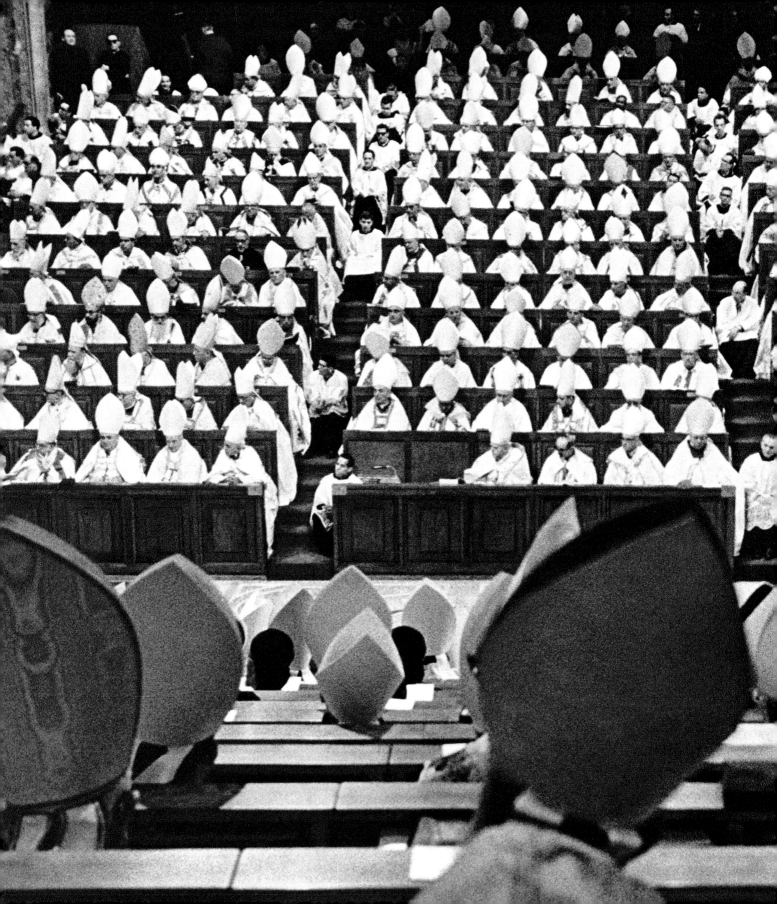

At the time of his first Council address, which initiated a new Council style, Pope John already seemed tired and worn out. Death looked over his shoulder. This had moved him to get the Council going before 'preparations' had been concluded. He wanted to get the Council off to a proper start: Don't issue condemnations, he said; use language everybody can understand, and don't lose track of the problems of the world amid your theology. 'Whenever I see a theologian, I have to ward off a slight feeling of mistrust,' he once said. Anyway this Council was supposed to be the first to avoid scholastic language and theological jargon; it was supposed to speak to all mankind.

There is another point, Venerable Brothers, which will help you understand. . . . In the daily exercise of our pastoral office, we often have to listen, with sad ears, to the voices of persons who, though burning with zeal, are not overly endowed with a sense of discretion or judgment. In these modern times they see nothing but calamity and ruin. They say constantly that our era, in comparison with the past, is growing steadily worse; they behave as if they have learned nothing from history, the teacher of life. They act as if former councils were evidence of complete victories for the Christian ideal of life and for true religious liberty. We, however, are of a completely different opinion from those prophets of doom who are always forecasting disaster as though the end of the world were at hand. In the present development of human events, through which mankind appears to be entering a new order, one must, rather, discern a hidden plan of Divine Providence. This plan, in the course of time, throughout man's works and way beyond his expectations, pursues its own end, and wisely it leads everything, even opposing human interests, to the salvation of the Church.

This truth is plainly evident when we think attentively about the world's serious political and economic problems, as well as the glowering controversies. Mankind is so preoccupied by these worries that he can find no time to take care of the spiritual realities which are the concern of the teaching authority of the Church. This way of life is certainly not right and must be justly condemned. Nobody can deny, however, that these new conditions of modern life have eliminated many obstacles that at one time were used by the worldly-wise to impede the free action of the Church.

A casual glance at ecclesiastical history immediately reveals that the ecumenical councils themselves, although a series of glories for the Church, were often accompanied by serious difficulties and sufferings caused by the undue interference of civil authorities. It is true the princes of this world probably intended in all sincerity to protect the Church. But too frequently they were guided by selfish motives and risky policies, and the Church suffered spiritual damage and danger....

Principal Duty of the Council : The Defense and Advancement of Truth

The greatest concern of the ecumenical council is that the sacred deposit of Christian doctrine should be guarded and taught more effectively. That doctrine embraces the whole of man, body and soul. And, since man is a pilgrim on this earth, it commands him to move steadily toward heaven. . . .

In order, however, that this doctrine may influence the many facets of human activity and be meaningful to individuals, to families, and to societies, it is necessary that the Church should never depart from the sacred treasure of truth inherited from the Fathers. But at the same time she must ever look to the present, to the new conditions and new forms of life introduced into the modern world, which have opened new avenues to the Catholic apostolate.

The Church therefore has watched with interest and awe the wonderful discoveries of human genius and has attempted to evaluate them rightly. But in fullest concern over these developments, she has never neglected to admonish men and to direct their attention beyond empirical things to God . . . otherwise the fleeting fascination of visible things might impede genuine progress.

How the Christian Doctrine Should be Spread Today

Having established the manner in which sacred doctrine is spread, we must make clear how much is expected from the Council in regard to it. This twenty-first Ecumenical Council, which can draw upon the support of highly qualified and experienced juridical, liturgical, apostolic and administrative experts, wishes to transmit the Church's doctrine pure and complete, without any attenuation or distortion. This doctrine, despite the difficulties and controversies of twenty centuries, has become the common patrimony of men. Although it is not well received by all, it remains a rich treasure offered to all men of good will. It is not our duty just to guard this precious treasure as though our only concern were for that which is old. Rather we must dedicate ourselves joyfully and courageously to advance the work which the Church has followed for twenty centuries. . . .

The principal work of this Council is not a discussion of one article or another of the well-known fundamental doctrines of the Church that have repeatedly been taught by the Fathers and by theologians, both ancient and modern. A council was not necessary for this. But watching us proceed with a calm adherence to the Church's complete and precise teaching (still clearly seen in the work of the Council of Trent and the First Vatican Council), the Christian, Catholic and apostolic spirit of the whole world expects us to take a step forward. We are expected to move and mold consciences with perfect fidelity to the true doctrine that must be studied, taught and made known through modern methods of research and literary forms. The substance of the ancient doctrine of the Deposit of Faith is one thing, but the way in which it is presented is another. It is the latter that must be given much consideration. Everything, with great patience, must be related in form and measure to a teaching authority that is predominantly pastoral in character.

How to Repress Errors

At the beginning of the Second Vatican Council it is as clear as ever that the truth of the Lord will live forever. We see, in fact, as one age succeeds another, that the opinions of man succeed and oppose one another. Often errors vanish as quickly as the morning fog before the sun.

The Church has always opposed these errors. Frequently she has condemned them, sometimes with the greatest severity. Today, however, the Bride of Christ prefers to use the medicine of mercy rather than the weapon of severity. She believes it more fitting for needs of the present time to demonstrate the validity of her own teaching rather than to condemn those of others. Certainly there is no lack of fallacious teachings and dangerous opinions which one must be on guard against and destroy. But they are so obviously in contrast with the right norm of honesty and have produced such lethal effects that men of themselves are inclined to condemn those errors. . . . But above all, experience has taught men that violence inflicted on others, the might of arms and political domination are of no help at all in finding a happy solution to the grave problems which afflict mankind. . . .

The Unity of the Christian and Human Family

The Church's solicitude to promote and defend truth is rooted in the fact that God wills all men to be saved and to come to the knowledge of the truth. But without the assistance of the whole of revealed doctrine man cannot reach a complete and firm unity of minds. This unity is linked to true peace and eternal salvation.

Unfortunately, the entire Christian family has not yet fully attained to this visible unity in truth. The Catholic Church, therefore, considers it her duty to work actively for the fulfillment of the great mystery of that unity which Jesus Christ himself asked from his heavenly Father in fervent prayer on the eve of his sacrifice. The Church rejoices in peace because she knows that she is intimately associated with that prayer. She rejoices greatly that this prayer is extended in an efficacious and salutary way to those who are outside her fold. Indeed, if one considers well this same unity which Christ implored for his Church, it shines, as it were, in a triple light: the unity of Catholics among themselves, which must always be a radiant example; the unity of prayers and ardent desires which suggest how much those Christians separated from this Apostolic See hope to be united with us; and the unity of esteem and respect for the Catholic Church which animates non-Christian religions.

Venerable Brothers!

This is the aim of the Second Vatican Ecumenical Council which unites the greatest efforts of the Church to persuade men to welcome the good tidings of salvation more favorably. At the same time she prepares and consolidates the path toward that unity of mankind which is necessary before the earthly city will resemble the heavenly city. . . .

The Council now beginning rises in the Church like daybreak, the forerunner of a more splendid light. . . . Let us contemplate the stars which augment the majesty of this temple with their brightness. These stars, according to the testimony of the Apostle John, are you, Venerable Brothers, and with you we see shining around the tomb of the Prince of the Apostles the golden candelabra, meaning that the Church is entrusted to you. We see here men of high rank, waiting with great respect and cordial expectations; we see you who have come together in Rome from the five continents to represent the nations of the world. We might say that heaven and earth are united in the convocation of this Council. May the saints of heaven protect our work; may the faithful of the earth continue in prayer to the Lord for it; and may you who are present respond to the inspiration of the Holy Spirit so that the work of all will correspond most exactly to the expectations and needs of the many peoples of the modern world. This means that you must act with serenity of mind, brotherly concord, moderation in proposals, dignity in discussion and wisdom in deliberation.

God grant that your labors and your work, toward which the eyes of all peoples and the hopes of the entire world are turned, may abundantly fulfill the aspirations of all.

Chronicle
of the Second
Vatican Council

Drawing: St. Peter on his throne.

'The brightest aspects of the history of all centuries justify the hope that through this Ecumenical Council ... even in its preparatory stages, the areas of love will broaden, ideas will become clarified, and genuine magnanimity will manifest itself in all bishops.' (*John XXIII, on April 23, 1959.*)

JANUARY 25, 1959   The first announcement of the Council. On the last day of the customary octave of prayer for Christian unity, in the Church of St. Paul-Outside-the-Walls, Pope John XXIII surprises the cardinals present with the news that he intends to convoke a council. Only the Secretary of State had previously been told of his intention. Pope John later repeats time and again that he was following 'a sudden inspiration'. He said this, for example, in a message to the clergy of Venice on April 21, 1959, and in the first words of his papal directive (technically called a MOTU PROPRIO) of June 5, 1960.

First phase of preparation

MAY 17, 1959 (PENTECOST)   A preparatory subcommission under the direction of Cardinal Tardini is appointed. Pope John wants to sound out the wishes and expectations of the entire Church. More than 3,000 letters are dispatched to major ecclesiastical superiors, universities, scholars and important personalities of Roman Catholic life throughout the world. More than 2,000 replies are received from bishops alone in the course of a single year. Sixty universities supply detailed opinions.
Msgr. Felici, with a team of four clerics, sifts through the correspondence. The first general report is prepared, which will be the basis for further groundwork. On June 5, 1960, this task is finished.

JUNE 29, 1959   Encyclical AD PETRI CATHEDRAM ('To the chair of Peter'). The Pope outlines the Council's aim when he writes: 'The principal purpose will be to encourage the growth of Catholic faith, to renew the life of the Christian people and to adjust the norms of ecclesiastical law to the needs and thought of our times. It will be a marvelous spectacle of truth, unity and love; a spectacle which we hope will also shine out as a gentle invitation to those separated from the Apostolic See, to seek and to reach out toward that unity for which Jesus Christ so insistently prayed to his heavenly Father.'

AUGUST 30, 1959   During an audience the Pope declares: If the separated brethren wish to participate in the Council, 'it is only common sense for us to receive them since the Church is always their home'. (OSSERVATORE ROMANO, the semi-official Vatican newspaper, never mentioned this audience.)

OCTOBER 30, 1959 Cardinal Tardini's well-known address to the international press on the meaning of the Council and the progress of the preparatory work. Asked whether the Council should be considered a continuation of the First Vatican Council (which defined papal infallibility) or as a new council, Tardini answers that the main goal of this Council is to renew Christian life and to adjust ecclesiastical policy to the demands of the times. The proposals received to date extend 'from the development of dogmatic definitions to the condemnation of the most important errors of the times'. They want a reform of ecclesiastical discipline for the clergy and the people and a reform of the liturgy, among other things. Providence, he said, had a way of playing stupendous jokes. At Vatican I papal infallibility had not been on the agenda of the fifty projected schemata, but had been introduced from the outside, by France, to counter Gallicanism. Regarding the separated Christians, Tardini observed, it was not impossible that they would participate as Council observers. Finally he noted that Pius XII, working with certain experts, had already done some groundwork in preparation for a Council.

One year later—Reaction of non-Catholic Christians

WORLD COUNCIL OF CHURCHES: 'The initiative of the Pope met with general interest in 72 Protestant, Orthodox, Anglican and Old Catholic Churches from 83 countries. But the lack of precise information about the Council has prevented their taking a stand.'

ORTHODOXY: Msgr. Siméon, First Secretary of the Synod of Constantinople: 'The Patriarchate welcomes the message of His Holiness the Pope, and considers it the first step toward rapprochement and future cooperation between the two churches—from which the entire Christian world will profit.'

REFORMED CHURCH: Pastor Boegner, President of the Reformed Church in France: 'The Council could mean a real step forward if all major confessions separated from Rome are invited.'

LUTHERANS: Bishop Lilje, President of the Lutheran World Federation, thinks it improbable that separated Christians will be invited since the scope of the Council reaches only the churches under the authority of the Holy See.

ANGLICANS: Dr. Joost de Blank, Archbishop of Capetown: 'Whatever can help to end disunity is welcome.' Canon H. M. Waddams, former secretary for external affairs of the Anglican Church: 'Should observers be invited, we should accept the invitation.'

JANUARY 25, 1960 Cardinal Tardini states that he believes representatives of other confessions could come to the Council if they wish; not as members, but as observers—'for we have nothing to hide'.

JANUARY 31, 1960 In concluding the Roman Synod, the Pope announces that the Council will be called the 'Second Vatican Council'.

It is therefore not to be considered a continuation of the First Vatican Council which was never officially terminated.

MAY 30, 1960 In a public consistory, the Pope announces to the cardinals his intention to establish nine preparatory commissions and one special secretariat for Christian unity. Before the meeting, Pope John whispers to Cardinal Bea, the future head of the secretariat: 'I am calling it a secretariat, and not a commission, so that we may be freer in organizing it.'

Second phase of preparation

JUNE 5, 1960 (PENTECOST) The Pope, through his papal directive, SUPREMO DEI NUTU ('with divine inspiration'), establishes *ten* preparatory commissions and *two* secretariats. Their task will be to work out 'schemata' based on the suggestions of bishops and universities and the advice of Roman congregations (the Vatican's equivalent of ministries). 'Schemata' (singular, 'schema') are drafts on specific themes—for instance, on liturgical reform. Most preparatory commissions correspond to Roman congregations whose traditional responsibilities include the subject assigned to the commission; but the commissions are supposed to work independently. Originally Pope John did not intend to appoint heads of congregations as presidents of commissions. But pressured by the Curia, he finally did so anyway. As a result, for example, Cardinal Ottaviani, Secretary of the Holy Office, is also president of the preparatory commission on problems of faith and morals. This unified, personal control by one man of both conciliar and curial administrative offices is to prevail throughout the entire Council period. Many difficulties will ensue from this original birth defect. No Curia members belong to the commission for problems of the laity, nor to the secretariat for mass media. These last two were added to the list of commissions and secretariats by Pope John, under prompting by Msgr. Achille Glorieux and others. The founding of the Secretariat for Promoting Christian Unity is an epoch-making innovation which will be of decisive importance for the course of the Council. The secretariat's first task is to inform non-Catholic Christians about the work of the Council. The secretariat is responsible for invitations sent to the observers, but even in the very preparatory stages of the Council it is already developing into a general point of contact between Christian churches and the Holy See.

The preparatory commissions consist of 30 to 50 members each, including both bishops and clerics, plus an approximately equal number of specialists and advisors. While the commissions are made up of members from all over the world, their work method depends on the president and secretaries in charge. In some cases, members and advisors from outside Rome have little or no influence whatever.

A central commission in theory will coordinate the work of these subject-area commissions. Because of lack of time and internal difficulties, it will be able to do its job only very imperfectly.

NOVEMBER 14, 1960 The Pope solemnly announces the beginning of the preparatory commissions' work.

NOVEMBER 16, 1960   Despite resistance from the Holy Office, the Pope hints at the possibility of a Council role for non-Catholic Christians.

DECEMBER 2, 1960   Dr. Geoffrey Fisher, Archbishop of Canterbury and primate of the Anglican Church of England, pays a visit to Pope John as well as to Cardinal Bea and Msgr. Willibrands, president and secretary of the Secretariat for Christian Unity. On his return next day, Dr. Fisher states at London airport that one purpose of the visit was to prepare the way for 'frequent informal and formal exchanges of interest and understanding between the two churches'. For some time, he said, it had been possible to move toward such an exchange—but only, so to speak, silently. Now this could be done openly and publicly. This kind of rapprochement, he continued, is the natural result of the teachings of the gospel, and whoever objects to such meetings thereby identifies himself with outmoded ideas. To object is to show you are a bit out of date—you are B.C. instead of A.D.

DECEMBER 3, 1960   Press conference of Msgr. Pericle Felici, Secretary General of the Central Preparatory Commission. He asks that reporting of the Council, 'apart from all rhetoric and journalistic embroidery which is not always necessary, but on occasion quite useful', be exact on essential questions of faith and of morals, and that it fully correspond to the teaching of the Church. 'Lapses excusable in non-Catholic or ordinary news reporting will not be tolerated in the Catholic press. Therefore contact with the official or at least semi-official organs of information is mandatory. Before a sensational bit of news is passed on, one must find out how much truth there is in it.... I wish all to conform to this and to control their desire for what is surprising and sensational. It is better to be a minute late with an accurate report than a minute early with an inaccurate one.'
Felici says that a press bureau will be set up at the Council. 'It will from time to time distribute useful and true information which will as far as possible meet your needs. I remind you, gentlemen, of the Latin proverb, "From friends we demand only what is honorable". Don't get involved in matters which are either closed or forbidden to you. Only on these conditions are we going to become good friends.'
Felici admonishes the journalists to lead irreprochable personal and family lives as a preparation for Council accreditation.

JANUARY 16, 1961   At a consistory, the Pope names four new cardinals, of which three are Americans. The most prominent among them is Joseph Cardinal Ritter, Archbishop of St. Louis. Pope John reiterates the importance of the Council for South America. Later developments prove him right.

JANUARY 30, 1961   In a meeting with journalists, Cardinal König of Vienna stresses the importance for the Council of the press and mass media. 'Outwardly, the Council appears to be the business of the Pope and bishops. In reality it is the business of the entire Church—which means all the faithful. It depends on you, the Catholic journalists, whether it will be that. I'm thinking here especially of journalists who do not write for the Catholic press. The task of the journalist is to be the public conscience of Catholics. If you have something to say about the Council, do not wait for word from the bishop, nor for news from Rome. Warn where you feel you must warn, proceed courageously where you feel you must. Inform the world at every occasion about the Council. If journalists make the Council their concern, then the Council will become the concern of all Christians. Report all public opinion and all that the faithful expect of the Council.'

MARCH 29, 1961   Osservatore Romano publishes a long report on the now completed fifteen volumes of the *first* preparatory period of the Council (Acta et Documenta from January 25, 1959 to June 5, 1960). These are divided into *four* parts totaling 9,520 pages. The *first* part had already been published in July of 1959. It contained the Acta of Pope John XXIII in regard to the Council (one volume of 168 pages). The *second* part contains the requests and advice of bishops and prelates. The first three of ten volumes comprising this section contain letters of the European bishops: 762 letters in all, the most voluminous collections coming from Italy (1,900 pages), France (400 pages), Spain (350 pages), Germany (200 pages), and Belgium (50 pages); most of the countries behind the Iron Curtain are missing except for Poland, Yugoslavia, and Latvia. A fourth volume relates to the bishops of Asia, a fifth to Africa, a sixth to North and Central America (694 pages), and a seventh to South America and Oceania. An additional volume contains suggestions from superiors of religious orders (109 letters). Then follow two volumes which organize all the material by subject and divide it into 8,972 proposals. The *third* part presents the 'proposals and admonitions' of the Roman Curia: a volume of 412 pages. Finally there is the *fourth* part in three volumes. This part contains the suggestions of Catholic universities. Apart from the Roman universities, which fill two volumes, 37 others throughout the world are here. This documentation is likely to be of outstanding value long after the Council. The public will have access only to the first volume, but the other two volumes have been put at the disposal of members of the commissions.

APRIL 16, 1961   In the Greek rite, the Pope consecrates as bishop the Basilian monk Cousa (Syrian) of the Melchite Church. John hopes this will have 'far-reaching consequences for the Council'. From now on he will frequently make such symbolic gestures, with the result that the Eastern bishops speak boldly in the Council, and the Western ecclesiastical advocates of uniformity will be thwarted.

MAY 7, 1961   In an apostolic letter to the entire Church the Pope urges the whole Church to pray for the Council on Pentecost. 'The preparatory labors of the Council are becoming more intensive and the need of prayer is ever more urgently felt.' This sentence points up difficulties which are appearing in the commissions. Cardinal König describes them as follows: 'There can be forces, influences may reveal themselves, which will seek to divert the course of events in line with all too narrow human desires. Perhaps certain commissions will be able, through their methods of working and organizing, to restrict the

Council's own orientation and way of working. Only later will this become obvious....'

MAY 21, 1961   Press conference by Msgr. Felici. Declaring that the press bureau will be organized 'according to need', he goes on: 'The need today is limited, and consequently so is the activity of the bureau. The public and the journalists must be patient. Even if the Pope has repeatedly declared that it is extremely desirable for the faithful to follow the Council with lively interest, it must not be forgotten that the Council is an act of the highest teaching and governing authority of the successors of the apostles under the authority of the Pope. All must look up to the Council in reverential silence and ask the Holy Spirit to illuminate the Father. All commission members are bound by strict secrecy which they must protect with utmost care.'

The third phase of preparation

JUNE 12, 1961   First meeting of the Central Preparatory Commission. On this occasion the Pope addresses them, asking them to see their work through to completion. The meetings of the central commission are held on June 12 to 20, and November 7 to 17, 1961; January 15 to 25, March 26 to April 3, May 3 to 12, and June 12 to 21, 1962. From the news released to the public the only thing that becomes apparent is that a certain confusion reigns in these sessions. Barely completed proposals are reviewed before similar or complementary proposals have been finished. By June 1962, 59 schemata will be more or less completely worked out. The question of inviting non-Catholic Christians is discussed. The Pope surprises the members by implying that he feels non-Catholic participation is most desirable.

OCTOBER 24, 1961   Moved by the violent reaction of the Catholic press throughout the world to the narrow directives of Msgr. Felici (directives evidencing a poor grasp of the importance of public opinion), Pope John gives a long speech to foreign correspondents. He emphasizes his complete sympathy with the problems of journalists and the importance of public opinion. The press bureau will be further expanded: 'We are vitally interested in facilitating your work. We are fully conscious of the valuable service the press can perform in presenting the Council in its true light, so that the public at large will understand and appreciate it properly.'

DECEMBER 25, 1961   The Council is formally 'announced and convoked' by means of the apostolic constitution HUMANAE SALUTIS ('human salvation'). Auxiliary bishops are also invited; in all, 2,908 persons will be entitled to participate. The Pope declares that non-Catholic observers will also take part in the Council.

FEBRUARY 2, 1962   In a papal directive Pope John sets the opening of the Council for October 11, 1962.

JULY 6, 1962   The first seven schemata are sent to the bishops. They concern (1) the sources of faith, (2) the preservation of faith, (3) moral-ity, (4) chastity, marriage, family, and virginity, (5) the liturgy, (6) the mass media, (7) Christian unity (the Eastern Churches). Texts 2, 3 and 4 are never fully discussed by the Council. They disappear. Only the text on the liturgy wins the approval of the fathers.

The First Session

OCTOBER 11, 1962   The solemn opening of the Council. Pope John gives his keynote address.

OCTOBER 13, 1962   The first plenary session (called 'general congregation'). Members of conciliar commissions are to be elected. Ten presidents appointed by the Pope are to preside in rotation. This meeting comes to a premature conclusion, because two of the presidents, Cardinals Liénart and Frings, reject the proposed nominations for commission members and demand time for the bishops to get acquainted and themselves draw up various lists of nominees. The whole praesidium approves of the proposal. And so on the very first day the dominance of the Roman officialdom is broken. The desire for genuine dialogue prevails.
The observers from non-Catholic churches—30 of them—are received by the Pope, along with eight special guests privately invited by the Secretariat for Christian Unity. Among the Churches represented are the Orthodox: the Patriarchate of Moscow, the Coptic Church of Ethiopia, the Armenian Orthodox Church, the Russian Orthodox Church in exile. Not represented here, however, are the very important Orthodox churches of Greece, Bulgaria, Yugoslavia, etc. The most notable absentee is Constantinople. Protestants represented include the Anglican union (United Kingdom, the United States, India), the International Lutheran Confederation, Old Catholics, Presbyterians, the German Evangelical Church, Congregationalists, Methodists, and the World Council of Churches.

OCTOBER 16, 1962   Election of the 160 commission members. Entirely new faces will now appear in the commissions. Forty-two countries are represented: 39 members come from central Europe, 31 from southern Europe, 27 from North America (United States and Canada), 27 from Latin America, 15 from Asia, 7 from Africa, 6 from eastern Europe, and 8 from England and Oceania.

OCTOBER 20, 1962   The third general congregation produces an unexpected message of the Council fathers to the world. It is a response to the opening address of the Pope. It bids farewell to any kind of triumphalism, and speaks of the *servant* Church. The dignity of man is its concern, and it particularly emphasizes the peace of nations and social justice. One may well consider this message as a kind of position paper for the Council. Without it, neither the declaration on Religious

Liberty nor the Pastoral Constitution on the Church in the contemporary World could have been formulated.

OCTOBER 22, 1962 The debate on the liturgy begins. It lasts until November 13. This long debate shows up the deficiencies of the agenda. Three hundred and twenty-nine Council fathers speak, endlessly repeating each other. Meanwhile nobody knows how many bishops support any given speaker. Great fatigue and irritation set in. There is talk of tactics of procrastination. Cardinal Cushing leaves the Council in protest. The main points discussed are the liturgy in the vernacular and the authority of bishops' conferences.

NOVEMBER 4, 1962 Cardinal Montini is celebrant at an Ambrosian Rite Mass on the fourth anniversary of the coronation of Pope John XXIII. The Pope again praises the manifold riches of the liturgy and liturgical reform.

NOVEMBER 14, 1962 The first great day of the Council. Voting starts on the main lines of the draft on the liturgy. The fog begins to lift. The main lines of the draft are accepted almost unanimously. The job of the commission is now to incorporate the bishops' recommendations in such a way that the improved texts will win approval. On the same day debate begins on the second item—the draft on the sources of revelation. The clash of opposing positions reaches a climax in the following general congregation. This topic is of the greatest ecumenical significance. Many observers stress that if the schema as drafted is accepted by the Council, dialogue between non-Catholic churches and the Catholic Church will come to an early end. Thus, the second (but by no means subordinate) goal of the Council is at stake. Many fathers demand that the present text be dropped from the agenda, others demand thorough revision; still others defend it obstinately. Cardinal Siri, president of the Italian bishops' conference, calls upon the Italians to 'defend the faith'. Brochures sharply attacking the Pontifical Biblical Institute, which opposes the draft, are distributed in the Council hall.

NOVEMBER 20, 1962 The presidents of the Council order a vote on whether to close debate on the draft. Result: 1,368 affirmative against 822 negative votes; this is 92 votes short of the required two-thirds majority.

NOVEMBER 21, 1962 The Pope himself steps into this desperate situation. He terminates the debate and assigns revision of the draft to a mixed commission whose membership is drawn from both the Theological Commission and the Secretariat for Christian Unity under the joint leadership of Cardinals Ottaviani and Bea.

NOVEMBER 23—27, 1962 Debate on the draft ON MASS MEDIA (press, film, radio, television). The fathers are tired and discussion flags. But on November 27 the main outlines of the draft are almost unanimously accepted. The commission is to condense the text; it is for too long and goes into detailed short-range prescriptions.

NOVEMBER 27—30, 1962 The schema ON THE EASTERN CATHOLIC CHURCHES comes up. Particularly its first part seems to many insufficiently ecumenical in language and attitude. Once more the discussion raises the question: What is 'ecumenism'? Cardinal Bea points out that the theme of ecumenism is dealt with in another draft prepared by the Secretariat for Christian Unity, and in Chapter 11 of the schema on the Church, prepared by the Theological Commission. The inadequacy of the Central Commission becomes obvious: three commissions have treated the same subject with absolute independence from each other. Consequently, on December 12, the schema is turned over to a mixed commission which is to work the two texts into one unified schema.

NOVEMBER 28, 1962 Cardinal Ottaviani requests, against the wishes of the majority, that the remaining days be devoted to debate concerning the schema on Mary. (He hopes this will achieve a peaceful and harmonious conclusion of the session.) The praesidium turns down his proposal and puts the schema on the Church on the daily agenda.

DECEMBER 1—7, 1962 Debate on the schema on the Church. Once again the question comes up: Do the fathers wish to reject a draft outright? Again the reason given for rejection is the basic lack of ecumenical, pastoral and biblical perspective. But the fathers have to content themselves with sharp criticism, because no vote is taken. Yet Cardinals Suenens, Montini and Lercaro develop an overall program for the Council in which everything will center on the theme of the Church. The 72 schemata are actually condensed to about 20 by December 5. The Pope sets up a coordinating commission of six cardinals, under the direction of Cardinal Cicognani, to integrate the Council's work. It has become clear that the present schemata do not reflect the spirit of this Council.

DECEMBER 7, 1962 The improved fourth chapter of the liturgy schema is approved, with 1,922 yes and 11 no votes; 180 fathers vote a qualified yes while 5 cast invalid ballots. The 180 votes with reservations need not be taken into consideration by the commission because they do not constitute one third. In subsequent balloting, only unqualified yes or no votes will be permitted. The result of this balloting (the first chapter contained the controversial questions) is that the entire schema on the liturgy is assured of success.

DECEMBER 8, 1962 Ceremony closing the first session. The Pope is very ill. He appears only for a very brief, encouraging address.

Between the First and Second Sessions

DECEMBER 12, 1962 In a general audience the Pope expresses his hope that the Council will finish its work by Christmas of 1963.

DECEMBER 19—23, 1962; JANUARY 21—23, 1963 In his regular general audiences and in addresses to special groups, John XXIII emphasizes again and again that the Council must not concern itself exclusively with the Church's intramural problems. It must be a council for all mankind.

JANUARY 6, 1963   Letter of the Pope to all Council fathers and 'to every individual person in particular' concerning the work between sessions. The Pope discusses the coordinating commission, announced on December 6, 1962, and set up on December 17. It is headed by Cardinal Cicognani, the Secretary of State. (Once more the same person is both head of a Curia office and presiding officer at the Council.) The rest of the membership has a mixed international character: It includes Cardinals Liénart (France), Spellman (United States), Lercaro (Italy), Urbani (Italy), Confalonieri (Italy), Döpfner (Germany), Suenens (Belgium), Agagianian (Syria), and Roberti (Italy). The idea is to have men who, for the most part, are 'readily accessible'.

The Pope declares himself against the introduction of new forms of devotion. He asks that all Council fathers remain in contact with the coordinating commission through correspondence. He asks that they discuss the Council in their individual dioceses, particularly with specially qualified experts. He regards the growing interest of the world as a seed of hope for Christian unity. He concludes from this that the Council must initiate dialogue with other Christians and with the world. He cites all the many biblical passages which present Christ as redeemer of 'the universe', of 'every individual man', of 'all flesh'; and as redeemer 'of all men ... without regard to persons'.

MAY 20, 1963   The last letter of Pope John to the bishops of the world, on preparation for Pentecost. Once more he emphasizes the 'essentially pastoral goal of the Council'. This was to be his legacy.

JUNE 3, 1963   (Monday after Pentecost) The death of Pope John XXIII. This legally interrupts the Council. Whether it is to be resumed will depend on the decision of his successor.

On June 3, 1963, Pentecost Monday, Pope John XXIII died. Since the end of the first session he had clearly been very ill. He had said in a parting audience to French bishops: 'I know what role I will have to play in this Council.' No one would know what the sacrifice of his life under these circumstances meant to him, for as late as December 1962, he had remarked: 'There are many who still do not understand me. There is too much talk for its own sake, and too little intercession on behalf of mankind.' It had been John who had opened the Council; his successor would not likely have done so. In his intuitive way, John gave the Council its direction and awakened hopes that soon became obligations. Two statements made in his picturesque biblical style will endure: 'We will have to unsettle the dust that has been gathering on the throne of Peter since Constantine,' and 'One must first see the good in every person.'

This picture of St. Peter's basilica was taken at midnight between June 4 and 5, 1963. It was the night before the funeral of the 'Universal Father', as Pope John was called. Only then was it evident how deeply his brief pontificate (less than five years) was written into the hearts of the people. And not only Catholic people: In a French city, Jewish school children raced into a classroom to learn more details from the teacher about the death of the good rabbi. And Protestant pastors Charles Westphal and George Casalis said, 'For the first time in history, Protestants mourn the death of a pope.'

Expectantly the crowd looked for the smoke, which rose twice a day from the conclave where the cardinals assembled to elect a new pope. If the smoke was black, a ballot had been in vain; if it was white, the oldest cardinal deacon, Ottaviani, would presently announce from the loggia: 'We have a pope.' Elections of popes in the past had lasted weeks and months. This time the election was short, and although some 'well-informed' circles pretended to know that Cardinal Montini would certainly not be elected, he was—this Archbishop of Milan who had been the candidate of the late Pope.

Pope Paul VI en route to his coronation. Nuns and devout women came running to the scene. The critical Romans were more reserved. The Roman Curia was afraid. For thirty years Montini had been active in the secretariat of state under Pius XI and Pius XII (from 1924 to 1954). He was familiar with the papal offices. A rumor circulated that he was supposed to have said at leaving: 'I will return with a broom.' Anyway, it was known that he had long considered various plans for reforming the Roman Curia, internationalizing it, and including in it bishops from places other than Rome.

Following page: The coronation of Pope Paul in St. Peter's square by Cardinal Ottaviani, eldest of the cardinal deacons. As early as the first session, Montini had in his letters criticized the preparations for the Council: 'An immense amount of material, but heterogeneous. It should have been courageously condensed and evaluated. But there was no central architectonic idea governing the work.' The collegiality of bishops? Or the dialogue with man? John had said: 'Communism is the enemy of the Church, yet the Church does not have any enemies.' From the new pope many expected another kind of 'politics'.

43

JUNE 21, 1963   Giovanni Cardinal Montini, archbishop of Milan, is elected Pope on the sixth ballot. He adopts the name of Paul VI.

JUNE 22, 1963   In the Sistine Chapel the new Pope addresses a radio message to the world in the presence of 79 cardinals. 'The continuation of the Second Vatican Council will be the focus of all our efforts. This will be the first thought of our pontificate, so that the whole world will hear ever more clearly the long-awaited message that salvation is to be found only in the gospel of Jesus.' The Pope intends, among other things, to 'work for the revision of canon law', to further the goals of 'the great social encyclicals—the consolidation of justice, in truth and freedom, in civil, social and international life, and the recognition of the mutual duties and rights of men'. New consideration must be given to 'underdeveloped countries where standards of living are often unworthy of human dignity'. The new age of mankind, heralded by space exploration, 'will be singularly blessed by the Lord if men truly recognize one another as brothers rather than competitors'. The Pope then speaks of international peace. He urges all nations to use resources for the salvation of mankind and the peaceful development of God-given human rights: 'There have been many recent encouraging signs from men of good will. We thank the Lord for them and offer to all sincere and steadfast cooperation for the preservation of the great gift of peace in the world.' He then emphasizes the theme of Christian unity. 'We open our arms to all who glory in the name of Christ. We call them brothers. They will find in us constant understanding and good will. They will find in the Roman Church the treasures of their historical, cultural and spiritual heritage preserved, as it were, in new splendor in the house of the Father.' The Pope concludes with a special greeting to the Church of silence.

JUNE 27, 1963   The Pope calls for the next session to begin on September 29, 1963.

JUNE 30, 1963   The coronation ceremony of Pope Paul VI. The Pope speaks in several languages. First, in Latin, he says that God has entrusted him with the Church that he may bring her ever closer to mankind. Next, in Italian, he states that the Council must strengthen the moral forces of the Church, rejuvenate its forms and bring it up-to-date to meet the demands of the age. The Council must make the possibility of sincere reunion attractive to the separated brethren—so that being reunited in the love for the mystical body of the one universal Church will seem to them easy and a source of joy. Speaking in French, the Pope turns to the Eastern Churches: They have a double claim to fame—their great loyalty to the primitive Church, and their devotion to the successor of Peter as the living apostolic center of the mystical body of Christ. Again in French, he addresses separated Christians: 'We do not deceive ourselves about the scope of the problem and the obstacles which must be overcome. We want, however, to continue the dialogue that has been begun and, as far as it is in our power, to further this work using only the weapons of truth and of love.' Pope Paul adds a few remarks about dialogue with the world. He intends to advance it to give just recognition to the finest efforts of contemporary man on behalf of justice, human progress, mutual trust and peace. In such efforts 'the world shows amazing energy, courage, ambition, dedication and willingness to sacrifice. We say without hesitation that we will cooperate with all these efforts.' Then he adds: 'We hear these continual pleas from the world and, following the example of our great predecessor, we offer contemporary man the cure for his weaknesses and the answer to his pleas—the unsearchable riches of Christ. Will our voice, however, be heard?' In English, the Pope praises the English language for the laudable way it has contributed to greater understanding and greater unity among people of all races, across all continents, to every corner of the earth. Once more he stresses world peace.

SEPTEMBER 12, 1963   The Pope writes to Cardinal Tisserant, Dean of the College of Cardinals. The Pope announces in his letter he has dissolved the former secretariat for extraordinary affairs and transferred three of its members to the Council presidency—Cardinals Wyszynski of Warsaw, Siri of Genoa, and Meyer of Chicago. The praesidium will supervise the carrying out of the agenda and solve any questions and difficulties that arise. The remaining four cardinals of the former secretariat are appointed Council moderators. Their task is to supervise preparation of the documents and to coordinate the debates. The Council drafts, in the meantime, have been reduced to 17. To make the journalists' work easier a bishops' press committee (like that of the World Council of Churches) will be established under the direction of the American Msgr. Martin O'Connor. Laymen, representing recognized international Catholic organizations, will also be admitted to the general conferences. At the right time a special secretariat for non-Christian religions will be established.

SEPTEMBER 14, 1963   The Pope addresses two letters to all the bishops of the world. In the first, he definitely convokes the second session for September 29, 1963. In the other, he asks everyone to engage in repentance and prayer in preparation for the Council.

SEPTEMBER 21, 1963   Before the entire Roman Curia the Pope announces that the Curia will be reformed. While stressing that the Curia is needed, he notes critical opinions, rejecting some but agreeing with others. The Curia will be simplified and decentralized, but at the same time it will be enlarged to include local bishops in order to take care of the Church's growing responsibilities. He hints at the possibility of a bishops' synod to supervise the Curia. The Pope urges the Curia to set a good example. It isn't supposed to be an anonymous corporation nor a bureaucratic machine.

The Second Session

SEPTEMBER 29, 1963   The second Council session opens. The Pope insists that the Council must be oriented exclusively toward Christ. 'May no light shine above this Council except Christ, the Light of the World. May no truth concern us except the words of the Lord, our only master.

May no desire guide us except the desire to be absolutely faithful to Him. May no hope sustain us except His strengthening word, "Behold, I am with you all days, even to the end of time". . . . You, Christ—only You do we know. . . .' This theme has deep appeal for the separated Christians yet it disturbs many Catholics, who find the emphasis on Christ alone too strong. 'Wherever the guilt for separation can be attributed to us, we humbly ask God's forgiveness and also pardon of our brethren who feel they have been hurt by us.'

SEPTEMBER 30, 1963   The first general congregation begins the debate on the completely revised schema on the Church. Several suggestions are made that the Marian schema be incorporated as the last chapter in *this* schema, so that Mary will have her place in the *Church*. Eleven laymen visit the Council for the first time as auditors ('listeners'). Archbishop Morcillo of Saragossa, one of the Council undersecretaries, suggests that representatives of non-Christian religions also be invited as observers.

OCTOBER 1, 1963   The schema on the Church is accepted by the fathers as a basis for discussion. Debate on the first chapter (The Church as Mystery) begins. The Church and the Kingdom of God are sharply distinguished by the English Benedictine, Christopher Butler. The difference in the concept of the Church as presented here and in the schema on the liturgy is pointed out.

OCTOBER 4—14, 1963   Discussion of the second chapter (Structures of the Church) begins. A vigorous battle ensues on the issue of whether Christ founded a college of apostles and (by extension) the college of bishops succeeding it. The sacramental consecration of bishops appears to meet little resistance. The permanent diaconate is brushed aside by Cardinal Spellman as 'the romanticism of liturgists', but Cardinal Meyer and many others contradict him. The proposal for a married diaconate meets with much more vigorous opposition. Voting begins on the revised liturgy schema.

OCTOBER 15, 1963   The moderators, anxious to get an idea of how the vote on crucial issues is going to be divided, announce that five questions (on controversial topics such as collegiality) will be read out and voted on during the next two days. The second chapter of the schema on the liturgy does not win the two-thirds majority required for approval and is returned to the commission for revision.

OCTOBER 16, 1963   Cardinal Agagianian announces the postponement of the five directive questions. Rumors spread. Impatience and defection spread among most of the bishops and among the public at large.

OCTOBER 16—25, 1963   Discussion continues on the third chapter of the schema on the Church (The People of God and Particularly the Laity). Debate is diffuse and listless since the moderators' five questions have not come up during the entire period and many rumors are circulating as to why. It is clear that many bishops want a special chapter on the People of God to include both laymen and priests. This is important for the Church's new self-awareness.

OCTOBER 18, 1963 The Secretariat for Christian Unity announces that a chapter on the Jews may be added to the schema on ecumenism. The third chapter of the liturgy schema does not attain a two-thirds majority vote. The Council is in a gloomy mood. The five questions are reformulated but are still to be submitted.

OCTOBER 23, 1963 The 'three heads' of the Council, i. e., the three directive bodies (coordinating commission, moderators and presidents) meet with the Council secretaries (who have no vote) in order to solve the dispute about who has jurisdiction over the five questions. Cardinal Ottaviani, the moderators (October 17) and Cardinal Suenens (October 21) have all successively seen the Pope. There still are no results.

OCTOBER 24, 1963 Cardinal Döpfner of Germany, a Council moderator, announces that a vote will be taken whether the Mary schema will be included in the Church schema or not. Two cardinals will argue: one for, and the other cardinal will present the reasons against. Cardinal König of Vienna speaks for the former and Cardinal Santos of Manila for the latter. Finally, the fourth chapter of the schema on the liturgy is accepted with 552 reservations.

OCTOBER 25—31, 1963 The fourth chapter of the schema on the Church is debated. Discussion covers the Christian vocation to holiness and the place of religious orders in the Church. Although a debate similar to the one on the third chapter might be expected to develop here, there are only faint rumblings: the bishops are exhausted.

OCTOBER 26, 1963 The Council moderators hold their weekly meeting with the Pope. He seems to approve of the form of the five questions. But on the issues themselves he seems to favor Cardinal Ottaviani's views. The vote on the Marian question is postponed one day.

OCTOBER 27, 1963 Memorial ceremony for Pope John XXIII. Cardinal Suenens' major speech helps revive the Council's spirits. He makes several allusions to the Council's 'unresolved crisis' and is greeted with lively applause. The Cardinal is received by the Pope.

OCTOBER 29, 1963 At last the five questions designed to clarify opinion on the second chapter of the schema on the Church are submitted. A vote is taken on the Marian question. A scant majority votes to include the Marian schema in the schema on the Church. Confusion! What will happen in the case of the five questions should the ratio of votes be equal? The entire text might be rejected. The fifth chapter of the liturgy schema is accepted with only 16 reservations.

OCTOBER 30, 1963 Voting on the five questions begins. (1) Is the consecration of bishops a sacrament? 2,123 yes, 34 no. (2) Is every regularly consecrated bishop a member of the body of bishops? 2,049 yes, 104 no. (3) Does the college of bishops as successor of the apostolic college have supreme power in the total Church? 1,808 yes, 336 no. (4) Does the college of bishops have its power by virtue of divine law (established by Christ)? 1,717 yes, 408 no. (5) Is the diaconate a permanent state? 1,588 yes, 525 no. The results are transmitted to the commission, so that they will be taken properly into account in revision of the text. The sixth chapter of the liturgy schema is approved with only 9 reservations. The bishop's change of attitude is completed.

NOVEMBER 1—4, 1963 The Council rests.

NOVEMBER 5—18, 1963 Discussion continues on the schema ON THE BISHOPS. Despite sharp criticism, due to insufficient consideration of the still unfinished text ON THE CHURCH, the schema is accepted after two days with 477 negative votes.

NOVEMBER 6, 1963 At the opening of debate on the first chapter (Relations between the Bishops and the Roman Curia) Patriarch Maximos IV Saigh delivers an important speech, in French, on the structure of the Church.

NOVEMBER 7, 1963 Due to the abrupt conclusion of the debate on chapter four of the schema on the Church, seventeen fathers have been prevented from participating. There are two schools of opinion, and the views of each on holiness and religious life are presented to the Council by Cardinal Döpfner. Now the bishops concerned feel that their opinion has not been presented correctly.

NOVEMBER 8, 1963: The text of the chapter on the Jews is distributed. Cardinal Frings sharply criticizes the methods of the Roman Curia, especially those of the Holy Office. Cardinal Ottaviani loses his composure. Cardinal Lercaro points out the organizational defects of the Curia. Debate begins on the second chapter of the schema on bishops. Cardinal Browne of Ireland contests the validity of the moderators' five questions.

NOVEMBER 11, 1963: Cardinal Döpfner (moderator) defends the five questions.

NOVEMBER 12, 1963 Cardinal Suenens (moderator) pleads for a maximum retirement age for bishops. Debate on the question of bishops' conferences begins, and by vote the fifth chapter of the schema on the bishops is separated and given to the Commission for Renovation of Ecclesiastical Law. The main concern of this commission is the establishment and delimitation of parishes.

NOVEMBER 13, 1963 Bishop Carli of Segni (Italy) contests the value of the vote on the five questions. This is the last objection from the minority for the time being.

NOVEMBER 14, 1963 The schema ON MASS MEDIA (which has two parts) wins a decisive majority. Debate on the fourth chapter on the schema on the bishops begins in a more relaxed atmosphere.

NOVEMBER 15, 1963   Once again the 'three heads' of the Council meet with the Pope. Cardinal Lercaro presents an important summary of the work of the Council to date.

NOVEMBER 18, 1963   Cardinal Lercaro reports to the Council on the highly satisfactory and efficient work of the Liturgical Commission, · with the intention of spurring other commissions on. The revised first chapter of the schema on the liturgy is approved, with only 20 negative votes. Debate on the schema ON ECUMENISM begins, although the Theological Commission is holding back the fifth chapter (On Religious Freedom). This angers the bishops and the press (especially the delegation from the United States).

NOVEMBER 19, 1963   The fathers finally receive the fifth chapter of the schema on ecumenism.

NOVEMBER 19—DECEMBER 2, 1963   Discussion of the schema on ecumenism continues in an atmosphere that is somewhat dispirited once more. Cardinal Cicognani, in an introductory address on November 19, tries to explain why the chapter on the Jews has been included in this schema. In the process he adds a passage on non-Christian religions which later develops into almost a whole schema. The chapter on the Jews, and particularly its treatment in the context of ecumenism, meets with determined resistance, especially from Middle Eastern bishops. Rumors spread about interference from Arab nations. Many Italians and Spaniards join in with a barrage against the statement on religious freedom. Here, too, political motives play an obvious part. This leads the moderators to decide on November 21 to call for a vote on the three first chapters only: are they acceptable as a basis for discussion? Surprisingly the three chapters are accepted almost unanimously. The influence of the observers is noticed during the debate.

NOVEMBER 21, 1963   Many of the national bishops' conferences insist on new elections for commissions. They want new presidents and new secretaries elected by the bishops. The Pope meets this request halfway. As a matter of fact, it turns out that this change is sufficient to give the great majority of the Council fathers a bare plurality on the commissions (including the Theological Commission).

NOVEMBER 22, 1963   On this, the sixtieth anniversary of the *motu proprio* of Pius X which pioneered the beginning of liturgical reform, the last vote is taken on the completed liturgy schema. Today 2,158 out of 2,178 fathers vote acceptance of the four chapters. Cardinal Tisserant recommends that the other commissions follow the example of the Liturgical Commission.

NOVEMBER 25, 1963   Last vote concerning the schema on mass media. Three of the bishops have recognized the weakness of this text too late. The fear of self-repudiation gets the better of the fathers. On the day of the vote itself these three bishops have pamphlets distributed in a last-minute effort to stop the fathers from approving the schema without adequate reflection. Cardinal Tisserant censures this action as

illegal, and Msgr. Felici moves forcefully to have it stopped. Later on the tribunal will reprimand both the cardinal and the general secretary. The negative ballots on this final vote reach a total of 514, the highest total of the entire Council.

NOVEMBER 28, 1963   Cardinal Frings speaks on the question of mixed marriage. Four other bishops have discussed this issue earlier and three more bishops will speak on it later.

NOVEMBER 29, 1963   A text on the priesthood is distributed. It seems to the bishops to be theologically inadequate, hardly cognizant of the true condition of priests and altogether too paternalistic in its tone. It is withdrawn even before it comes up for discussion.

DECEMBER 3, 1963   Through a papal directive of Pope Paul, the bishops receive some of the prerogatives which until now have been vested in the Holy See.

DECEMBER 4, 1963   Final ceremony. The CONSTITUTION ON THE LITURGY and the DECREE ON THE MEDIA OF SOCIAL COMMUNICATIONS are approved by the Pope and the bishops. The Pope in his speech uses a new mode of address for the bishops, one more in keeping with the concept of collegiality. At the close of the address the Pope announces his impending trip to the Holy Land.

Between the Second and Third Sessions

DECEMBER 23, 1963   The Pope broadcasts a Christmas message to the world. He shows his concern for problems—hunger, birth control, underdeveloped countries, the tasks of missions, and peace—to be dealt with the Council's text ON THE CHURCH IN THE CONTEMPORARY WORLD. On birth control, he says: 'Instead of providing more bread for hungry human beings—this is now possible through modern methods of production—some seek to reduce the number of people by dishonorable means unworthy of human culture.'

DECEMBER 25, 1963   The coordinating committee meets. They resolve to abbreviate the Council texts and to limit discussions so the Council can be concluded in the third session.

JANUARY 4—6, 1964   The Pope's pilgrimage to the Holy Land. He sends greetings to countries flown across enroute: Greece, Cyprus, Lebanon and Syria. King Hussein of Jordan greets him personally, as does the president of Israel, while both Muslim and Jewish populations (respectively) greet him enthusiastically. The entire trip is religious in purpose; the Church is seeking self-renewal by reaching back to its sources. His visit centers on the sacred places where Christ walked. The whole trip is symbolic and reflects the Pope's message in his opening address to the second session (September 29, 1963), when he proposed as the keynote for the Council: 'You, Christ—only You do we know.' It is in this light that the dialogue with all peoples and all religions must be understood, as well as the efforts toward Christian reunification. The Pope's meeting with Patriarch Athenagoras on January 5 is the climax of this striving.

JANUARY 13, 1964   Experts, including laymen, work out proposals for the text ON THE CHURCH IN THE CONTEMPORARY WORLD.

JANUARY 25, 1964   The Pope issues a papal directive on the liturgy. On February 16, certain directions go into effect which alter the mass and the sacraments in line with the new liturgical constitution.

JANUARY 27—FEBRUARY 4, 1964   The commission on religious orders meets with six other subcommissions to consider the schema ON CONTEMPORARY RENEWAL OF RELIGIOUS LIFE.

FEBRUARY 1—4, 1964   A mixed commission (i. e. one composed of the members of two or more commissions) meets in Zurich to discuss Schema 13—THE CHURCH IN THE CONTEMPORARY WORLD.

FEBRUARY 14, 1964   The coordinating commission meets once again. The inaccurately titled 'Döpfner Plan' is drafted. Besides the six major constitutions and decrees—revelation, the Church, the bishops, ecumenism, laity, and Church and world—some short texts are to be drafted as 'guidelines'. These deal with the Eastern churches, the missions, religious orders, priestly ministry, priestly formation (training), Catholic schools, and the sacrament of marriage. Religious liberty and the text on the Jews are not yet considered as declarations independent of each other.

FEBRUARY 24—March 7, 1964   After a whole series of meetings with experts (February 3—23), the Secretariat for Christian Unity meets in plenary session to work on improving the schema on ecumenism as well as the declarations on religious liberty and the Jews.

MARCH 2—8, 1964   The commission on the sacraments changes the schema on marriage into a draft.

MARCH 2—10, 1964   The commission on faith and morals meets. It still has two chapters to go in its schema on the Church: *eschatology* and *Mary*. It must also approve the texts on religious liberty and the Jews. The schema on revelation has to be prepared for a mixed commission as does the text on the lay apostolate. Mixed commissions will have four meetings on Schema 13.

MARCH 2—10, 1964   The commission on bishops meets to discuss the schema on the bishops' pastoral office. Further consultations will be necessary to incorporate the most important sections of a similar schema on the care of souls which the commission for clergy and people has worked out.

MARCH 3—10, 1964   The commission for seminaries meets to change into 'drafts' its schemata on the training of priests and Catholic schools.

MARCH 4—9, 1964   The commission for religious orders changes its text to a draft.

MARCH 10—16, 1964   The commission for Eastern churches reviews its draft schema.

MARCH 11, 1964   First meeting of the new commission on the liturgy, under the presidency of Cardinal Lercaro. This is not a curial commission but rather (at first) a planning agency under the Congregation of Rites. The commission's purpose is reform and modernization of the liturgy, its members are drawn from every continent. This marks the beginning of universal episcopal participation in the governing of the whole Church. The commission decides to create fifteen special groups of experts, each to work on a specific topic. Actually this commission is already functioning as a post-conciliar institution. Its secretary is Msgr. Bugnini.

MARCH 26, 1964   On Maundy Thursday the Pope commemorates the institution of the Eucharist with a greeting to the whole world. The Pope says that in the 'college of bishops' the pope is 'president of a community of love'. He also salutes the separated brethren, saying that the road of Christian reunion will be a long one but that 'from now on, we shall strive for mutual respect and through this mutual respect we will reduce the distance that separates us, so that love can work, as we hope, for that victory which will one day be won'. The whole transformation which the Council has effected in the Catholic Church is expressed in this frequently quoted address.

APRIL 2, 1964   In a directive the Pope establishes a pontifical commission for the communications media—press, radio, film and television.

APRIL 14, 1964   The Pope addresses the Italian bishops. He asks that they take an 'absolutely positive' attitude toward the Council and 'enter into intelligent and brotherly dialogue with bishops of other countries'.

APRIL 16—17, 1964   The coordinating commission again checks on whether the individual commissions have been following instructions.

APRIL 17—18, 1964   Plenary meeting of the new liturgical commission. It reviews the work done thus far.

APRIL 18, 1964   Letter from the Pope to Ecumenical Patriarch Athenagoras.

APRIL 21, 1964   The Pontifical Biblical Commission publishes an instruction on the historical truth of the Gospels. This instruction will smooth the way for the Council's text on revelation.

APRIL 25, 1964   The Roman Congregation of Rites (actually a purely executive agency) enters into competition with Cardinal

Lercaro's liturgical commission by changing, on its own authority, the rite for distributing communion.

APRIL 26, 1964   The Pope appoints 70 consultors to the commission on canon law to institute changes in line with conciliar decisions.

APRIL 27, 1964   The Pope sends special greetings to the Patriarch of Moscow on the occasion of the Orthodox Easter. On May 13 the Patriarch cordially reciprocates.

APRIL 30, 1964   In preparation for Pentecost, Pope Paul addresses an apostolic letter to the bishops of the world. Again he emphasizes the need for improved and more intensified preparation for the third session. He praises the work of Council theologians.

MAY 4—13, 1964   The commission on missionary activity wants to submit a major schema, a kind of Magna Carta for the missions, but fails to win approval from the coordinating commission. Many preliminaries were already completed by special commissions but now the commission reluctantly gives in and decides on a 'draft' text.

MAY 7, 1964   Archbishop Heenan, speaking in behalf of the English bishops about the schema On the Church in the Contemporary World, say that it is necessary for the Council to take a stand on the question of war and peace. But, he adds, the Council can in no way approve artificial contraceptives because these are contrary to the law of God. He cites Pius XI and Pius XII in support of this warning that the Council must not be like 'the blind leading the blind'.

MAY 17, 1964 (PENTECOST)   Paul VI announces that he will establish a secretariat for dialogue with non-Christian religions. Cardinal Marella will be president.

JUNE 1—22, 1964   The various Council commissions resume their meetings. Their work is approaching completion. On June 6, Patriarch Alexis of Moscow sends the Pope a letter on the first anniversary of the death of John XXIII. Pope Paul replies, June 9.

JUNE 23, 1964   Pope Paul VI gives an address on his name day (the feast of St. John the Baptist). The Pope announces that at the beginning of this session he will return the reliquary containing the head of St. Andrew the Apostle, now in Rome, to Patras, Greece—a token of reconciliation with the Orthodox Church. The Pope also announces that the problem of birth control is being studied by a commission which he has appointed. With the cooperation of many important scholars, he hopes to finish the study soon. 'However, we admit frankly that up until now we do not see sufficient reason for regarding the norms declared by Pius XII as superseded and therefore no longer binding.'

JUNE 26, 1964   The coordinating commission checks the completed schemata.

AUGUST 8, 1964   Pope Paul's first encyclical sums up the Council in the single word—'dialogue'.

SEPTEMBER 1, 1964   The Pope writes to Cardinal Tisserant, the oldest of the Council presidents and the dean of the College of Cardinals. His letter reconvenes the Council on September 14.

Third Session

SEPTEMBER 14, 1964   The Pope, in his opening address, is concerned almost exclusively with the role of bishops in the Church and their relationship to the Pope. He emphasizes that the First Vatican Council is over, and that the most important task of the third session of the present Council will be to vote on the schema On the Church. The pastoral accent seems to be fading into the background.

SEPTEMBER 15—18, 1964   The chapters in the schema on the Church which deal with eschatology and Mary have not been discussed so far. Now the discussion makes it clear that there are two distinct notions of eschatology: the idea of 'the last things' (death, last judgment, purgatory, heaven, hell); and the idea of an inner direction toward a final goal, which is at work here and now in every individual. Still, there is a certain consensus of opinion. Only in regard to the Marian title, 'Mother of the Church', does a profound difference of opinion persist.
There are only 9 yes-with-reservations votes in the vote on chapter one of the schema on the Church. In the second chapter the hierarchy is treated as 'service'. The theology of the ecumenical attitude and of missionary activity are dealt with. There are 9 no votes and 13 qualified yes votes. The first and second chapters have been accepted. The commission will review the reasons for qualified yes votes, and then the suggested improvements will be approved or rejected on a strictly yes or no basis.
Once again laymen are present as auditors at a general congregation, They will be joined after a few days (beginning September 23) by the first laywomen auditors. There are 21 laymen and 15 laywomen at the start, representing various international Catholic organizations.
The list of observers now totals 61 names but some of these are substitutes. Not all are able to interrupt their normal activities at home in order to attend the whole Council. There seldom are more than 50 observers in actual attendance.

SEPTEMBER 18—23, 1964   Debate on the revised sections of the schema On the Pastoral Office of Bishops. The material connecting this schema theologically with the third chapter of the Church schema has been improved as well as condensed. The duties of bishops are treated in great detail. At the last moment the commission inserted into the second chapter two paragraphs; they deal with the Church's freedom vis-à-vis the State. Discussion is temperate and calm. The speakers find the schema altogether too juridical; it takes contemporary man too little into account. The language used to describe the relations between bishops, priest, and lay people must be improved. A reform of the Curia is needed. Lay-councils are needed at both the diocesan and parish level. Something must be done to improve the text's treatment of relationships between secular and religious clergy.

Voting begins on September 21 on the third chapter on hierarchical structure of the schema on the Church. Because of its importance as doctrine, the chapter is divided into 39 sections. Before September 21, four 'reports' were made to the fathers. The first report (on sections 1—7) is made by Cardinal König, whose main topic is the founding of the college of apostles and the sacramental character of episcopal consecration. The second 'relator' is Archbishop Parente, assessor of the Holy Office, whose topic is the college of bishops: he defends the prepared text. A third report is submitted by Auxiliary Bishop Jimenez (Venezuela), who deals with the section on priests and the restoration of the office of deacon (including married ones). The fourth and final report is submitted by Bishop Franic, who presents the objections to all three parts of the chapter. Since Franic represents the viewpoint of the minority, his report comes first.

None of the first seven sections draws more than 200 negative votes. But negative votes show a sudden increase on September 22 and 23 when sections 8—14 come up for decision, averaging roughly 300 negative votes for each section. This is far below the one-third needed to reject the text: that would require about 749 votes. But the voting does show the strength of the minority on this issue.

SEPTEMBER 23—25, 1964 Debate on the DECLARATION ON RELIGIOUS LIBERTY. Bishop De Smedt (Belgium) presents the text. He explains why the text retains a statement on the *principles* of religious liberty. Vehement debate follows. Some ask why it is necessary to go beyond Pius XII's statement on toleration. Would this not only contradict the idea that the Catholic Church is sole possessor of truth, and also previous papal statements? Even Cardinal Ritter of the United States is ready, if need be, to permit deletion of the passages stating the principles of religious freedom. Archbishop Parente and other southern Europeans promptly concur; but Bishop Colombo, 'the Pope's theologian', saves the situation with a well-balanced concluding speech, probably inspired by the Pope himself.

Voting continues on the third chapter of the schema ON THE CHURCH.

SEPTEMBER 26, 1964 This is the date of a brief from Pope Paul VI, ordering the return of the reliquary containing the head of St. Andrew the Apostle which had been kept in Rome since 1462. In Patras, the brief is read by Father Duprey. Cardinal Bea, also in Patras, speaks before Metropolitan Constantine of Patras, Princess Irene, President Papandreou and a large audience of Orthodox believers. The day is declared a religious holiday throughout Greece.

SEPTEMBER 26, 1964 An instruction on the liturgy prepared by Cardinals Lercaro (president of the liturgical commission), and Larraona (prefect of the Congregation of Rites) is published. In it considerable changes are made regarding the use of the vernacular, the form of the mass, the administration of the sacraments and the liturgical training of priests and lay people. All are in line with the Council's constitution on the liturgy. It goes into effect on March 7, 1965.

SEPTEMBER 28—29, 1964 Debate on the so-called 'Jewish declaration'. Cardinal Bea has already read the text on Friday, September 25. He stressed that the wish of some fathers to have the declaration deleted from the Council's agenda could not be granted because the overwhelming majority wanted such a declaration, and public opinion expected the Council to make a statement. The Cardinal begged that the crime of deicide not be attributed to the Jews. This passage is in fact stricken from the schema, so that Bea's report constitutes in effect the first vote against the prepared schema. Bitter debate follows, but it produces a deepened understanding of the issue through the interventions of Cardinals Cushing, Liénart, Frings and especially Lercaro. Meantime individual voting continues on the third chapter of the schema on the Church, reaching a climax on September 29, when the question of the diaconate (subsections 37—39) is discussed. The question of whether conferences of bishops can grant the conferral of the permanent diaconate gets 702 negative notes. Thus the proposal is almost rejected. Slightly more favorable is the vote on whether the Church's supreme authority (the Pope or the college of bishops with the Pope) can grant ordination as deacons to more mature married men. This gets 629 no votes. Finally comes the question: can the Church's supreme authority grant ordination as deacons to young married men? More than half the fathers (1,364) are against this. So this section is dropped from the text.

SEPTEMBER 30—October 6, 1964 Debate on the schema ON DIVINE REVELATION. The violent argument about whether there are two separate sources of revelation—scripture and tradition—each with its own independent and exclusive value—has been shelved. The text stresses instead the close connection between scripture and tradition. The Bible is presented as a book which cannot be 'replaced' by good religious instruction, but must be studied seriously by every Christian: This represents a practical but profound revaluation of scripture. Scientific methods of studying scripture are sanctioned—if they are used responsibly. The discussion proceeds calmly and on a high level.

Meantime the vote on the schema on the Church continues. September 30 is awaited with great excitement: that is the day when the summary vote on chapter three (hierarchy, especially the bishops) is scheduled. Despite violent protests from the minority, a two-part vote is taken. The first section, on the college of bishops, is approved with 1,624 yes votes, and 572 reservations. The ice seems to be broken. The second section, which deals with priests and the restoration of the diaconate, is approved with 1,074 yes votes, and 491 yes-with-reservations. The no votes (42 and 53 respectively) are of no consequence. On the same day (September 30) chapters four, five and six (on lay people, holiness and religious) come to a vote after only one question period. The total of qualified yes votes is respectively 76, 302, and 438 (these 'yes-but' votes reflect the comparative worth of the chapters; they gradually decline in quality). Voting resumes on October 5. The topic is now the considerably revised schema on ecumenism. The first chapter is no longer titled 'Principles of Catholic ecumenism' but 'Catholic principles in regard to ecumenism'; the idea is that there are not many ecumenisms but only one. The text emphasizes, moreover, that ecumenism is a movement continually in progress; therefore no rigid rules can be laid down for ecumenical conduct. The balloting on individual questions never reaches more than 60 no votes. The chapter as a whole is approved with only 209 reservations.

OCTOBER 12, 1864 Debate on the schema ON THE LAY APOSTO-LATE. The bishops evidence a certain disappointment: the schema lacks depth; it appears too clerical; it seems in fact to have been conceived in original sin—the sin of clericalism. Nonetheless it has certain advantages in that it speaks not only of the lay apostolate in the narrow sense, but also of lay witness in family and public life and of vocation. Its structure is clear.
Voting is concluded on the text dealing with ecumenism; the text is approved. There is to be another vote on improvements made in this text.

OCTOBER 9—24, 1964 Amid all these peaceful developments come two letters addressed by the general secretary, Msgr. Felici, to the Secretariat for Christian Unity. The letters, which are sent in the name of 'higher authority', threaten the two declarations on religious liberty and on the Jews. On October 13, Cardinal Frings, with 16 other cardinals, writes a letter to the Pope which is released to the press on October 17. As a result of this awkward incident, public opinion about the Council is on the downswing.

OCTOBER 12—15, 1964 Discussion of the draft schema ON PRIESTLY LIFE. The draft as such is not supposed to be debated, but the bishops demand debate. The so-called Döpfner plan has failed. The fathers are highly dissatisfied with the schema on priestly life. They say it fails to give sufficient consideration to the actual situation of priests; its style is extremely paternalistic. The draft is rejected with 1,199 no votes, as against 930 yes votes; therefore it has to be revised.

OCTOBER 15—19, 1964 A second draft schema is presented—that dealing with Eastern Catholic Churches. During debate, Cardinals König and Lercaro, and Abbot Hoeck argue for a breaking up of the monolithic uniformity of the Latin Church, in line with the example of the Eastern Church. They therefore reject the schema in its prepared form. The Eastern bishops themselves, however, say they are satisfied with their improved situation as reflected in the schema. And so this schema is accepted by the majority. Only the point dealing with particular churches fails; it gets 719 reserved votes.

OCTOBER 20—23, 1965 General delay on the schema ON THE CHURCH IN THE CONTEMPORARY WORLD. Discussion stays on a high level. Only three speakers completely reject the schema though all agree it must be fundamentally changed. The attempt to get away from a 'dualism' of natural and supernatural is well-received. Cardinal

Meyer of Chicago points out a biblical way of overcoming this dualism. The schema is approved as a basis for discussion with 1,579 yes votes and 296 no votes. With this the need for a fourth session is clear.
Voting continues on other matters. The seventh chapter of the schema on the Church (on eschatology) which had been discussed at the beginning of the present session is ready for presentation on October 18. On October 20 the whole chapter is accepted (with 238 reservations). Voting begins next day on the guidelines for relations with the Eastern Churches, but the second text is rejected with 719 reservations.

OCTOBER 23—27, 1964 Debate on the first three chapters of the schema ON THE CHURCH IN THE CONTEMPORARY WORLD. These chapters deal with the theoretical part of the schema and treat the vocation of man, the Church in the service of God and of man, and the situation of the Christian in the world. The fathers seem to find the presentation confused. There is no clear analysis of what the 'contemporary world' is. They want an anthropology—a treatment of the nature of man. Again and again the problem of atheism comes up.

OCTOBER 29, 1964 Pope Paul sends a greeting to Metropolitan Meliton, president of the Third Pan-Orthodox Conference of Rhodes, which is meeting from November 1 to 12.

OCTOBER 28—NOVEMBER 5, 1964 Debate on the first four topics in the fourth chapter of the schema on Church and world. This deals with specific problems of the present day. In the debate on the dignity of the human person, racial discrimination comes up for discussion, along with other questions, like the changed status of woman. A very animated discussion ensues on the marriage question. Cardinals Ruffini and Browne profess themselves 'shocked' that the text on this point is not a mere repetition of the encyclicals of recent popes. However, Patriarch Maximos IV Saigh and Cardinals Léger and Suenens energetically argue for a deepening and updating of moral doctrine in line with present-day knowledge, and for a pruning away of elements drawn from non-Christian philosophies of an earlier age. As to the third problem—cultural development—we can mention only two addresses of real importance: the speech of Cardinal Lercaro (which was afterward very often called the best intervention of the entire Council), and the remarks of Bishop Elchinger, coadjutor of Strasbourg. Voting during these days is carried forward on: (1) the as-yet-undiscussed chapter on Mary at the end of the schema on the Church (521 reserved votes, 10 no votes). (2) The beginning of the second series of votes on the schema on the Church (only yes and no votes are permitted); the first and second chapter get only 17 and 19 no votes respectively. (3) The sections of the schema on the bishops' pastoral office not previously discussed in this session: the work of the bishops; their independence of the state; bishops' retirement; diocesan boundaries; auxiliary bishops and coadjutors; the bishops' synod; the work of the parish priests; the assistance of religious orders in the work of the diocese. Here the respective no votes are: 22, 8, 57, 12, 22, 25, 14, and 172. Among those dissatisfied with the text are some members of religious orders and a few bishops who refuse to give up.

NOVEMBER 6—9, 1964 Suddenly and with no reason given, the almost-concluded debate is interrupted. The Pope appears in the general congregation and opens discussion on the draft schema on the missions. Although he himself finds weaknesses in the text, he urges its acceptance. The draft is debated for three full days. The central issue at first is whether the committee of scholarly experts mentioned in the schema should serve as an advisory board for the Congregation of the Propagation of the Faith. Many speakers thank that this panel should be a directive body rather than an advisory board. Then Cardinal Frings gets up and proposes that the draft be rejected. He argues for a decree which will really come to grips with the actual needs and problems of the missions. Result: 1,601 fathers call for a new schema; only 311 want to accept the present draft after revision. The Pope is disappointed; he weeps.

Voting also proceeds on November 6 on the second chapter of the schema on the pastoral office of bishops. There are only 19 negative votes but there are 889 reservations. This is more than a third, and consequently the commission must review the proposals for improving the text. There is also a vote on the third chapter, on episcopal cooperation. The chapter as a whole receives 469 reserved votes. On November 9 the fathers review the revised schema on ecumenism.

NOVEMBER 9—10, 1964 The interrupted debate on the schema on Church and world comes to an unsatisfactory conclusion. Many fathers want a clear and vigorous condemnation of atomic warfare. But some fathers, particularly English and Americans, do not want to see the right to defense jeopardized—even atomic defense.

A second series of votes begins on the third chapter of the schema on ecumenism. The first chapter receives 147 no votes and 2,064 yes votes.

NOVEMBER 10—12, 1964 Three brief schemata remain to be voted on for the first time. Of these, the first to be brought before the Council is the draft On Contemporary Renovation of Religious Life. Cardinals Döpfner and Suenens demand a throughgoing reform, a return to the sources, a discarding of 19th century moralisms, a new view of the vows of poverty and obedience, and serious attention to contemporary problems. This schema, like that on the priesthood, seems destined to fail. Nevertheless there are a great many fathers and members of religious orders. As a result, despite 882 (more than a third) no votes, individual balloting proceeds. (Here a simple majority will be decisive.)

Further voting continues on the second and third (last) chapter of the schema on ecumenism.

NOVEMBER 13, 1964 In place of a general congregation, Patriarch Maximos Saigh and various bishops as well as archimandrites celebrate a Byzantine liturgy. The Pope solemnly carries his tiara through St. Peter's and lays it on the altar as a gift for the poor.

NOVEMBER 14—17, 1964 Text on priestly formation. Despite radical revision, the schema is well received by the majority of bishops. They even want to go further: They want seminary training to be more integrated, forming the whole man and preparing him for life in the world. More serious controversy arises over the issue of the importance of scholastic philosophy and the value of St. Thomas Aquinas. But all are agreed that training in scripture is of first importance in priestly training. There is general satisfaction with the idea that the bishops should have much greater freedom in directing the seminary program. Confusion comes with the second voting on the third chapter of the schema on the Church, dealing with episcopal collegiality. On November 16, Secretary General Felici prefixes to this chapter an 'explanatory note' which appears to interpret the statements on collegiality in such a way as to weaken them. This note apparently originated in the complaints of 'some fathers' to 'higher authority'. Felici declares that this 'higher authority' wants the third chapter voted on 'in this sense'. Bishops are bitter about this procedure. Nevertheless the chapter receives only 46 no votes. On the same day a vote is taken on the fourth (lay people) and the fifth (holiness) chapters of the Church text. The respective no votes are only 8 and 4.

NOVEMBER 17—19, 1964 Debate on the Declaration on Christian Education. Things proceed now with great speed, not to say haste. But the bishops are not disturbed by this, because a fourth session is now a certainty. The bishops are obviously not very happy with the draft. As a consequence, there is a call for a post-conciliar commission, to study all these questions in depth. Partial voting leads to approval, with a total of 1457 yes votes and 419 no votes. In the voting on individual sections the total of reservations only once goes as high as 280.

The electoral center of gravity is steadily shifting. Apart from the votes already mentioned in the text on priestly formation and education (14 separate votes!) suggestions for improvement (modi) in chapters 6, 7 and 8 in the text on the Church come to a vote. The no votes total 12, 4 and 23, respectively. Finally the schema on the Church is voted on as a whole: 2,130 fathers vote yes and 10 vote no. All that is necessary now is the solemn promulgation of the document by the bishops together with the Pope. Then the text will become official teaching. But on November 17 the revised text on the Declaration on Religious Freedom is presented. It has been radically reworked. Then on November 18, Felici announces that 'many' fathers have demanded a new debate on this radically changed text, or at least they want longer time for reflection (the 'many' fathers total about 130). So he says that the next day, November 19, a preliminary vote will be taken to find out whether the fathers approve this new version. On November 19, Cardinal Tisserant, as president of the praesidium, announces that this preliminary vote will *not* take place. (Only the 'report' of Bishop De Smedt will be read.) As a matter of fact, this is a decision of the tribunal, but this is not mentioned by Cardinal Tisserant. The fathers are terribly agitated. Even the presidents leave their places. In the excitement the voices of the speakers on Christian education are drowned out. It is 11 o'clock—the coffee bars are opened. Within fifteen minutes, 441 protest votes are gathered by Cardinals Meyer, Ritter, and Léger (all North Americans) and, against all rules and regulations, are taken to the Pope before the end of the day's debate. But the Pope does not veto the praesidium's decision. Only later does he mention that this decision comes from the tribunal. As if that weren't enough, on November 19 19 'improvements' are inserted 'at the direction of higher authority'. Some of these 'improvements' obviously weaken the ecumenical character of the whole text. All in all, November 19, 1964 turns out to be the blackest day of the entire Council.

NOVEMBER 19—20, 1964 On that same unfortunate 'black day', debate begins on the marriage text, which contains the extremely important passage on mixed marriage. The most controversial point here is the possibility of dispensation from ecclesiastical form in the marriage ceremony, in consideration of the conscience of the non-Catholic party. Although Cardinal Ritter is for this change, the auxiliary bishops of New York protests the change in the name of Cardinal Spellman and 100 other bishops from the United States. This problem is also turned over to the Pope after a vote of 1521 in favor and 421 against. The idea is for him to settle the issue through a papal directive which would reflect both the text and the suggestions made during the debate.
Lively voting continues on November 20. The schema on ecumenism as a whole is approved by the fathers with 2,054 yes votes as against 64 no votes. The text on the Jews and non-Christian religions is first voted on in two parts. Here there are only yes and no votes. No votes total 146 and 247 respectively. Then the text as a whole is voted on. Recommendations for improvements total 242. Then come three votes on the text on Eastern Churches. In final voting there are still 150 no votes.

NOVEMBER 21, 1964 Solemn closing of the third session. The great CONSTITUTION ON THE CHURCH, the decree ON ECUMENISM and a second decree ON EASTERN CATHOLIC CHURCHES are the tangible results of the session's work.
In the balloting before promulgation, there is a slight improvement in the voting ratio. The text on the Church receives 2,151 yes votes, 5 no votes; the text on ecumenism, 2,137 yes votes, 11 no votes; the text on Eastern Catholic Churches, 2,110 yes votes, 14 no votes. The Pope is in high spirits as he gives his final address, but for many the day is darkened because in the second part of the address the Pope solemnly confers on Mary the title 'Mother of the Church'. To many this seems like a last-minute 'correction' of the chapter on Mary: In discussing this chapter the fathers had deliberately stricken this title from the text.

Between the Third and Fourth Sessions

DECEMBER 2—5, 1964 The Pope visits India for the Eucharistic Congress in Bombay. Although he does not go, as he originally intended, as a 'missionary', his manner is wholly in keeping with the spirit of the new constitution on the Church. This is the manner in which Paul VI greets the representatives of Indian non-Christian religions. He praises Gandhi and Nehru in the presence of Premier Radakrishnan, but also expresses his joy that 'in this country Christ is respected not only by the Christians who represent a minority but by millions who have come to know him and love him as an example of love and renunciation'. For the Catholic Church this is an entirely new approach to non-Christian religions, an approach which will be echoed during the fourth session in the decree on missionary activity.

DECEMBER 8, 1964 A brief of the Pope to all bishops of the world on the theme of the unity of bishops. Basing his remarks on the Constitution on the Church, whose 'clear doctrine' on collegiality is emphasized by the Pope, he asks them to reconsider the responsibility each of them has toward all the others. 'It seems to us that the teaching on episcopal collegiality, which has only now been authoritatively proclaimed, is not without reference to a mysterious plan of God: Our time is very much in need of an example of genuine and complete spiritual unity. . . .'

JANUARY 12—21, 1965 The Central Committee of the World Council of Churches meets in Enugu, Nigeria. On the very first day the secretary general Visser 't Hooft declared: 'The acceptance of this decree on ecumenism creates an entirely new situation. The Roman Catholic Church no longer stands apart.' On the last day of the meeting plans are made for a joint 'working group' to study principles and methods of cooperation with the Catholic Church.

JANUARY 13, 1965 The liturgical commission publishes practical directives for the so-called 'prayer of believers' to be used at Mass and on other occasions.

JANUARY 20, 1965 During a general audience, Paul VI issues directives for an *honorable* ecumenical dialogue. Only a superficial person would believe that reunification could be accomplished rapidly and easily. The attempt to minimize doctrinal differences by watering down final statements of the magisterium or ignoring them, is no help to the cause of reunification.

JANUARY 25—30, 1965 The Council's commission for the lay apostolate discusses Schema 13 (the Church in the contemporary world). A special commission is appointed to handle this subject.

FEBRUARY 1—13, 1965 The subcommission responsible for working out schema 13 meets. Its president is Bishop Guano, its vice-president Bishop Ancel. Twenty-nine clergy and six lay people, including four women, attend. The version is to be prepared by the following: the canonist Haubtmann, Father Riedmatten, O.P., Msgrs. Philipps and Moeller, Fathers Tucci, S.J., and Hirschmann, S.J.

FEBRUARY 15, 1965 Metropolitans Meliton of Heliopolis and Chrysostomos of Myra, official delegates of Ecumenical Patriarch Athenagoras of Constantinople, present to the Pope the proceedings of the Third Pan-Orthodox Conference of Rhodes (held in November 1964).

FEBRUARY 18, 1965   Cardinal Bea conveys to the World Council of Churches, meeting in Geneva, the Pope's approval of the 'mixed committee'. The objective of the committee is not to make decisions but to 'sound out' approaches to genuine dialogue and the possibility of cooperation.

FEBRUARY 22, 1965   The Pope names 27 new cardinals. He gives the following principles of selection: (1) the need to consider the variety and remoteness of the particular countries; (2) the need for visible variety in the Church's leadership, dictating the choice of some Eastern patriarchs; (3) the need to especially honor representatives of the suffering Church (in Communist States); (4) the need to underline the pastoral character of the College of Cardinals by singling out the most important dioceses; (5) the need to recognize the loyalty of the Roman Curia; (6) the need to have men especially expert in theology or in pastoral work place their experience at the service of the college. In general the idea is to represent the universality of the Church in various ways. Does this constitute a beginning of the synod of bishops working together with the Pope, called for by many fathers?

MARCH 7, 1965   The reform of the liturgy (ordered by the new liturgical commission in its instruction of September 26, 1964) takes effect.

MARCH 12, 1965   The CATHOLIC HERALD (of London) publishes a letter from Msgr. Vagnozzi (the Apostolic Delegate to the United States) in which he criticizes 'certain excesses' in joint religious gatherings of Catholics and non-Catholics. He says that people should wait until the Council commission has published its definitive rules on joint religious worship. But the bishops of New Zealand have already decided to regulate this matter themselves.

MARCH 17—22, 1965   Two congresses on Mary, one of the theologians and one a public congress, meet in Santo Domingo. Their aim is to work out the place of Mary in scripture and to implement the chapter on Mary contained in Vatican II's Constitution on the Church.

MARCH 19, 1965   The Pope, in a talk to workers, speaks of the limits of dialogue with Marxists: 'The dialogue cannot be a tactical maneuver—this would be a trap; Catholics cannot make concessions at the cost of their principles.'

MARCH 27, 1965   Pope Paul addresses the special papal commission for the study of birth control, at the opening of their fourth work session. Archbishop Binz (United States) is in charge of the plenary meeting of the commission; Father Riedmatten, O.P., is general secretary. Lay people are in the majority on the commission. Three married couples are included. Some members' names are known: the Redemptorist Häring, the Jesuit Fuchs (Gregorian University), Canon Janssens (Louvain), Nalesso (Milan), Msgr. Lambruschini (Lateran University), and the psychiatrists Ibar (Spain), Cavanagh, and Ayd (United States) and the gynecologist Helligers (United States).

MARCH 28—April 1, 1965   An unofficial conference of about 25 experts, including Roman Catholic theologians and sociologists from the Roman Catholic Church and the World Council of Churches, meet to discuss problems in the schema ON THE CHURCH IN THE CONTEMPORARY WORLD.

MARCH 29—APRIL 8, 1965   The Council subcommissions are meeting again on Schema 13. Canon Haubtmann's plan is now definitely accepted. A plan worked out by the Poles and presented by Bishop Wojtyla does not win majority approval. The Council commission on missionary activity, and that on clergy and people, meet during the same period. The first commission is working out an ambitious new schema; the second is considering additions to the schema on bishops. The rest of the work is consigned to the commission for renovation of canon law.

APRIL 3, 1965   A papal delegation visits Patriarch Athenagoras of Constantinople, reciprocating the visit of the Orthodox delegation on February 15.

APRIL 8, 1965   A secretariat for non-believers is created by the Pope. Dialogue with atheists will also be initiated. Cardinal König of Vienna is president and the secretary is Father Miano, dean of the philosophical faculty of the Salesian University in Rome.

APRIL 9, 1965   Through the intercession of Cardinal Alfrink, charges brought by the Holy Office against the reputation of the Dutch theologian, Anna Terruwe, are dropped. The trouble had resulted from a condemnation of eight points of doctrine falsely attributed to her, and because of the dismissal of a professor of moral theology at Nijmegen who had been her advisor.

APRIL 18, 1965   The Pope in his Easter message emphasizes the problems the fourth session of the Council will consider—peace, hunger, racism, and freedom of conscience.

APRIL 24, 1965   On their way to a Holy Land pilgrimage, the Anglican bishop Mortimer (Oxford) visits the Pope along with 350 pilgrims, mostly Anglicans. On the same day, the Anglican bishop of Crediton is also received by the Pope. Three days later the Anglican bishop Tomkins (Bristol) spends time with the Pope. He is the president of the Faith and Order Conference of the World Council of Churches.

APRIL 26—MAY 4, 1965   The Council's commission for seminaries completes the revision of its text on the formation of priests.

APRIL 27, 1965   A Dutch pastoral letter on good and harmful aspects of liturgical reform and new interpretations of the Eucharist.

APRIL 27—MAY 4, 1965   The commission on religious orders reworks its draft, turning it into an impressive schema.

APRIL 29, 1965 Encyclical letter, MENSE MAIO ('In the Month of May'). The bishops are asked to pray for the success of the Council.

MAY 7, 1965 The Pope receives the Jesuits who have gathered to elect a new general for their order. The problem of atheism is the problem that most occupies him at the moment, and he asks the order to make a special study of this issue.

MAY 11—12, 1965 The Council Coordinating Commission meets with its secretary, Felici, and subsecretaries. Msgr. Le Cordier (Paris) replaces Msgr. Villot, who has been named a cardinal. Schema 13 and the text on the missions still present problems. However, a calendar for the final session is worked out.

MAY 22—24, 1965 The mixed commission of World Council and Catholic representatives, initiated in Enugu, Nigeria, in January, meets in Geneva for the first time. Among the participants are the following: from the World Council, Vitaly Borovoi, Edwin Espy (American Baptist), Nicos Nissiotis (layman), Edmund Schlink (Germany), Oliver Tomkins (Anglican bishop), Paul Verghese (Syrian Orthodox), Lukas Vischer (Reformed), and W. A. Visser 't Hooft. From the Catholic Church, Msgr. Holland (England), Msgr. Willibrands (titular bishop), Msgr. William Baum (United States), Msgr. Karl Byer (Caritas International), Father Pierre Duprey (White Fathers), and Jerome Hamer, O.P.

JUNE 12, 1965 Five texts prepared by the commissions for the fourth session are dispatched to the fathers of the Council.

JUNE 24, 1965 The Pope addresses the College of Cardinals on his name day. He is clearly concerned about 'unrest' in the world: 'The world plunges ahead, the little bark of Peter is crossing a stormy sea, everything is in motion, everything stirred up. You are well aware of this.' The question of mixed marriages needs 'further study'. On the subject of birth control, the Pope says: 'We hope to be able to make some kind of declaration on this soon. . . . We pray the Lord for the light of his wisdom on this vitally important topic.'

JUNE 30, 1965 Cardinal Lercaro, president of the liturgical commission, writes to Cardinal Siri, president of the Italian bishops' conference, describing the work of the commission. He says among other things: 'For the last fifteen months, the liturgical commission has been busy with its forty study groups made up of experts, as well as with the forty-three bishops who form the heart of this enterprise.'

JULY 10, 1965 Cardinal Shehan (Baltimore) takes the place of the late Cardinal Meyer of Chicago as member of the Council praesidium.

JULY 15, 1965 The Secretariat for Christian Unity announces the formation of a mixed study group in conjunction with the Lutheran World Federation (53,000,000 members). Seven members from each group will study together the possibilities of cooperation. The Catholic

side is represented by Volk, Willibrands, Baum (United States), Blaeser (Paderborn), Witte (Rome), Martensen (Copenhagen), Congar (Strasbourg). The Lutherans are represented by Dietzfelbinger (Munich), Brauer (Chicago), Skydsgaard (Copenhagen), Quanbeck (United States), Vatja (Strasbourg), Schmidt-Clausen and Mau (both of Geneva).

AUGUST 25—27, 1965 The members of the mixed working group of the Catholic Church and Lutheran World Federation meet for the first time.

SEPTEMBER 3, 1965 Encyclical letter MYSTERIUM FIDEI (Mystery of Faith). Addressed especially, but not exclusively, to the Dutch, this encyclical warns of exaggerated theological conclusions drawn from the reform of the liturgy. The reform of the liturgy has obviously not been a complete waste!

SEPTEMBER 12, 1965 Pope Paul VI returns from Castel Gandolfo for the opening of the fourth session of the Council. He makes a visit to the catacombs to demonstrate, as he says in his talk, that he will obviously not refuse to give his help and support to 'the Church of Silence', but that he nevertheless does not consider it appropriate to make a new condemnation of Communism, and that he will not stop trying to pursue an honest dialogue with Communist countries.

The Fourth Session

SEPTEMBER 14, 1965 Solemn opening of the last session of the Council. Pope Paul's speech is a kind of personal revelation of his thoughts on the Council's problems, which he believes can only be solved through love. 'A person only really knows a thing if he loves it.' He urges the fathers not to forget this during their debates.

SEPTEMBER 15, 1965 In a directive Pope Paul establishes a synod of bishops. The majority of members are to be drawn from bishops' conferences. It is up to the Pope to convoke the synod and to select its theme. Besides the synod, which deals with the problems of the Church as a whole, he also envisions 'regional' synods which will deal with problems pertinent to a specific continent. In addition to these synods dealing with general problems, there will also be special synods to deal with special problems. The statutes of the synod are very elastic—as a matter of fact, intentionally vague, so that the way is not closed to future development.

SEPTEMBER 16—22, 1965 Debate on the text ON RELIGIOUS LIBERTY. The controversial issues remain just about the same. But everyone wants a declaration, and almost all are ready for a statement of *principle*. Here, however, comes the first point of disagreement: The text has the right of freedom based on man's objective dignity, but many speakers do not want to go beyond a positive juridical conception of freedom, based on 'tolerance'. They cite the teaching of 18th and 19th century popes. (So argue Siri, Ruffini, Morcillo, Ottaviani, Velasco, Gabarri, Lefebre and Dante.) But they are answered by others (Urbani, Shehan, Hallinan) who argue that the teaching of the popes clearly shows development. The text contains two lines of argument: one based on natural law and another on scripture. But thinking is divided on this. Cardinal Frings declares that a Council has no business issuing a statement based on natural law. But Bishop Elchinger doesn't want an argument based on scripture. Any such argument seems to many completely and totally insufficient (Carli, Morcillo). Strong witnesses (Beran, Cardijn) move in to boost the stock of religious freedom. But others only deflate it. Finally Cardinal Journet (probably at the behest of the Pope) smooths over the situation with a carefully balanced intervention.

The fathers vote on the prodigious formula, 'Do the Fathers approve for completion the newly revised text as a basis for a final declaration, as being in conformity with Catholic teaching on true religion, and as reflecting the suggestions for improvement made in Council discussion, and as a text to be approved according to the regulations for the Council agenda?' The declaration is accepted with 1997 yes votes against 224 no votes.

SEPTEMBER 20—22, 1965 The first of a series of votes on the schema on revelation. What is significant in the improvements offered here will emerge in the next series of votes, dealing with suggestions for improvement. The 'improvements', whose intent is to change the substance of the text, have to be rejected by the commission: The text has already been accepted in its basic outlines.

SEPTEMBER 22—23, 1965 The revised text on the schema on Church and world comes up for debate. It begins with a kind of sociological report on the hopes and anxieties of contemporary man. Two main sections follow. The first is a four-chapter theoretical treatment, developing first a kind of teaching on man as an individual and man in community; the focus then shifts to the work of man in the world; and finally (in the fourth chapter) to the work of the Church in this world. During the discussion of the anthropological part of this section, atheism also comes up for discussion. The five chapters of the second part deal with some critical problems in the contemporary world. Debate centers at first on whether the text can be accepted as a basis for discussion. No one is entirely opposed. Quite a few feel that sin has been dealt with superficially; the draft contains no theology of sin; the basic tenor is too optimistic (Siri, Döpfner, Vinney, Rusch, Shehan, Renard).

SEPTEMBER 23—28, 1965 Voting on the schema on lay people. Many bishops would like a completely new discussion of this text, arguing that the document had been totally reworked since its discussion last year (1964). But debate is not permitted because the bishops had received the revised text in early July. Therefore they had been given ample time to forward proposals for improvement, but had clearly neglected to do this.

What is particularly new is the rewriting of the theological foundation of the text and a section on lay spirituality. Most of the suggestions for improvement (there are 311 of them) apply to the third chapter which deals with the various fields of the apostolate. No chapter is rejected.

SEPTEMBER 27—28, 1965 Debate on the first main section of the schema on Church and world. Almost all the interest centers on the problem of atheism. Despite a stronger treatment of this theme, the draft meets general disapproval. Two tendencies are plainly evident. One group wants a more profound treatment of the roots of modern atheism and the cure for it (König, Seper). Others want a new condemnation of Marxism, not a condemnation of atheism alone (Ruotulo). Only a few criticize the statement as inadequate in its teaching on man (Garrone, Schick). Bishop Bengsch declares his opposition to the inductive approach of the whole first part. The German bishops seem to want a rearrangement of the plan, but the majority are not in favor of this.

SEPTEMBER 29—OCTOBER 1, 1965 Voting on improvements made in the schema ON THE PASTORAL OFFICE OF BISHOPS. Those reporting on the schema cite the following specific improvements. The desired reform of the Curia is extended to include expressly the papal nuncios. Their powers are to be limited, and an international point of view is to govern their selection. Diocesan boundaries are to be 'subject to review' by the bishops' conferences. Cathedral chapters are to be adjusted to 'present day requirements'. Besides old age, there are other 'grave reasons' why pastors should retire. Nuncios and papal legates are not automatically to be members of the bishops' conferences. Parts of the schema are accepted by an overwhelming majority. The vote on the entire text on bishops will take place on October 6, producing 2,167 yes votes and 14 no votes.

SEPTEMBER 29—OCTOBER 1, 1965 Debate on the first chapter of the second part of the schema on Church and world. The discussion brings out the old familiar counter-positions. Some are 'dismayed' that the text does not distinguish between the primary and secondary ends of marriage (Ruffini, Browne, Nicodomo), while others want the importance of married love still more strongly underscored (Léger, Urtasun, Reuss). The first party wants the express citation of the statements of Pius XI and Pius XII on forbidden means of contraception (Heenan, Da Silva, Conway), while the second party wants responsible parenthood emphasized and also wants more detailed treatment postponed until the results of the papal commission on the birth control problem are announced. Bishop Colombo, 'the pope's theologian', takes a position between the two sides.

OCTOBER 1—4, 1965 Debate on the proper development of culture (chapter 2). There is clearly a feeling that the Church is in a sense isolated from the cultural life of today. The French are especially disappointed with the text (Elchinger, Blanchet, Veuillot) and are anxious to promote a better understanding of historical science (Pellegrino, Blanchet). The role of woman in modern culture deserves greater attention (Frotz). To some the text appears excessively optimistic

(Veuillot, Spulbeck), and so Morcillo (Madrid) again proposes that the entire second part of the schema be left to post-conciliar commissions.

OCTOBER 4—5, 1965 The Pope visits the United Nations with a select group of international cardinals and gives a very significant address in support of the UN. Despite its difficulties, the UN holds much promise for the future. On October 5, Paul VI returns to Rome and goes directly to St. Peter's where the 142nd general congregation (daily session) is about to close. After a short address by the Pope, Cardinal Liénart moves that the UN speech be included among the official acts of the Council. This is approved by the fathers with enthusiastic applause.

OCTOBER 4—5, 1965 Meantime, debate proceeds on economic and social life and the life of the political community. The fathers greet the prepared text with rather sharp criticism. Some find it capitalistic in orientation (Bueno y Monreal). Others think it does not measure up to the standards of the papal social encyclicals; that it shows a naive faith in progress; that it pays too little attention to the importance of private property, exaggerating the possibility of employee participation in industry; that it equates work with the production of goods and overvalues 'planning' (Siri, Hengsbach, Höffner). Garcia says there is even a certain 'demagoguery' in the text. Another group of Council fathers regret the lack of concrete proposals to solve the problems of developing countries (Cardjin, Mahon, Eccheverria, Anoveros). Still others want more attention paid to agriculture (Matrelli, Castellano). In the face of such confusion, an increasing number of voices are heard in favor of a post-conciliar planning bureau. The discussion of political life is surprisingly dull and uninteresting.

OCTOBER 5—8, 1965 Debate on the community of nations and on peace. Many fathers want a stronger, more decisive condemnation of total war—indeed of any war (Alfrink, Butler, Wheeler and others want disarmament). But some argue that the possession of such armaments is necessary as a 'deterrent' (Beck, Castan). Some want the 'justification' of willingness for military service stricken from the record. Some (especially the French) would like to see Council give special approval to conscientious objection. Quite a number are interested in removing causes of war (Ottaviani, Liénart, Duval, Simons, Wheeler, Grant, Gaviola, Klepacz, Rupp and others). They see these causes as stemming from international social injustice, from history instruction which glorifies war, from the current population explosion, from hunger and racism. The need for a strong international authority is repeatedly stressed (Léger, Duval, Wheeler, Ottaviani, Goujon, Beck, Ancel). Some call for the creation of a central ecclesiastical agency for study and action on the problem of peace; a variety of names for such an agency is offered, such as a bureau for social justice (McCann), a bureau for international justice (Wheeler), a war cabinet (Grant), a central organization to work for peace (Brezanoczey).

OCTOBER 6—11, 1965 Voting on the schema ON THE RENEWAL OF RELIGIOUS LIFE. According to the report of Bishop Compagnone,

14,000 suggestions for improvement have been submitted since the original vote (November 15, 1964), which rejected paragraphs 1 to 13. The new text is drastically revised. It recommends among other things that all members of religious orders become aware of the condition of man in the contemporary world, not only of the needs of the Church. It also recommends that superiors consider the suggestions of their subordinates in the renewal of religious orders. All religious orders should understand the Church's service function; they should adjust to the needs of contemporary man; they should not shy away from new forms of poverty. Yet they should contribute collectively toward the alleviation of poverty; they should cultivate a conception of obedience befitting human dignity; they should minimize class distinctions within the individual orders. The vote produces almost unanimous approval on all points. So the final result (2,126 yes votes and 13 no votes) comes as no surprise.

OCTOBER 8—13, 1965 Debate on missionary activity. Many bishops find the text of the schema unsatisfactory in the way it explains the need of missions. Many think it too little in line with the decree on ecumenism and with proper procedure in dialogue with non-Christians (König, Alfrink, Degrijse). The difficulty of cooperation with mission institutes and young native churches is made clear (Zoungrana, Sobornana, Gahamanyi, Nujahaga and others). The text is deemed inadequate in the way it deals with the missionary activity of the people of God as a whole (Alfrink, Gonzalvez, McGrath, Corboy, Grotti). Only one bishop (Martin) expresses dissatisfaction with the formulation of the powers of the newly constituted commission on missions. For the first time the rest are aware that the text has been watered down.

OCTOBER 11—12, 1965 Voting on suggestions for improving the schema ON PRIESTLY FORMATION. This was already debated (November 12—17, 1964) and accepted in a first balloting. The new text on the responsibility of bishops and priests emphasizes more strongly the need to recruit 'vocations'. The responsibilities of seminary superiors are spelled out in great detail. Still greater emphasis is given to the need to develop strong and well-developed personalities—people who will make good pastors, meaning people who can talk to men of today and guide their spiritual development. On October 12, the schema as a whole is pronounced satisfactory. The total is 2,196 yes votes as against 15 no votes.

OCTOBER 11, 1965 A papal brief is read to the Council. The Pope says he understands that during the pending debate on priestly life some fathers intend to discuss the obligation to celibacy in the Latin Church. Without wishing to curtail the Council's freedom on this matter, he wants to express his own opinion. He would consider a public debate on celibacy out of order. He wants to strengthen the traditional law. But if some wish to express an opposite view they should do so in a written communication addressed to the praesidium. The Pope promises 'to examine such communications before God and with the greatest conscientiousness'.

OCTOBER 13—14, 1965 Voting on improvements for the text on Christian education. The text has been considerably expanded. According to the report of Bishop Daem, the declaration confines itself to general outlines, in view of greatly varying situations throughout the world; practical applications are left to regional conferences of bishops. More no votes (between 75 and 132) appear than in the case of other recent texts. Voting on the text as a whole—time pressures have cut discussion short—results in acceptance, with 1912 yes and 183 no votes.

OCTOBER 14—15, 1965 Balloting on improvements for the Declaration on Non-Christian Religions. The commission reflects the suggestions of one group (of about 250) who want to establish the guilt of all Jews in the death of Christ. The voting reaches a relatively high total of negative votes: One statement—'the Jews must not be presented as rejected by God or as accursed'—is rejected by 245 fathers. Final voting on the text as a whole produces 2,023 votes; of these 1,763 are yes votes and 250 are no votes, with 10 null ballots. Many think the Pope, in order to obtain greater unanimity, will order a further watering-down of the text, but actually he will not.

OCTOBER 15—26, 1965 Debate on Priestly Ministry and Life. A very lengthy discussion reveals two tendencies. The first group (Döpfner, Léger, and others) is satisfied with the text, because it does not view priests in a purely ritual light and does stress priestly service. But the other group think the draft too 'superficial'. They want everything centered on the priest's sacramental function (Shehan, Richaud, Charue, d'Avac). There is much talk—especially in connection with obedience—of a spirituality suited to the priest in the world, to be worked out in line with biblical counsels. Notwithstanding the Pope's caution, Döpfner and Bea touch on the problem of the celibacy obligation in the Western priesthood. Despite many objections, and even before debate is completed, the text is approved by the fathers with 1,507 yes votes against 2 no votes. The total of votes is comparatively small: Many fathers have already left the Council.

OCTOBER 17—24, 1965 No voting takes place.

OCTOBER 26—27, 1965 Voting begins on the religious liberty declaration. The text is considerably revised. The declaration opens with a section asserting that revealed truth has been entrusted to the Church by Jesus Christ. All men are bound to search for God and his Church, and to confess the truth when they see it. There is no contradiction between recent and earlier popes, so the Council can simply follow the line of recent popes to its logical conclusion. Specifics are worked out in terms of human dignity. The section on scripture has been thoroughly reworked. The basic theme has been stated more clearly, and now deals only with civil and legal liberty. And so the step beyond Pius XII's declaration on tolerance has finally been made, despite attempts at compromise. Of course the opposition party remains the same. Negative votes on individual paragraphs average about 200. On four questions concerning improvements of larger passages,

reserved ('yes-but') votes vary from 543 to 307. But none of the texts is rejected. There is great rejoicing among the bishops and lobbyists. But what about the Pope? He wants—he must want—the greatest possible unanimity. What will he do?

OCTOBER 28, 1965 In a public congregation, five documents are solemnly approved by the Pope and bishops. (1) The decree On the Pastoral Office of Bishops: 2,319 yes votes, 2 no votes, 1 null ballot. (2) The decree On the Contemporary Renewal of Religious Orders: 2,321 yes votes, 4 no votes. (3) The decree On Priestly Formation: 2,318 yes votes, 3 no votes. (4) The Declaration on Christian Education: 2,290 yes votes, 35 no votes. (5) The Declaration on Non-Christian Religions: 2,221 yes votes, 88 no votes.

OCTOBER 29, 1965 Voting on suggestions for the improvement of the schema on revelation. The substance of the disagreement centered on three points: (1) the relationship between scripture and tradition; (2) the kind of inspiration found in Holy Scripture; (3) the historicity of the gospels. The commission has been under considerable pressure from a powerful group of bishops who are trying to use papal influence to change the treatment of these three points. The Pope has passed along the commission's request and has added his own choice of possible formulations. The commission has very skillfully solved the problem of all three points in a way that leaves the door open on those questions disputed among contemporary Catholic scripture scholars and theologians. The text clearly states the minimum teaching held in common by all. The relationship between scripture and tradition receives the highest total of no votes: 55. A vote on the text as a whole follows with 2,081 yes and 27 no votes.

OCTOBER 30—NOVEMBER 8, 1965 Once again there is a period with no daily general congregations. The Pope decides on a procedure to fill the time gap between balloting. He asks the presidents of the bishop's conferences to submit memoranda on proposed papal decrees dealing with certain disciplinary questions that could later be formulated by Roman congregations. The first proposal deals with new regulations on fast and abstinence. The recommendations prepared by the bishops and submitted to the Pope during the first week of vacation (October 17—24) turn out to be quite negative. For example, the collective episcopate of the United States says the new regulations are trivial. Unless modified, they would be entirely out of keeping with the needs of the times. These answers seem hardly appropriate for public consumption, so the Pope turns immediately to the second question—a new regulation on indulgences. Cardinal Journet forecasts basic general agreement on this.

NOVEMBER 9, 1965 The suggestions for improvement on the text On the Lay Apostolate come to a vote. Numerous small modifications have been worked out. There is almost complete agreement on all parts of the whole schema which is approved by a total of 2,201 yes votes and only 2 no votes.
On the same day, during the intervals between six votes, Cardinal

Cento reads a declaration on new regulations on indulgences and Msgr. Sessolo gives a three-part reading of the document. The key to the changes lies in a radical simplification so the 'inflation' of indulgences will be minimized.

NOVEMBER 10—11, 1965   The debate on the missionary schema, which has been going on since October 13, is submitted to a first balloting. The recommendations expressed at this time are largely reflected in the text. Especially noteworthy is the detailed treatment of local churches as well as the expanded statement on ecumenical problems which the Council observers had hoped for. Despite some resistance, the schema is accepted. Only the fifth chapter, dealing with the proposed commission on missions, to be established by the Pope, receives 712 reserved votes (votes with suggestions for improvements). The first request of the fathers is that the bishops' conferences be consulted on the membership of this commission; the second, that meetings of the commission be held at regular intervals to make decisions by deliberative balloting.

At the same time, during the voting intermissions, representatives of bishops' conferences speak on the reform of indulgences. The first is Cardinal Patriarch Maximos IV. He emphasizes that the 'calculated balancing' of intercessory prayer against the remission of punishment due to sin had no theological basis whatever, and therefore should be completely dropped. But this is precisely what the project does not provide for. After various other opinions have been heard, Cardinals König and Döpfner speak for Austria and Germany. Without totally rejecting the system of indulgences, they nevertheless submit it to a historical and theological criticism which concludes that any 'measuring' of punishment due to individual sins, and of the remission of this punishment, is inadmissible. The fathers and the observers respond with prolonged applause. No other bishop is permitted to express his opinion. The experiment is cut short with the explanation that expressions of opinion take too much of the time needed for voting; yet the planned revision of indulgences appears to be temporarily shelved.

NOVEMBER 12—13, 1965   First vote on the schema ON PRIESTLY LIFE AND MINISTRY. The new text is sharper in outline. The commission has tried to harmonize the two views on priestly life which have predominated during the debate. It has also worked out more clearly the relationship between practical responsibilities and priestly holiness. The role of the priest in the world defines the way in which his spiritual perfection is linked to his three-fold office. On the question of celibacy, the Pope himself has suggested a special section on Eastern Churches which would prevent downgrading of married priests. Nevertheless, the reserved votes—suggesting improvements—reach a high total (568, 95, 630, 544).

NOVEMBER 15—17, 1965   The schema on the Church in the contemporary world, revised in line with a previous debate, goes through 33 individuals ballotings. The improvements deal especially with the text on anthropology in which the attempt was made to reinterpret the theology of sin. In regard to atheism, a new commission has been formed under the direction of Cardinal König. On the commission are names like Seper (Yugoslavia), De Lubac and Daniélou (France), and Bishop Kominek (Poland). They have, in fact, succeeded in working out a very well-balanced three-paragraph text. The language of the text on marriage is much clearer. Married love and its significance is presented without equivocation. On the question of atomic war, the extremely detailed distinctions have been eliminated. The same thing is true of the section on legal justification of military service. Conscientious objection to military service is treated with greater understanding. On the whole, there is growing disapproval of nuclear and other warfare. As a result, this chapter draws the highest number of reserve votes (523). In the chapter on marriage, the section on procreation in marriage receives 140 no votes, while the chapter as a whole receives 484 reserve votes. The first main section on atheism receives only 74 no votes, and the first chapter as a whole draws 453 reserve votes. The chapter containing the second principal section on culture receives gentlest treatment: only 185 fathers submit recommendations for improvement.

NOVEMBER 18, 1965   In a public congregation two schemata are approved and promulgated by Pope and bishops: (1) The Decree ON THE LAY APOSTOLATE: 2,340 yes and 2 no votes; (2) the dogmatic constitution ON DIVINE REVELATION: 2,344 yes votes and 6 no votes.

NOVEMBER 19, 1965   Suggestions for improvement in the DECLARATION ON RELIGIOUS FREEDOM are voted on. Despite heavy attacks, pamphleteering and various proposals, neither the commission (the Secretariat for Christian Unity) nor the Pope have been persuaded to make further concessions. Balloting on the text as a whole produces 1,954 yes votes, 249 no votes and 13 void ballots. It is obvious an influential Council group considers the text a failure.

NOVEMBER 20—29, 1965   Interval. Proposals for improvement still have to be worked into the three final texts.

NOVEMBER 30, 1965   Voting on improvements in the mission schema proceeds. The section referring to ecumenical spirit has not been watered down, as 58 fathers had requested. Changes in the passage on the new central authority have been made in line with suggestions. A new attempt has been made to reformulate the real essence of missions. Everything is accepted almost unanimously. The vote on the text as a whole produces 2,162 yes and 18 no votes.

DECEMBER 2, 1965   Voting on the improvements in the schema ON PRIESTLY LIFE AND MINISTRY continues. The result of the vote on the text as a whole is 2,243 yes, 11 no, and 3 invalid ballots.

Bishop Garrone reads a report on the schema ON THE CHURCH IN THE CONTEMPORARY WORLD. Supplementary last-minute petitions come from about 200 bishops demanding an explicit new condemnation of Communism. But the commission has not granted their request. And the Pope also has been pressured for a clearer statement on birth control. So the commission now cites the texts of Pius XI and Pius XII;

and it also cites Paul VI who is setting up a papal commission on the problem. This makes it impossible to take a more definite position on this issue. But there has been a certain weakening of the text on war due, especially, to the pressure from American bishops. A group of four Americans (Spellman, Shehan, O'Boyle and Cody), two Mexicans, the Australian Elyde Young, the Argentine Tortolo, the South African Hurley and a Marionite, circulate a statement which asks that the voting on September 4 reject the chapter on peace and the community of nations. The signatories take exception to the statement that any possession of 'scientific' weapons constitutes a cause of war.

DECEMBER 4, 1965 Twelve votes conclude the balloting on the improvements made in the schema ON THE CHURCH IN THE CONTEMPORARY WORLD. The no votes are still less than 110. The chapter on atheism receives 131 no votes; the chapter on marriage, 155; the chapter on freedom, 483. The schema as a whole is approved with 2,111 yes votes against 251 no votes and 11 invalid ballots.
During the afternoon the Pope, the bishops and non-Catholic Christian observers meet in the Church of St. Paul Outside the Walls for a common prayer service, in which representative observers take an active part by reading passages from scripture. Even English hymns are sung. The Pope delivers a long address.

DECEMBER 7, 1965 Solemn 'public congregation'. The last four documents are promulgated by the Pope and bishops: (1) the DECLARATION ON RELIGIOUS LIBERTY: 2,308 yes, 70 no, 8 null; (2) the decree ON MISSIONARY ACTIVITY: 2,394 yes, 5 no; (4) the decree ON PRIESTLY LIFE AND MINISTRY: 2,390 yes, 75 no, 7 null.
In an apostolic brief the Pope deplores all the dissension and hatred which led to the excommunication of Patriarch Michael of Constantinople in the year 1054, and which Michael answered with an excommunication of the Pope. The Pope deletes the excommunication 'from the memory of the Church', and with an embrace, presents the brief to Metropolitan Meliton, delegate of Patriarch Athenagoras. Meanwhile in Constantinople, Athenagoras issues a statement in which he cancels the excommunication of Pope Leo IX. A joint declaration is then read in both places to explain the meaning of these proceedings. This is not as yet an act of reunion, but an act of 'purification of hearts' which should serve as a first step toward rapprochement. The Pope gives an address—perhaps his most important one. He deals with the Church's concern to serve man in all his problems.

DECEMBER 8, 1965 Ceremonial closing of the Council. Various cardinals address Council messages to rulers, scientists, artists, women, workers, the sick and suffering, and to young people. The Pope himself hands these messages to representatives of each group. After a short speech, Pope Paul in a brief officially closes the Council. He says that this Council has tried to consider the needs of the times, especially by giving attention to pastoral problems, and to 'nourish the flame of love by endeavoring to meet with Christians still separated from communion with the apostolic see—in fact to meet the whole human family in a spirit of brotherhood.'

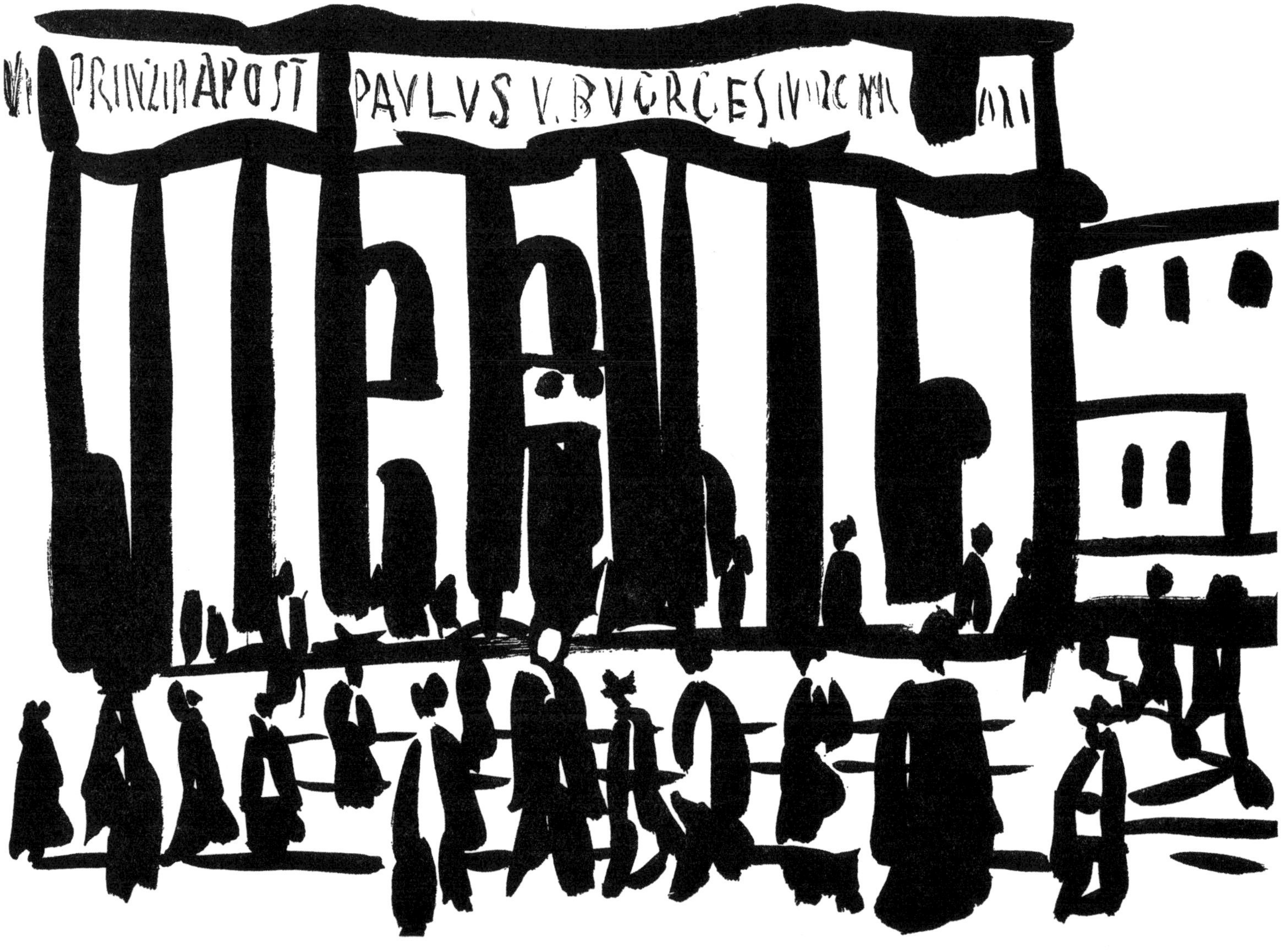
PRINZIPAPOST
PAVLVS V.

Three trends of the Council:

From a law-centered to a life-centered Church
From defensiveness to dialogue
From fixed ideas to historical change

Drawing: On St. Peter's Square

So it is that this messianic people—although it does not actually include all men, and may very often look like a small flock—is nonetheless the indestructible seed of unity, hope and salvation for all mankind.

(Dogmatic Constitution on the Church, ch. 2: 'The People of God')

What follows is not a history of the Second Vatican Council. That history with its dizzying twists and turns is told in the Council Chronicle.

Plan or Spirit

We know that some readers now expect that in orderly and tidy fashion we will discuss the sixteen texts which the Council promulgated. That would of course be a possibility. But the argument against it is that, while there is a certain logic in the way these documents are linked, they are really not logically connected: not all of them follow a Council plan.

When the text on the liturgy came under discussion there was yet no overall plan. Nor can it be claimed that later developments grew logically out of a plan. This becomes even more obvious when we examine the document on revelation. This text met with bitter opposition during the first session. (At the time it was still titled 'Draft on the Sources of Revelation'.) Pope John XXIII had it struck from the agenda. Many (including the theologian Karl Rahner) then felt that it had been removed once and for all, and that this Council would have nothing more to do with it. We agreed, because it did not really seem to fit into the 'plan' put forward at the end of the first session. These are two of the most significant Council documents, but neither fits into an overall picture. Then there is the decree on communication, which we can read today only with the embarrassed smile of a poet leafing through one of his

very early works. Anyway, there is nothing in the decree directly related to a plan of the Council.

Even if we examine the official 'plan', some things are still not easy to explain. The plan places the constitution on the Church (DE ECCLESIA) squarely in the center. Everything else is supposed to be a kind of practical application of that central document.

In part this is true. The decree on the bishops extends into practice the third chapter of DE ECCLESIA, which presents the Council's theology of bishops. The decree on the lay apostolate points up the realistic consequences of the doctrine on lay people in chapter four of the Church text. The decree on renewal of religious orders puts the principles of religious life (set forth in chapter six) into practice.

The decree on priestly ministry is an extension of the paragraphs in the constitution on priests. Yet the decree is not merely a practical application but actually a kind of correction, since the treatment in the constitution is so jejune, and does not really correspond to the 'spirit of the Council'. The bishops tried in the most varied ways to correct this. A 'message' was prepared and then withdrawn. A second effort met the same unhappy fate. Then many saw the solution in some kind of pastoral letter issued by the Council. This idea also was abandoned. Eventually came this 'decree', which is much more, really, than a disciplinary, practical decree. Much the same thing can be said of the decree on ecumenism. Undoubtedly it is related, like the declaration on non-Christian religions, to paragraphs in the constitution on the Church. But both of these decrees go beyond the constitution's paragraphs, and beyond them in doctrinal content. They simply cannot be dismissed as mere 'practical applications'.

Finally, the decree on the missions has far greater significance than the plan seems to permit. Here again the plan envisioned the constitution as an adequate outline, needing only the complement of a few practical 'guidelines.' But the spirit of the Council broke the bonds of the plan.

The minor documents on the training of priests and on Christian education do partially develop the constitution's themes of priests and lay people, but the declaration on religious freedom wrecks the plan entirely. It does fit in naturally with the decree on ecumenism but it really goes beyond it. It is certainly not a disciplinary text. So it was no surprise that the fathers argued back and forth where it should fit in: in the text on the Church or in the text on Church and World? Finally it became an independent 'parallel' document, after being detached (more by accident than by design) from the decree on ecumenism.

Finally—contrary to all logic and custom—comes the constitution on the Church in the World. How does this unprecedented document tie in with the constitution on the Church? Oh, but they talked and talked about that at the Council! 'Chapter two', some said. 'Maybe it's supposed to develop the schema on non-Christian religions?' the others asked in return. As if the problem of the Church in the world would not be exactly the same if all men were Christians! How about connecting it with the paragraph on the missionary character of the Church? Obviously the Church in the world had something to do with missions. The con-stitution on the Church says that through the Church's work 'whatever good is in the minds and hearts of men, whatever good is latent in the religious practices and cultures of different peoples, is not only saved from ruin but also cleansed, raised up and perfected.' There are similar, almost identical statements in the text on the Church in the World. Nevertheless, the focus there is somewhat different.

So others claim that the schema on the Church in the World belongs with the chapter on lay people: After all, the commission on the laity excused the incompleteness of its text by claiming that it thought lay people were to be treated in the text on the Church in the World. And surely lay people are 'secular', if anyone is. We might say that lay people *are* the world. But it makes a great difference whether we speak of the lay person *in* the Church and *in* the world, or lay people *as* the Church and *as* the world.

Yet another group wanted the Church and World text coordinated with chapter seven of DE ECCLESIA, which deals with the eschatological ('end-times') aspect of the Church. Certainly: At the end of time there will no longer be any difference between the world and the Church—not only because the world passes away, while the Church remains, but because the world, which until now 'has been groaning in travail', will then be 're-newed'. No doubt this is one way of looking at the Church and World text: That the Church is 'in the world without being of the world' is now—in this time of pilgrimage—an essential feature of the Church.

The Church cannot be conceived except as 'in the world', and so the text on Church and World seems a kind of ninth chapter of, better, a *second part* or the constitution on the Church, balancing the first eight chapters, which form *part one*.

This rapid review of all the schemata of the Council makes it clear that the division of the Council's achievements text by text cannot bring its particular genius to the fore. The 'plan' wasn't the 'soul' of the Council, not its guiding light. A real plan should have been developed. Before he became pope, Cardinal Montini rather pointedly criticized the absence of a plan. But contemplating with hindsight one may well exclaim: What luck! A plan should have been made, but what was even more important was the all-pervading 'spirit' of the Council. Born during the first session, this spirit pervaded all the texts, sometimes shattering the plan, sometimes throwing it into confusion. The plan naturally defended itself. Had the spirit not been born first, perhaps the plan would have swallowed it up. But there stood the texts fathered by that free spirit—the text on the liturgy, the outlines of texts on the Jews and on religious freedom, and the 'message of the bishops to the world'. They were there. They could not be stricken from the record, nor could they be left standing like primeval rocks. And so the spirit triumphed. It overcame the plan, pressed it into service, permeated all its parts—some more, others less—and whenever the plan ran too confining a course, the uninhibited spirit ran over the banks. This drama, which the press took little notice of, was far more interesting and exciting than the struggle between progressives and conservatives. This latter struggle was, and remains, very real. Furthermore, the drama and the struggle partially over-lapped; but by no means entirely, nor in every instance. More on this later. Here it will suffice to explain why this book does not follow a text-by-text pattern, but wants to point out the Council's fundamental spirit.

What was changed by the Council is interesting today *and* tomorrow. But the principal change was this of the spirit. From it come practical changes, which will be followed by more. It is not important to know how many. There will be a lot. Nobody will count them. It seems strange where some people focus only on concrete, if overdue, reforms. Obviously not everything has happened yet that ought to. But it is certain that without a preliminary conversion of the spirit, the consequences of the Council might only have been confusion. Given this transformation of the spirit, however, concrete reforms will come, sooner or later. They will come.

One example: mixed marriage reform. If a generous reform in this area had been decided upon without a renewal of spirit—'conversion' is the word used in the decree on ecumenism—then a kind of mediocrity and indifferentism would have been the almost inevitable result. But once a genuine and profound ecumenical spirit has established itself, deeper Christianity rather than compromise can be expected to follow. This reform should and is being gradually worked out. We want to speak first about this spirit. This won't make things clearer, but it will help keep the essential from getting lost.

The Pope and the Spirit of the Council

We do not want to disagree with the many Council theologians (Hirschmann, Küng, Congar, and others) who at the end of session four warned against the horrible oversimplification of all the attempts to package the whole Council under one label or motto, saying, for example, that it was 'an opening to the world', or 'charismatic rather than juridical', or 'ecumenical', and so on. Even Paul VI, whose mind has a systematic bent, finally gave up the idea of finding a single comprehensive motto. From his coronation to the end of the second session, Paul had such a motto in mind. It recurs in many of his addresses and is a motif of his first encyclical: it was 'dialogue'.

Then his attention is diverted due to powerful pressure from his former Curia associates. They feel that the projected teaching on the bishops and the episcopal college would compromise or even undermine papal primacy and infallibility. There are at the same time difficulties in the dialogue, and danger in other areas. Here and there the liturgical enthusiasts are giving the prescribed rules for the conduct of services rather cavalier treatment. There is friction between bishops and priests. The Pope now speaks of contemporary 'crisis of obedience'. Italian Communists especially seize upon the word 'dialogue' with enthusiasm and use it for their own political ends. Now the Pope's theme is the 'limits of the dialogue'. He never quite gives up on the word 'dialogue' but it begins to be slightly uncomfortable to him.

For a while it seems that he is under a spell, so preoccupied is he with the question of the bishops: 'This Council will undoubtedly go down in history as a complement to Vatican I. While the earlier Council formulated the pope's role, this present Council will indicate the scope and dignity of the office of bishop.' He speaks in this vein at the beginning of the third session and on many other occasions. He does not deny that there are many other questions for the Council to examine, but he mentions them only casually.

Again the scene changes. The Pope is worried about the troubles of the times, especially atheism. How is the Church to survive in this unprecedented situation in which atheism is the air everyone breathes? So 'openness to the world' becomes the focus of his thoughts. With prudence and circumspection but also with remarkable resolution, he begins to guide the Council. Due in no small measure to his efforts, the declaration on religious liberty emerges intact from the labyrinth of votes and opinions.

Against the wishes of a grumbling Curia he visits the United Nations. The world—this unbelieving world, which achieves such greatness yet suffers and is in such danger—this now appears to be the most important theme of the Council. It is Pope Paul who eventually speeds the action on Schema 13, especially in the period between the third and fourth sessions. Without his special assistance the members of the commission would hardly have lasted through the final weeks. This important text could easily have been split up into one or more small declarations; the Council might have got away with a few harmless generalities. Paul VI did not want this.

A rereading of his closing address shows clearly that the Council's main theme now (December 7, 1965) seems to him to be 'man as he really is'. He distinguishes clearly between two principal and intimately interrelated aims. The Church is seeking, first of all, to know itself better in order to better understand 'God's plan for the Church and His presence in her'. This first aim is a prerequisite for the second—the Church in today's world. And how does Paul VI see the world of today? 'A time in which forgetfulness of God has become habitual and seems apparently to be demanded by scientific progress . . . a time marked by upheavals and a hitherto unknown decline in the great world religions. It was at such a time as this that our Council was held.' The Council seems, says Pope Paul, almost like an act in 'defiance of the charge of anachronism and irrelevance levelled at the Church by the world.

But what was the Council's answer? It was first of all the study of the modern world, the taking of it seriously. 'Never before, perhaps, has the Church so strongly felt the need to become acquainted with the society in which she lives—to draw near to it, to understand it, to penetrate it, to serve it and bring to it the message of the gospel; to come to grips with society; to run after it, almost, in its rapid and continuous change . . . so much so that some have been inclined to suspect (the Council) of an excessive responsiveness to the world, to passing events, cultural fashions . . . at the expense of fidelity to tradition and to the detriment of religious goals. . . .' The Pope, however, does not find the reproach justified. 'Whoever does not love his brother, whom he has seen, what love can he have for the God he has never seen?' He stresses, moreover, that the Church, in trying to approach modern man, has struggled to achieve an attitude of service: 'All this rich teaching is channeled in one direction—the service of mankind.' In order to know God, he says, we must understand man.

I have followed the words of the Pope closely, so that no one can say I am giving a purely subjective and one-sided interpretation. After all, he is the man most qualified to comment on the Council and its spirit.

The Meaning of the Spirit of the Council

Let me try now to describe in my own words the spirit of the Council. It cannot be captured in a single catchphrase. Yet it is untrue to say that the Council was swayed by separate and unrelated currents. Rather, the various tendencies joined together from the first, distinctively different yet interwoven like the strands of a rope—each one separately visible and detachable, but all reinforcing one another.

It was not necessary that all the bishops always shared equally in weaving the fabric of the Council's spirit. For example, Cardinal Spellman was an energetic opponent of liturgical reform and at the same time was an advocate of the text on religious liberty. All in all, he was rather distrustful of this 'spirit of the Council'. Archbishop Hurley of Durban, South Africa, surely one of the most open-minded personalities at the Council, was wholly imbued with its spirit. His work on the commission for priestly training is responsible for most of the good beginnings made on the eventual decree on the seminaries. He was displeased with the efforts to minimize scholasticism, yet he took an especially positive stand on Teilhard de Chardin. In the debate on nuclear weapons toward the end of the Council he was one of the signers of the letter that nearly jettisoned the last chapter of the text on Church and World. Archbishop Parente, assessor of the Holy Office, fought very skillfully against the text on religious liberty. Though he was one of the most dangerous opponents of that text, he spoke on behalf of collegiality. He even acted as 'relator' for this text, defending it against Bishop Franic of Yugoslavia.

Many concluded that there never had been anything like a 'Council spirit'. Everything (they said) had been decided case by case, on the basis of what seemed best under the circumstances. It is true that this Council was not a battleground where closed theological systems waged war. Theological 'schools' still exist today if not perhaps as in the past. These 'schools' are, of course, all Catholic in their approach, but they differ radically in theories, positions and practical conclusions. But the Council moved on a much higher plane. It stayed clear of scholastic quarrels. In this it followed an ancient conciliar tradition. A council is supposed to present a doctrine of the whole Church without canonizing some particular school of Catholic thought. Time and again during the debates, one side would reproach the other for voicing 'party-line scholasticism'. This is how the 'two-source' theory of revelation got shot down in the first session. Bishop Carli used the same tactic against collegiality and religious liberty. It was also used by the bishops who tried to eliminate the chapter on war. But in no case was it ever that simple. A particular view

might at first be merely the opinion of an individual 'school'. But its acceptance depended upon broad support and this, in turn, called for up-to-date scholarship and solid proof. In such a case an opinion could no longer be considered that of an individual school but would be acknowledged and recognized as the 'official' viewpoint of the Church as a whole—not because the Council raised the opinion of a particular school of universality, but because the view of a school had become universally accepted before it came up at the Council. For example, it was precisely because Alfonso Maria Buteler Mendoza, the 75-year old Argentinian archbishop, was out of harmony with the official orientation of the Church as a whole, that the 27 Argentinian clergy were justified in reproaching him during and after the Council for refusing to introduce liturgical reform in his diocese and to set up the council of priests provided for in the decree on bishops. In fact, he refused to make any changes whatsoever. The newspapers reported the archbishop as saying that after the Council, the Pope would reestablish order wherever the Council had 'spread disorder'. He did not preach a single sermon nor issue a single pastoral letter touching the Council. In this case, hardly an isolated one, neither the 27 young clergy nor the laymen supporting them are in rebellion; the archbishop is. They acted properly in appealing to Rome—to the Secretary of State and the Pope. From now on, Rome *has* to give them its support. Of course the Council's doctrinal statements, to say nothing of its disciplinary decrees, are not to be considered unchangeable definitions. Nevertheless, no bishop, priest or layman is absolutely free to take a position against them. On the contrary, it may be necessary for one to go beyond these statements if the 'spirit' which created them is to be fullfilled. It is entirely possible that a bishops' conference might, for some special reason, carry out the Council's decrees only gradually, and yet be completely faithful to the spirit of the Council. The opposite is also true. Someone might follow the decrees very strictly but still be out of step with the Council's 'spirit'. Here, once again, we see the importance of clearly understanding the spirit and its basic purpose.

That what is said here is not a subjective view is proved by Pope Paul VI himself: during the second week following Easter 1966, the post-conciliar commissions met in Rome; it was their task to work out a clean, juridical formulation of the decisions taken by the Council fathers. The commissions were charged to complete their work before the end of that period following the Council called *vacatio legis*—the period during which the decisions taken at the Council would not take effect. Although the members of all of these commissions worked zealously, the Pope was not satisfied with the results brought in by two of them. He sent their work back with the annotation: 'The commission's work should not only correspond to the words, it should also comply with the spirit of the Council.' The two commissions in turn replied that it was impossible for them to terminate this work by June 29, 1966, the end of the *vacatio legis*. However, the 'spirit of the Council'—which should emanate from the compilation of all decrees and debates—seemed of such importance to the Pope that he abruptly prolonged the life of the two commissions and proposed a new deadline. Ignoring the real facts, the newspapers of course wrote that 'the Pope delays the application of the Council's decrees,' and other reflections of this kind. Such reports did not noticeably disturb the Pope.

Dejuridification

The first of the Council's fundamental tendencies to be considered here is a certain dejuridification ('de-legalizing') of the Church. This is an ugly and even misleading word, but we lack a better one. One of the most frequently heard remarks during the debates was: 'The prepared text is too juridical.' This accusation was first heard during the discussion on mass media. It was voiced again even more emphatically in connection with the Eastern Uniates during the first debate on Church unity. We must remember that the Uniates had an important contribution to make in this regard. After all, they had preserved original Christian forms far better than the Western Church had; and for them, law has always played a far less significant role than for the Western Church. Little wonder, then, that the Council fathers, when looking back on the origins of Christianity, as any reform has to do, were amazed at how legalistic the Church had subsequently become. Eastern Catholics have a canon law of their own, but they have not succumbed to law in the way the Western Church has.

Eastern Catholics give far greater priority to the spirit.

Certainly if the Church is the continuation of the incarnation of God, it must naturally produce some kind of law. A purely spiritual Church would be a one-sided Church, out of line with the intention of its founder; and yet Christ clearly left his Church very little in the way of law. He fought against a kind of Judaism which emphasized law at the expense of the intent of the law. The entire Sermon on the Mount testifies to this. This is why the Church of the first centuries tried to keep legal prescriptions to a minimum—so the Spirit would not be snuffed out. At the Council, the Eastern fathers represented the early Church on this kind of issue; and it gave them an influence all out of proportion to their small numerical strength. No one at the Council would have denied the legitimate development of law within the Church. The law left us by Christ was developed in the course of centuries. It was not clearly defined at the very beginning. Then, too, the Church was entitled to establish her own norms and laws whenever the need arose. No one denied this. Yet it seemed that now and then juridical thinking had superceded the Spirit of God. Pope John had specified adjustment of the Church to modern conditions as one of the Council's goals. The world changes rapidly; conditions change from decade to decade even in the most remote hamlet. Situations arise that cannot be treated in old, habitual ways suited to a different time and place. The Church, with its impressive law, is armored like Goliath. It has become immobilized and unwieldly. It looks like an anachronism; and since people often do not distinguish the temporary and changeable from the imperishable and everlasting, they have come to regard it as out-of-date and old-fashioned—even in its Creed and testimony to Jesus Christ. I am not saying that this explains the phenomenon of present-day atheism. This has other, deeper roots. But one of the causes is certainly to be found here, and that is why Pope John always spoke of the Council and reform of canon law in the same breath. For him, these two things were inseparably linked.

Most of the bishops agreed with Pope John. They wanted, insofar as possible, to avoid excessively juridical language and to stress the inner meaning, the core, of their message. Paul VI, by training a jurist, nevertheless understood this tendency very well. In his closing speech on December 7, 1965, he said, in summation: 'The Church has gathered together in spiritual awareness . . . not to dedicate herself to reaffirming her rights and explaining her laws, but rather to rediscover in herself, in her activities and her life, the Word of Christ in the Holy Spirit, and to explore still more deeply her mystery.'

There is in these words of Pope Paul an unmistakable allusion to the battle on the schema on the Church. The first draft submitted to the Council was a juridical masterpiece. The legal aspect of the Church was formulated with all possible precision—her order, her hierarchical structure, the prerequisites for becoming a member of this Church. The fathers rejected this text as 'too juridical', even though Cardinal Ottaviani had remarked before the debate: 'I know, venerable fathers, that all the guns have already been moved into position to shoot this text down. It will be said that it is too juridical, not ecumenical enough, not pastoral enough. But I pray you, first read the text in peace.'

They did read it, and the text was gunned down. Another text takes its place. The title of the first chapter proclaims 'The Mystery of the Church'. This begins with the Father sending the Son. The text then speaks of the Spirit who makes the Church holy, who fills it with all truth, who 'rejuvenates' it at all times and is the inner principle of its unity, who adorns it with priestly and charismatic gifts. Then comes a section on the kingdom of God—a kingdom not identical with the Church; the Church is its 'seed and beginning' on earth. Then the Church is described in various scriptural images. This implies that the substance of the Church cannot be confined within nice sharp concepts and polished formulations. Through various biblical images which illuminate first one side of it and then another, the 'mystery' of the Church becomes visible—obscure in outline, but certain in its substance, with one image complementing and correcting another.

Obviously a jurist for whom the legal aspect of the Church is the main thing, and in any case the most important in practice, could only shake his head at this chapter. Here we touch upon one of the painful points of this Council. Most representatives of the Roman Curia are eminent jurists. This is certainly to their honor and credit; it is nothing of which to be ashamed. But just as any profession is subject to a certain one-sidedness, particularly in its most eminent representatives, so also here. The scholar is, after all, a favorite object of caricature. The Americans call them 'eggheads', the Germans ridicule the 'distracted professor', the French speak of 'professional deformation'. This last perhaps most accurately expresses what we are driving at. A quality which within limits is genuinely advantageous to the specialist becomes a deformation when it transcends these limits, invades other areas, and becomes a general way of life.

So it was inevitable that the tendency toward dejuridification met opposition from many representatives of the Roman Curia during this Council. All the presidents of the Council commissions were members of the Curia. During the preparatory period they were setting the style. But apart from the schemata worked out by the Secretariat for Christian Unity, not a single prepared text was accepted. In fact, after the fathers themselves had elected new commission members, the commissions and their presidents were perpetually in conflict with one another. Not a single one of the later, and now official, texts corresponds to the mind and intention of the president of the commission in charge.

A possible exception to this is Cardinal Cento, the president of the commission on lay people. Without indicating his own views, he allowed the other members to work on their own. So the initiation and formulation of the texts were entirely the work of men who were not members of the Curia. The members of the Curia, in turn, put the brakes on this development. Now braking is definitely a necessary function, but it is certainly not the most important one.

One can understand why the Roman Curia found this Council little to its taste: It was forced to play a role which did not correspond to its status. After the death of Pope John, the word went around that 'he would have to remain in Purgatory until the Council he had sponsored was finished'. This is typical curial humor.

But it must be admitted that on the whole the presidents of the commissions loyally abided by the decisions of the majority—as long as the majority clamored for its rights.

There is only one text that the Council needs to thank the Roman Curia for. This is the famous 'explanatory note' prefixed to the third chapter of the schema on the Church. In this note, where the rights and duties of the College of Bishops are described and formulated, the tendency to dejuridification did not prevail. The effort to use language that would be widely understood and to avoid purely legal expressions as much as possible—to define with all possible clarity the inner meaning of collegiality that undergirds and precedes legal aspects—necessarily produced many ambiguous and inexact statements. Obviously the fathers did not want to shut the door to possible further development, but there wasn't even a clear-cut division between certain debatable statements and doctrines. This is exactly the point where the jurists went to work. Naturally they found some other dangers (e. g., the threat to dethrone the Pope) lurking in this 'pastoral' language. So the jurists gave the Pope many a sleepless night. They badgered him continually until they finally got their 'note' which never came up for debate in the Council and was never submitted to a vote. In that sense, it can be considered an authentic pronouncement of the Pope. But it can hardly be regarded as a conciliar act even though it made the text on the bishops more exact and was even indirectly accepted by the college in subsequent voting. As a matter of fact, the non-juridical language proved to be a boomerang in this case. It would undoubtedly have been better to use strictly juridical language in dealing with a juridical theme. More progress might have been made this way.

But another aspect of the tendency to dejuridification must be discussed here in connection with the signs of the times. The Council wanted a change of attitude, not only in view of the need for reestablishing the right relationship between Christian substance and law in line with the teaching of scripture, and not only to 'catch up', as Pope Paul put it, with the rapidly changing times and do justice to their complexity. From a broader perspective, the Church had to realize that the times really were changing. During the Reformation period when Christendom split in two, the practice of Christianity was often only very superficial. It was precisely those who were suffering most from the emphasis on the superficial and external who separated from the Roman Church and took refuge in a kind of purely spiritual Church. At such a time the importance and need of the juridical element had to be given special emphasis. Surely, even then, the main stress should not have been given to law. For genuine reform could come only from inner spiritual renewal and not from norms and rules. This is precisely what the best minds of the Council of Trent saw. Any reform in the Church since that time, owes far more to this inner renewal than to any necessary emphasis on the legal defenses of the Church. In fact, the 'easier' way more often prevailed, and this was the way of external legalism. It prevailed to such an extent that a legalistic form of Christianity made itself at home in the Church—a milieu Christianity. Today, this is beginning to crumble more and more as shifting populations continue to merge and fewer predominantly Catholic areas are left.

In such a situation, the emphasis on the juridical actually turns into an obstacle that threatens to extinguish the spirit. In contrast, the emphasis on the spirit can liberate new forces to create new initiatives.

Here we finally touch on the positive aspect of dejuridification. Despite its hierarchical structure, the Church is in no sense a kind of supernatural super-state ruled by the Pope as absolute monarch, with a nice, neat aristocracy of bishops and their priestly helpers, and finally a great mass of subjects who have nothing else to do but to obey and follow laws. The Church is not primarily a 'salvage operation', a kind of huge international sanitarium. Rather, it stands, wholly and in every part, as a witness to the redemption and elevation of mankind. The hierarchy is therefore merely a necessary administrative function, whose task is service. This wholeness originates in the Eucharist. All are nourished by the body of Christ, all are joined together in a unity. And in all, the Spirit works as he wills.

This is how the Council came to speak of the unerring sense of faith of the People of God as a whole and of the charismatic gifts which spring up everywhere. Not all initiative is channeled from top to bottom through the hierarchical leadership of appointed officials. More often than not it rises instead from the bottom and is only subsequently approved and incorporated by the leadership. This is not surprising. Rather it is likely to be expected, because the hierarchy are so busy ordering, serving and judging, that it would be largely beyond their power to provide initiative as well. But the over-emphasis on legalism, which had its day in times of upheaval, had formerly received little attention. It was typical that resistance to statements in favor of charismatics came from countries like Sicily with a strong tradition of dug-in, milieu Catholicism; whereas countries which are in the midst of revolutionary upheavals were most strongly in favor of the charismatic statements. While exercising all necessary prudence toward alleged charismatics who are nothing but 'screwballs' or fanatics, the Council nevertheless adopted a statement on charismata. This motif also recurs in many other texts. It should also be mentioned here that the main stress of innovation in the post-conciliar period should not be placed on the new juridical dispositions. It is of course impossible to do without them. There are for instance regulations for the formation of a council of bishops around the Pope; for the conferences of bishops which are to be established everywhere on national and continental bases; for the councils of laymen, men and women, belonging to the various organizations; moreover every bishop should create a council of laymen, and such a council should be established in every parish. Despite such provisions, one should not forget that these groups, *per se*, offer no guarantee that the Council's intentions will be fulfilled. As Karl Rahner the theologian says, they could also bring into being an organizational wasteland. Thus such structures represent only *potential* aids for a true dialogue (of which we will speak in the next section). They are not the dialogue itself, for which they can serve only as a facilitation. Therefore a certain bishop was wrong when he said after the Council that he was glad the

Council had recommended laymen councils, because his word would penetrate, as carried by the wind, as far as the farthest family in his diocese. This is not the contribution expected from the laymen councils. The bishop should instead be glad now to be able to learn about the needs, the anguishes and the suggestions that *come to him* from his 'farthest family'.

On balance one should accordingly expect a reduction of constricting regulations and of organizations rather than an increase. Already, for example, the annulment of the rule on putting forbidden books on the Index has been decreed; of it Cardinal Ottaviani said, 'It died a natural death in the spirit of the Council.' Again it is the intention of a special commission to renovate the canon law and reduce to approximately one fourth the present 2414 canons. Thus in the end there would be left only skeletal regulations, which could be supplemented in details by each bishop according to the needs of his particular region. And finally there may be expected a loosening up of the crowded network of Catholic organizations, or better, of their over-detailed prescriptions, yearly programs, and their monthly, weekly, even daily directions. The Council speaks specifically, as already noted, of the 'small' charismatic gifts which are given to many if not most of the laymen; one wonders how these gifts can indeed unfold considering the countless restricting regulations of the devout societies. Yet, one cannot say that for the spirit of God the Almighty this is an insuperable impediment. When Jesus was crucified his tormenters said: 'If you truly are God's son, descend from the cross.' He could have done it of course, but he did not. Thinking of the dejuridification of the Church undertaken at the Council, do we not indulge in an abundance of individual prescriptions simply because we suffer from a lack of trust in the power of the Spirit?

Dialogue

A second surprising feature, important throughout the Council to the future of the Church, is 'dialogue'. Dialogue was not on the program. That's not surprising in a council. In the First Vatican Council (1869–1870) infallibility wasn't on the program either. The almost impossible actually happened at Vatican II. The demand for dialogue did not spring so much from any theoretical consideration; it was instead the result of real experience, and it was precisely this experience that appeared highly improbable before the Council began.

We know that both Pius XI and Pius XII had considered the idea of convoking a council. Pius XI was waiting for 'a more definite sign' that would have shown him the need for undertaking such a difficult enterprise. Pius XII, however, quite in keeping with his character, had made extensive secret preparations. Not the least of his worries was the question of how a council of this size could engage in a reasonably productive 'dialogue'. He saw no other solution but to ruthlessly limit the number of participants. There were 774 bishops in all who took part in the First Vatican Council. Sometimes the total attendance fell below 650. Even then a genuine discussion with arguments and counter-arguments was very difficult in view of the increasing number of dioceses. So there could now be no possibility for any real dialogue. Consequently Pius XII was thinking of a carefully balanced system of representation. But he found little positive response from those he consulted. John XXIII invited not only the local bishops, but also the titular bishops, the auxiliary bishops, and the suffragans. This meant about 2200 voting participants—three times the number at Vatican Council I. Actually 2540 fathers took part in the opening ceremony. No dialogue was possible. Speaking time had to be limited to ten minutes (later eight). No Council father was allowed to speak more than once on the same topic and had to register for this three days in advance. The actual effect of these rules was to prevent a dialogue.

Nevertheless, it was the unanimous opinion of the bishops at the end of the first session that the main achievement of this period, which had passed not a single Council text, had been precisely their experience of dialogue. Many observers expressed the same opinion: 'Undoubtedly the wonderful atmosphere of dialogue was the thing that made the deepest impression on us.' How was this possible? The dialogue took place outside the Council aula, and under conditions which no one could have anticipated. Bishops came from all over the world. At home, in their own dioceses, it was every man for himself. There most of them were like little kings. Everyone approached them with the greatest respect, ready to satisfy their every wish. Their relationship to their environment was that of commanders to obedient subjects. When they appeared in public, they radiated dignity and grandeur. They were like lonely mountain peaks. But now in Rome they had plenty of peers. They were, so to speak, demythologized. Many, for reasons of economy, had to travel alone and to cope by themselves with the most common ordinary things. There were no valets to help them or to dress them in their prescribed robes. They stood, awkward and unassisted, in some corner between two pillars of a colonnade, changing into their robes in full view of the whole world. As many publicly said: 'Finally we have become completely ordinary human beings.' They lived together in large hostels, convents and houses of religious orders. There was soon plenty of conversation between South Americans and Africans, between Germans and Poles, Frenchmen and Spaniards. The longer it lasted, the surer they became that the conversation was highly productive.

At first the bishops of the United States were an exception. They were located, lonely and isolated, at the Rome Hilton, or at one of the 'better accommodations'. They soon became somewhat envious: 'You won't find me checking into some hotel next year', one of them said to me during the first session. 'I'm completely out of touch here, and I'm missing the best part of the whole Council.' But that was not all. In the very first Council meeting, elections for commissions were to take place. The bishops did not know one another, so the secretary general made a proposition which in essence boiled down to confirming members of the preparatory commissions that had already been set up by Rome. Cardinal Liénart, one of the Council presidents, immediately opposed this, saying it was tantamount to a farce. The fathers must have a few days to become acquainted; then there could be an election. He was supported by another president, Cardinal Frings. The whole praesidium agreed. The first meeting was the shortest of the entire Council. It was brought to a sudden halt under the sign of 'getting to know one another'.

Bishops' conferences were hurriedly formed without any preparation. The Roman Curia disapproved of such gatherings from the beginning. One example: The bishops of the United States wanted to hold their annual bishops' conference at the Council. They notified Rome of this intention before the Council began. Permission was refused 'so that no factions and nationalisms should arise'.

This decision appears downright grotesque in retrospect. The belief apparently had been that during the Council each bishop would express his own opinion on each topic, and that from the total of these opinions the Council majority would result. No one had even considered the possibility that the bishops might form lateral connections. Obviously no one had anticipated that this kind of exchange might change the minds of certain groups of bishops, and that it would be precisely here that the real gain of the Council would lie. Yet this is just what did happen during the first days of the Council.

So the bishops' conferences, whenever such conferences existed, convened in a great hurry. Others, such as the Africans, gathered in hurriedly improvised groups. Each conference chose the most capable of its members and made the names known to others. International lists resulted, which already revealed certain tendencies. Every bishops' conference was visited by 'observers' from other conferences.

Then an intensive search was made for important theologians. There was no shortage of them in those days, but there were some theologians who had to give twenty lectures a week at various bishops' conferences. Previously they had perhaps been known in one country but they suddenly became 'international'. It is impossible to explain how this informal dialogue, which grew with great spontaneity and became increasingly lively, circulated new blood throughout the entire body of the Church, purged it of dregs, and influenced its changing opinions.

An example of this: At the beginning of the debate on the liturgy the bishops of the United States, under Cardinal Spellman's leadership, were united in their opposition to liturgical changes of any kind. When, at the end of the second session (December 4, 1963), the text on the liturgy was solemnly approved, there were but four votes against the schema. What had happened to the approximately 200 bishops of the United States? They had all changed their minds—thanks to dialogue. ('Except for two', one of them whispered.)

We have to keep in mind just what this experience meant for the bishops. Until this time each of them had been isolated, or at best linked with one another through national bishops' conferences held once a year. Even neighboring countries had practically no communication. All of them were, of course, joined vertically with Rome, the center of the Catholic Church. Rome guarded the unity of teaching and discipline. All roads led to

Rome. But there were hardly any horizontal connections. Soon after the Second World War, for example, there were any number of political and cultural ties between Germany and France. There was the Common Market; cities were sponsored by other cities; children crossed national borders in trainloads; student exchange programs flourished. But with rare exceptions the bishops had never seen one another. Here at the Council it became evident how much every bishop had missed.

More than that, there was a recommitment to original Christianity. Wasn't its hallmark the collegiality of bishops, their fellowship—their sense of community—along with the liveliest exchange? This was based on eucharistic communion. And what a lively exchange took place even in the middle ages! The bishops were perplexed. Didn't technology offer opportunities for travel and communication throughout the whole world such as were never known before? And didn't travel and migration make communication necessary from a pastoral point of view? In short, something seemed to be lacking in the realization of Christian ideals, despite community in faith. In addition, the attendance of observers from non-Catholic Christian churches led to a further development. Through dialogue with them, which began in Rome, whole new worlds were opened up to many bishops. They had surprising experiences: 'Think of it,' a South American bishop remarked, 'I have talked to an observer, and the man is not only intelligent, but he is even devout!'

During the general congregations an argument arose over the question, 'What does it mean to be ecumenical?'

One group said it meant, 'Speaking the plain, unvarnished truth, and hiding nothing, because truth and love cannot contradict one another.' 'Certainly,' replied Bishop De Smedt on behalf of the Secretariat for Christian Unity. 'We should not conceal anything, but we should speak in a language which is also understood by others who have not had our scholastic training; and we should make an effort to learn the language of those whom we do not understand, so that we don't keep coming up with rash judgments.'

Another question arisen had been troubling the bishops for some time: Why are we so isolated from the modern world? Is it because we no longer know its language? Wasn't it wrong for Cortez, the conqueror of Mexico, to have the Catholic creed read to the Indians in Latin, and think that he had preached the faith to them? Isn't it wrong to think that we have satisfied our obligation to preach the faith when we speak in a language which our hearers cannot possibly understand because it has nothing in common with their real desires and hopes? What, then, is dialogue supposed to mean?

Suddenly there were lots of talks on this theme. We can summarize them by saying that dialogue has three stages. The first stage primarily involves getting to know the other person, studying him, putting ourselves in his position, trying to sense how much God has already worked within him, and where in him we can find points of departure—where he is open to the message of God. Undoubtedly we often fail to make even this first step. So what we actually do is deceive them, because they, from their perspective, often cannot possibly understand the truth which we speak in our own way; or they misunderstand it because of their natural misconceptions.

The second stage involves meeting the other person with a readiness to learn from him, too, to accept something from him. This is not in conflict with the fact that the Catholic Church is entrusted with all revealed truth. Not everything is in every way perfectly clear to everybody. And God, as mentioned before, has already acted in everyone before he encounters the Church or one of its representatives. Only at the second stage can genuine dialogue really begin.

The third stage involves two people discovering something through their common effort in something never before known to either of them, at least in this particular way. Isn't God himself, in his Trinity, an everlasting dialogue? Doesn't the Christian then—for whom involvement in the divine dialogue is a goal and a challenge—have the duty to cultivate dialogue on earth? Didn't God become flesh in order to encounter man face to face on the level of dialogue? Didn't he want, although he was Lord and master, to be recognized among men as one who serves? These are only hints, but here are the roots of all the criticism so often voiced at the Council against triumphalism, against clericalism, against the feudalistic Church. All these things—triumphalism, clericalism, and feudalism—contradict the attitude of dialogue, the only attitude proper to a Christian.

A few months after the first session, Dr. Michael Schmaus, the Catholic systematic theologian of the University of Munich, was asked what he thought was the greatest achievement of the Council so far. He replied without hesitation: 'The living recognition of the need for genuine dialogue.'

Dialogue can be difficult, not only dialogue between Christian and atheist, between Catholic and non-Catholic, but also dialogue between bishops, and dialogue between pope and bishops. The experience of the Council testifies to this. Readiness for dialogue is not the same thing as the beginning of genuine dialogue; we can say that a good start was made, but no more.

The Dynamic Church

Pope Paul said in his closing address of November 7, 1965, that the Council considered it its duty to follow modern society 'in its rapid and permanent transformation'. The Pope made two comments on this: first, that this attitude originates in the 'essentially salvific mission of the Church' and second, that it had been 'effectively and continuously operative' at the Council, so much so that some considered it an 'excessive relativism in the face of ever-changing historical progress'.

The subject is touchy and delicate and certainly did not come to full maturation in the Council. Nevertheless, in any enumeration of the crucial elements in the spiritual attitude of the fathers of the Council, it cannot be overlooked 'for the sake of simplicity', because it *was* 'effectively and continuously operative'. In addition, it was new in the history of the Church. If we really want to know what was different about this Council, we have to mention one of the main features—a certain relativism, partly due to 'ever-changing historical progress'. As a matter of fact, we can say that the so-called 'conservatives' (a shifting circle now larger, now smaller, which never formed a party in the sense of a parliamentary faction) were uncomfortable precisely because of their distrust of this 'new and different' factor. Its precise difference from the 'old' appeared to them extremely problematic and even dangerous. Of course this third attitude of the Council is closely connected with the second one, which we have called 'dialogue'. One could even say that this relativism is inherent in dialogue; that it can be traced back to it. If dialogue is supposed to be an essential mark of the Christian, then the Christian is constantly exposed to the necessity of always learning something new. He has not yet arrived at his destination. For the individual, this is something self-evident, a matter of everyday experience.

But when we speak of the Church as a whole, this might not be so readily admitted. Doesn't the Church teach that the official revelation of God to man was concluded with the death of the last eyewitness? So an end has been set. The only thing that remains to be done is to carry this revelation to all the world, to present it to mankind, and to find the best ways and means of penetrating all human culture and human activity with its spirit. We know that the Church will never be finished with this work until the end of time. There will be successes and failures, yet the Church will never perish. But it will unflaggingly try, since this is its divine mission, to proclaim the great facts of the salvation of all mankind by Christ, the elevation of man to divine son-

ship, and the promise of the transformation of the universe through him. Moreover, this kingdom of God is certainly already achieved; it is not only for the future, but it exists in believers even now. Even though hidden, it is real and visible at least in sign and symbol. These signs and symbols are actually nothing else but the continuation of the one and only sign which Jesus Christ himself was in his humanity. Not only do these signs convey the kingdom of God, but they also express it. And they do not change through the course of history. They must be present to show that in the final analysis Christianity does not tear man asunder, splitting him into a perishable body and a divinized soul. Rather the whole man and the whole creation are transformed.

Up to this point, the fathers of the Council were all in agreement. The first chapters of the schema on the Church present all this beautifully and plausibly. But now comes the real question. Is the Church really an imperishable complex, always the same throughout the course of a history in which only its members and the situations in which they find themselves change? Is the Church something like a garment of the Lord, handed on to each succeeding generation, yet always remaining the same? Or must it be said that the Church itself has a history too—not just an external history but a history like that of a human being who always remains the same, yet grows, learns, increases and develops in body and spirit? True, he is always trying to achieve the same identical personal goals, but he is constantly thinking up new methods, using them and discarding them as circumstances require. He also undergoes an interior change, not surrendering his objectives perhaps, but recognizing ever more profoundly and clearly his own real meaning, and increasingly identifying himself with his goal. He nears his goal, not only as the time of 'arrival' constantly shortens, but also as the goal becomes more and more actualized within him. So he is always continually 'arriving'; as long as he lives he has never completely arrived, yet he is always moving closer to his objective.

The application of this idea of growth to the Church gave the Council a most exciting issue. Admittedly, the idea of growth is not usually found in theological textbooks. Yet there have always been Christian thinkers—to mention only Newman—profoundly concerned with this problem. The idea of growth comes through in almost all the Council documents. It is something we will try to clarify later in the book. It will be enough to indicate here the two chapters in the schema on the Church that triggered animated debate about growth. Both chapters underwent a series of revisions. Let us begin with the seventh chapter, significantly entitled 'The Eschatological Nature of the Pilgrim Church'. When we compare its first two pages with what is customarily understood by the 'last things', we immediately see the difference. Father Yves Congar says: 'This does not deal with the last things as presented in theological manuals—things encountered at the end: judgment, heaven, purgatory, hell. Christian eschatology, although it involves all these things, is something different.' What is so different? The whole truth of things will be discovered at the end. Everything in history receives its meaning—the meaning of its dynamism—from this final truth toward which everything is moving and which has already had its beginning in time. And eschatology does not deal with things to be found afterward, but with the inner relationship things have now to final truth and final perfection. This also applies to the Church in its historical situation. As we read in the text of the Constitution: 'At that time (of restoration) the human race, as well as the entire world, which is intimately related to man and attains its end through him, will be perfectly reestablished in Christ.'

This view is not restricted to man as an individual. It goes beyond him and unites man with world and cosmos. They all have a common goal toward which they are moving. Obviously this is not something external and therefore disposable; it is something in the innermost nature of things—an innermost impulse of all creation toward this goal. This goal is involved in all the endeavors, actions and doings of man, and even in the very evolution of the cosmos.

A perspective like this evidently has special importance for our time. We need only think of all the messianic visions (including atheism and its interpretation of history) and the enormous attraction they have for people of our era. Each of these interpretations sees history in relation to a hope and a perfection to be achieved at the end. Seventeenth and eighteenth century Christianity did not conceive its ethics—the responsibilities of men toward society and God—in terms of history. Christians then did not think in terms of a universal history of salvation. They did not see Christian life as the hope of the world, as the answer to man's historical quest. The Church is now, in a sense, making reparation for this neglect; it is filling the void in its doctrine once again. We can say 'again' because these ideas could have been found in the scriptures, the Old as well as the New Testament, long ago. In addition, in the second section of the same second chapter, the text develops the idea further by showing that the final restoration has already begun in Christ and that this process continues in the Church.

The final, decisive passage is in the third section, where the whole idea is applied to the Church itself. On one hand, the end-times have already arrived and the renewal of the world is irrevocably determined—and is, in a certain very real sense, anticipated in this era of the world. On the other hand, 'until there shall be a new heaven and a new earth . . . the pilgrim Church with her present sacraments and institutions has a worldly and temporary appearance. She herself lives among creatures who still groan and travail in pain. What this means is that the spirit is concretely present in the 'flesh'. Flesh has not yet been transformed into spirit. In scriptural language 'flesh' refers not only to the material order, but also to the way in which man expresses himself as well as to his own language. So the Church will never exhaust its revelation; it will never be able to express with all fullness and profundity what revelation means. Why? Because the Church speaks in a language shaped by the thinking of a philosophy which is imperfect and in need of improvement—a philosophy which has the added disadvantage of never being quite accurate in everything or at least tending toward onesidedness.

So this seventh chapter, considering its implications, does go 'very far', as Father Congar has acutely observed. Our suspicions are confirmed by the second chapter of the same constitution, entitled 'The People of God'. Even in the revised version of the Council's second session both of these two chapters were missing. But at this time Council members who attributed special importance to the idea of the 'People of God' asserted themselves, and through their efforts this special chapter was included.

How was this done? The idea was already present in the Old Testament. The chosen people of Israel were called the 'People of God'. They had a special covenant with God and had been given the responsibility of pointing through their history—gradually but with ever-increasingly clear awareness—toward the promised Messiah. Then the new covenant fulfilled the promise and superseded the former covenant. This happened at the Last Supper. The new covenant established a new People of God and this is what is meant by the Church; they are the Church.

The intention of the text was, as Father Ratzinger has expressed it: 'As long as this world lasts, the Church is on a journey like the wandering people of Israel on their way from Egypt to the Promised Land.' Therefore, the Church must never think it has finally reached its destination. It must time and again uproot itself from particular historical errors and cultures. Thus the mission of the Church is not merely a tactical and pedagogical adaptation. Its mission includes an 'acceptance of man in his entire historical perspective . . . so much so that the "flesh" of mankind—man's earthly historical existence—truly becomes the flesh of the Word'. This will not be accomplished without painful transformation. 'Both sides will bear the cross', Ratzinger continues. 'A Church which undertakes a missionary venture of this kind will again and again undergo the crucification of its own habits and customs. In this way it will gradually be transformed—moving toward the fullness of the maturity of Jesus Christ.' Here again, then, we find the inner historical growth of the Church toward a goal.

Thus the text of the chapter says that the Church must 'never cease to renew itself until, through the cross, it arrives at the light that knows no setting'. And in another passage: 'The Church is at the same time holy and in need of purification; it is always in the process of renewal.' We must not forget it was only a few short years ago that this phrase, 'ECCLESIA SEMPER REFORMANDA' (the Church must always be in process of reformation) was still thought to be heretical! Now a Council has made this expression part of a doctrinal statement. The change is almost beyond belief. The cause for the change—as this book has perhaps shown—is the understanding of the historical dimension of the Church. Historical limitations are, despite the eternal and unchangeable elements, always present in the Church.

We have, of course, not exhaustively treated the spirit of the Council under these three headings, nor have we really defined its newness. This spirit and this newness did not, of course, affect fidelity to tradition and to the divinely given life of the Church. The new element was not something superadded from outside or something formerly nonexistent. Had that been so, the Church would have had to reject this new element. But what it has to do instead, is simply to find the half-forgotten or still undiscovered aspects of the ancient truth. This effort of discovery does not change the goal of its pilgrimage but rather brings it closer to the fulfillment of the petition in the Lord's prayer: 'Thy kingdom come.'

The Bishops

The first set of photographs will serve to introduce the men who were the Council. It is easy enough to say, 'Meet the bishops!' But what are bishops? Are they papal functionaries? The Pope's deputies around the world? Or the opposite? Are they delegates of the Catholic faithful, instructed by their constituencies on what stand to take at this international parliament called Vatican Council II? Both conceptions are wrong, but both contain some truth.

One of the tasks this Council set for itself was to decide precisely what the relationships were between bishops and pope, and bishops and their respective local churches. Terms such as 'theocracy', 'constitutional monarchy', 'oligarchy', 'democracy'—terms taken from political life—are unsuitable. For a while one or another of these pigionholes may seem useful, but all of them are ultimately unsatisfactory.

From the beginning there was a certain hierarchy among the bishops. First, the bishop of Rome convoked the Council; no one else had the right to, according to current law. The Pope also was a participant at the Council—in fact, its first and most important participant. The bishops, on the other hand, are no mere papal advisors. The Pope cannot abolish the episcopate. The bishops' views and opinions must be listened to, and the bishops together decide what is going to happen afterward in the Church. And here comes our first surprise. The Pope, who is legally president of the Council, never takes part in any debate. Neither John XXIII nor Paul IV did so. This holding-back may have some historical precedent, but it is unnecessary, and I believe the time will come when the unfortunate custom is abrogated. This overemphasis on papal remoteness—to appear in public only rarely, to always eat alone, and so on—is all too reminiscent of Chinese emperors or the era of Philip II of Spain. It also degrades the bishops,

implying that they would be afraid to speak up in the Pope's presence. And how much more human his contact with the cardinals would be, were the Pope to join them at the bar for a Coca Cola. On the other hand, the prevailing practice does show that there is true freedom at the Council. The non-Catholic observers were genuinely and pleasantly surprised.

Secondly, there were papally-appointed presidents and, later, 'moderators' to preside over the sessions. The principle became clear very early: no group was to be suppressed. Even small groups were to have their say, and nobody was to feel shunted aside. This may appear to be a rather liberal principle. But it really is more—it reflects a surprising confidence that the spirit of God is effective in all and that each individual group has a contribution to make. Or we can put it this way: It is the conviction that the whole Church really is one body inspired by the same spirit, no matter how varying and conflicting the prevailing views may be. This principle, naive or even insane as it may seem (it is guaranteed neither by reason nor faith), persisted throughout the Council and conversely was no obstacle to genuine progress.

Thirdly, the bishops, although more than 2,000 in number, managed to have dialogue with one another without doctrinaire quarrels or major breaches. And it was a productive dialogue which, without sundering all bonds with tradition, supplanted centuries-old traditions on many points. We can only say that the bishops abandoned all masquerade and tried to meet one another as genuine Christians and authentic human beings. Their talks were not collisions between opposing systems, but real human encounters. Thus they themselves offered an example of unity—a unity whose deficiencies make it something to be smiled at, but which was undeniably an inner kind of unity not evident elsewhere in this world of ours.

The photograph says two things: (1) At the beginning of the Council, nobody knew his fellow participants. Everyone silently and graciously went to his place. There were no contacts, no conversation. Everybody had his own little nook. The numbered seats indicate this. (2) The order of seating was determined by 'seniority in service'. In earlier councils participants were usually seated according to nationality. This custom had unfortunate consequences—the formation of 'national factions', for example. Now there was to be none of that. But this did not take into account the temper of the times. The seating arrangement here divided 'old men' and 'young men'. The young ones, by their concentrated applause or shows of displeasure, dominated the atmosphere. All pleas of the Secretary General against demonstrations were in vain.

These two men pioneered the way for dialogue in the Council: Cardinal Frings (Cologne) and Cardinal Liénart (Lille). The first was 75 years old and the second was 78; Frings was made a cardinal by Pius XII, Liénart by Pius XI. This Franco-German alliance was to play an important role in the Council. Both cardinals were among the Council presidents. In the very first general congregation, members of the ten new commissions were supposed to be elected. The Secretary General proposed that, since the bishops did not know one another, they confirm as choices for these commissions the members of the preparatory commissions appointed by Rome. But these two presidents did not share the Secretary General's view. The first to protest was Cardinal Liénart: 'First we must get to know one another', he said, 'and only then will we vote.' He spoke a French-accented Latin, and many missed what he said. So Cardinal Frings, enunciating clearly and precisely, repeated the same identical message. Later he was to introduce himself to a mixed gathering in Germany: 'Cardinal Frings, archbishop of Cologne, famous for repeated *faux pas* at the Council. However as is often said, I wasn't the first one. I only wanted to clarify the words of my co-president. It was necessary, you see, that fear of the Roman Curia be dispelled right from the start.' Actually, all the Council presidents approved the proposal. The vote was postponed and since the stunned Curia had no substitute proposal, the session was closed. The French newspaper, *France Soir*, headlined a report on this incident: 'French Bishops in Revolt at Council. Lead Fight Against Official Agenda.'

(Frings, *left*; Liénart, *right*)

Not until the second session were 'moderators' or papal 'legates'
appointed; they were supposed to guide the Council. Paul VI introduced these moderators so that the work would go more rapidly. Up to
then, the ten presidents had guided deliberations. Of these, only two
were slightly younger than 70, while two were already over 80. The
Pope wanted younger, more energetic men. He would have preferred to
have just one person in charge who would be invested with extensive
powers. But Cardinal Cicognani, the Secretary of State, thought
differently. So, as a compromise, four cardinals were appointed
moderators—Döpfner (49), Suenens (58), Agagianian (67), and Lercaro
(71). Their powers were never clearly defined, and consequently there
were constant jurisdictional quarrels—for instance, about the famous
five questions on collegiality, about the conflict on religious liberty, and
so on. Pictured here are the three progressive moderators (l. to r.):
Suenens of Belgium, a leading candidate for pope after the death of
John XXIII; Lercaro, archbishop of Bologna, the 'inspired one', a
white dove among the Italian bishops, who is later to become president
of the new liturgical commission which will supersede the old Congregation of Rites; and Döpfner, archbishop of Munich. A Bavarian
himself, Döpfner was first bishop of Berlin and became famous through
his efforts to make contacts with the Polish bishops; thus his work
anticipated the subsequent exchange of letters between the Polish and
German hierarchies in 1965.

These three moderators have been jokingly referred to as 'the synop-
tics', since the fourth, Cardinal Agagianian, stood somewhat apart as a
Curia cardinal. Agagianian is prefect of the Congregation of the
Missions; Romans call him 'the red Pope'. He is an Armenian, born in
Tiflis, also the birthplace of Joseph Stalin. Yet Agagianian as moderator
never quarreled with the other three—precisely because he was an
Armenian.

Upper left: Here are the Council presidents and (in front) the four moderators. At the middle of the presidential table stands the Dean, Cardinal Tisserant (with beard). In the beginning there were ten presidents; later on there were twelve. Except for the Dean, who is a member of the Roman Curia, all were local bishops. Of these, two each were from the United States and Italy, one each from France, Syria, Australia, Germany, Argentina, Poland and Holland. Spanish and African representatives were noticeable by their absence. Originally there was a Spaniard. When he died, he was replaced by the Italian Siri. Everybody asked what the presidents were supposed to do, once leadership in the Council had been given over to the moderators. The Secretary, Cardinal Lercaro, a noted jurist, answered: 'Flowerpots', he said, 'nothing but flowerpots, set up there to round out the picture of the assembly.' Yet he was mistaken. 'The twelve presidents are to remove any procedural doubts and difficulties which might arise', said the second edition of Council regulations. And that was frequently to be the case. For instance, there was the time when Bishop Reuss of Mainz distributed some handouts in front of St. Peter's and Msgr. Felici wanted to use force to stop him. Or the time when Msgr. Staffa, because of Council rules, wanted to postpone a vote contrary to the decision of the moderators.

Lower left: The controversial Secretary General of the Council, Msgr. Pericle Felici. Many thought him a man of intrigue. He was not. He was a conservative, and that is not the same

(continued overleaf)

thing. Often he would 'interpret' the wishes of the Pope in line with his own thinking, and this got Paul VI into some unpleasant situations. But on the whole Felici was a delightful bureaucrat, who charmed everyone. Once, for instance, at a public congregation during the fourth session, he declared: 'They reproach me for talking too much. Esteemed Fathers, I am well aware that God is found only in silence. But I am an official of the Church and, apart from a little embroidery here and there, I say only what I am told to say by higher authority.'

Page 91: The venerable fathers sat close together, listening for four hours every day to Latin monologues. No wonder that some of them got tired. At 11 they would arise and betake themselves to the 'bar'. There were two of these. The bar where the progressives met was called 'Bar-Jonah'. There the dialogue finally began over a cup of espresso. 'That's where the Council is really being decided,' an English bishop said in one of his lectures.

'You simply have to see this. Every morning, two hours before the general congregation, hundred of bishops go to confession in St. Peter's—that's where the penitentials have their confessionals.' So said a lady at a reception. She was right. 'The Church in pilgrimage' is no empty saying. The shepherds are human beings, too, and ornate robes do not make them any different. And they admit it; they do not hide it. Everyone can see for himself. They confess—that is, they confess that they know they are sinners, forever in need of reform.   *(Right)*

Above: The devil, too, was there at the Council. 'Sometimes you could almost pinch him,' a German theologian said in a lecture at the end of the Council. But he wasn't always so readily recognizable as here in this picture showing the devil cringing beneath the foot of St. Ignatius Loyola and biting his finger with rage. Some wanted to crush the devil everywhere, and stepped, instead, on people they were supposed to help. Then the roles were almost switched. . . .

Below: The telephone from heaven would ring again. The telephone stood right next to the Secretary General. 'Didn't I say there were to be no condemnations at this Council? Of course there are false doctrines and dangerous opinions. But men today judge doctrine by its results. And above all, they have learned from experience that the use of strong measures and inadequate to solve successfully the problems that plague them.' The little naked angel seemed to nod with satisfaction whenever such sayings of John XXIII were remembered. There too, the old era confronted the new.

What was all this whispering about, between these two great Council figures? On the left is Cardinal Bea, head of the new Secretariat for Promoting Christian Unity and intimate friend of John XXIII. At the right, Cardinal Léger of Montreal, perkaps the most courageous speaker at the Council. Except for Cardinal Ruffini, who was constantly protesting, no one spoke as often as Léger. Léger was not a member of Bea's Secretariat. Nonetheless, whenever these two men saw each other, the rest of the world seemed to disappear. They talked and talked—very quietly and for a very long time. Thus threads were spun across the ocean which would never appear in the Council records.

Roman Curia—Spain

Congo—Germany

France—Vietnam

Roman Curia—Mexico

India—United States

Tanzania—United States

Holland—Germany

How did the Bishops live in Rome?

Surely they didn't live in the same way as they did at home. They lived in a city which symbolizes the mingling of old and new. Rome would like to be modern, yet it carries its burden of history. It is a city of monuments. Almost every house has its memories. This is nice. It is valuable. Yet it is also an obstacle that stands in the way. Everything is relative and absolute at the same time. Every bishop brings with him a tradition—a divine tradition he must not change, and a human tradition he does not want to abandon. Now they are all uprooted from their home territory and wondering what meaning there may be in the Church's pursuit of 'aggiornamento'. Pope John has tossed this multicolored word to the Council. Perhaps that's what they're thinking about while this modern bus carries them past the old horse-drawn buggies on the Via della Reconciliazione, where drivers sit and debate, like everyone else, about how long Rome is going to see car and buggy side by side. What in the Church belongs to the horse-and-buggy era, what is automated—and what is non-negotiable? Everybody is supposed to be detached, yet authentically human. Yet even there a person can trip on the ecclesiastical skirts of triumphalism. One has to take the rain and strong wind in stride. Can't even a completely modern young woman be genuinely Christian? The walls that make the bishop seem a demigod—must they not fall? Shouldn't he be a man accessible to young and old, and not merely a signer of solemn letters? This is the source of the motto: 'Look for man as he really is, as he exists today.'

The coachmen of the old Roman carriages became accustomed to seeing the many modern busses which passed them every midday during the months of the Council sessions, fully occupied by purple coats and lace shirts: the bishops. The cars drove the Fathers from St. Peter's to their lodgings. For a group of Americans this meant the Hilton, Rome's most fashionable hotel; for a group of Indian bishops, a small, crowded hotel on the outskirts; and for many others, a modest student's room in one of the many homes of sisters.

In vain did many bishops protest against the prescribed ceremonial robes they had to wear day in and day out to the general congregations. Once the spirit of anti-triumphalism almost brought on a strike. But Pope John gave the high sign and the rebels fell in line. Then the weather saw to it that solemnity would not be overdone. A brisk wind swept over the rulers of the Church, revealing often enough what the long robes concealed, while they were all flailing about desperately for their headgear. In short, the bishops got used to looking comical on occasion.

Left: There was no dressing room around, so the bishops either had to climb in full battle array into one of the busses waiting to take them to their hostels—so they could retire to their (ordinarily very modest) cubicles —or else they had to stand there before the whole world while struggling out of their festive attire.

Right: Sometimes they would go to the Council in bright sunlight at 9 a.m., and when they left at 1 p.m., the rain would really pour down. This gave rise to some modern versions of the old parable of the wise and foolish virgins. Oil for lamps, in this case, meant raincoats.

There were receptions almost daily. They began with a lecture on a Council topic by one of the leading theologians. A person simply had to listen to it, because men so busy with all that governing of dioceses had often forgotten their theology. So theology boomed. After the talk there would be a repast—in hospitable surroundings—as here on the Piazza Navona in the Foyer Unitas. This place, operated by the pious 'Ladies of Bethany', offers the separated brethren a home and an introduction to the Roman world. These pious women are thoroughly modern in their dress. Young people are delighted at this, and many an older person is astonished.

And then, usually, came the main event when conversation started in small circles—circles, for instance, of fog from a good cigar. By the way, Dutch Catholics recognized *their* Cardinal, Alfrink, much more easily when he was hidden in the smoke of his cigar. Then he was entirely human, and they knew he would defend them if they were attacked by anyone. And attacks came; for instance, from certain controlled segments of the Italian press during the last session on the question of the Eucharist. 'It is not because they are godless that Dutch Catholics look for new explanations,' Alfrink said, 'but rather because these are vital questions for them. No people in the world goes as often as they do to the Lord's table. Indifferent people, of course, are content to let old formulas stand, precisely because they don't understand them and don't even care.'

The whole span of the colonnade area in St. Peter's square was blocked off by wooden barricades during and after the general congregations until all the bishops had left Vatican City by bus, car, cab or on foot. Only individuals with special identification, such as chauffeurs or bishops' theologians and secretaries, were allowed to pass. But if a bishop (in this case, Bishop Hasler of St. Gall) left the roped-off area on foot, he was done for. Like a film star or boxing champion, he would be surrounded by autograph-hunting youths, especially young students who had waited at the barricades since noon to see the exodus (nobody knew the exact time in advance). 'Oh', I was told by an American girl who happened to be standing there, 'there's nothing about this in the guidebook!' But anyway, the students knew; and the bishops established immediate contacts here—something that was simply impossible at home.

Message of the Fathers of the Council to all Mankind

(on October 20, 1962, first session)

We wish to convey to all men and all nations the message of salvation, love and peace which Jesus Christ, Son of the Living God, brought to the world and entrusted to the Church. This is why we, the successors of the apostles, 'united together in prayer with Mary, the mother of Jesus', and forming one single apostolic body whose head is the successor of Peter, are gathered here at the invitation of His Holiness Pope John XXIII.

The Image of God in Man

We want in this meeting to seek, under the guidance of the Holy Spirit, the most effective ways of renewing ourselves and of becoming 'increasingly more faithful witnesses of the gospel of Christ'.

We will try to proclaim to the men of our times the truth of God in its entirety and purity and in such a manner that they may understand it and accept it freely.

Conscious of our duties as pastors, we ardently desire to meet the expectations of all those who seek God 'and perhaps grope after him and find him, though he is not far from any one of us' (Acts 17: 27).

Faithful to the instruction of Christ, who offered himself to death 'in order that he might present to himself the Church in all her glory ... that she might be holy and without blemish' (Eph. 5: 27), we shall totally devote mind and strength to renewing of ourselves and the faithful entrusted to us, so that the gentle face of Jesus Christ (which illuminates our hearts with the knowledge of the glory of God) may appear to all people.

The Church was born to serve

We believe that the Father so loved the world that he gave his only begotten son to save it. Through this, his son, he freed us from the slavery of sin 'That through him he should reconcile to himself all things, whether on the earth or in the heavens, making peace through the blood of his cross' (Col. 1: 20), so 'that we should be called children of God' (I John 3: 1) and truly be so.

Moreover, we receive the Holy Spirit from the Father so that we might live the life of God, love God and our brothers, with whom we are united in Christ.

We as followers of Christ are far from being strangers to earthly labor and concern. Indeed, the faith, hope and charity of Christ urges us to serve our brothers and to imitate the example of the Divine Master who 'has not come to be served but to serve' (Matt. 20: 28).

And so the Church was born not to dominate but to serve. 'He laid down his life for us; and we likewise ought to lay down our life for the brethren' (I John 3: 16).

Because we hope that the light of faith will shine more clearly and brightly through the work of the Council, we also hope for a spiritual renewal. This may provide a fortunate impetus for the advancement of human dignity—for the achievements of science, the development of technology, and a broader diffusion of culture.

The dignity of man is the Council's desire

United here from every nation under the sun, we carry in our hearts the needs of all persons entrusted to us—anxieties of body and soul, sorrows and longings and hopes. The fears that burden men sear our soul. Our first concern, therefore, speeds to the humble, the poor, the weak. Following the example of Christ, we feel compassion for the many who suffer hunger, misery and ignorance. We identify constantly with those who, lacking the help they need, have not yet achieved a way of life worthy of human beings.

This is why, in performing our tasks, we are most specially concerned with whatever has to do with human dignity and whatever contributes to real brotherhood among nations. 'For the love of Christ impels us' (II Cor. 5: 14). In fact, 'He who sees his brother in need and closes his heart to him, how does the love of God abide in him?' (I John 3: 17).

In his broadcast message of September 11, 1962, His Holiness Pope John XXIII stressed two points. First of all, *peace among peoples:* There is no one who does not detest war, no one who does not ardently desire peace. This is the greatest wish of the Church as mother of all. Through the voices of popes, she has never ceased to proclaim her love for peace. She was always ready to support any sincere means to keep peace. And she wants to work with all her strength to bind all peoples together and to encourage them to give one another material help and human appreciation.

Does not this conciliar assembly—admirable for its diversity of races, nations and tongues—give evidence of a community bound by fraternal love as its visible sign? We proclaim that all men are brothers, regardless of the race or nation to which they belong.

Secondly, Pope John urges all to help realize social justice. The doctrine outlined in the encyclical letter MATER ET MAGISTRA clearly shows how the message of the Church is needed in today's world to denounce injustices and shameful inequalities and to restore the rightful order of property and economics so that, based on the principles of the gospel, the life of man may become more worthy of man.

Our hope in Jesus Christ

We have neither riches nor power on this earth. But we place our faith in the strength of the Holy Spirit promised by Jesus Christ to his Church. Therefore, we humbly and earnestly invite not only our brothers of whom we are the pastors, but all our brothers who believe in Christ and all men of good will, whom 'God ... wishes to be saved and to come to the knowledge of truth' (I Tim. 2: 4), to collaborate with us in building a more ordered way of life and wider brotherhood in the world. In fact, it is the divine will that through love the light of the kingdom of God shine even now upon earth, as a first revelation of the light of the everlasting kingdom. In the midst of this world—so far from the peace it longs for, threatened even by a wonderful develop-

ment of science, and not always oriented toward a higher law of morality—we pray that the light of our great hope may shine—the light of Jesus Christ, our only Redeemer.

The People of God

(from the Constitution on the Church, Chapter 2, sections 9, 10, 12)

At all times and in every nation, God has welcomed all those who fear him and do what is right. It pleased God, however, to call men to holiness and salvation not as individuals independent of mutual bonds, but to make them a people that would acknowledge him in truth and serve him in holiness. God selected Israel to be his people and made a covenant with them, and has taught them step by step; and did this by revealing himself and his will to them through Israel's history, making this people holy unto himself. But God's dealings with Israel were by way of preparation and served as a pattern on the new and perfect covenant to be ratified in Christ. God's revelation to Israel anticipated this fuller revelation given through Christ himself, God's word made flesh. 'Behold, the days are coming', says the Lord, 'when I will make a new covenant with the house of Israel and the house of Judah.... I will put my law within them, and I will write it upon their hearts; and I will be their God, and they shall be my people.... For they shall all know me, from the least of them to the greatest' (Jer. 31: 31—34). Christ instituted this new covenant, this new testament, in his blood: he called Jew and Gentile together to be one people, not bound by fleshly ties but united in the Spirit into a new people of God. Those who believe in Christ are reborn through the work of the living God —reborn out of deathless seed, not out of flesh, but out of water and the Holy Spirit, to become 'a chosen race, a royal priesthood, a holy nation, a purchased people ... who in times past were not a people, but are now the people of God' (I Pet. 2: 9—10).

The head of this messianic people is Christ, 'who was delivered up for our sins, and rose again for our justification' (Rom. 4: 25), who with a name above all names reigns in heavenly glory. The heritage of this people is the dignity and freedom of the sons of God, because the Holy Spirit dwells in their hearts as in a temple. Their law is the new law— to love as Christ loved us. The destination of God's people is the extension of his kingdom which he began on earth and will perfect at the end of time, when Christ, our life, will appear and 'creation itself also will be delivered from its slavery to corruption into the freedom of the glory of the sons of God' (Rom. 8: 21). So this messianic people— though it does not include all humanity and even at times appears rather small—is planted in the world as the sure and certain seed of unity, hope, and salvation for the whole human race. This people, established by Christ as a community of life, love, and truth, also is his means of redemption for all men. Christ sends forth his people into the world as the light and salt of the earth.

Just as that other Israel was already called the Church of God while it wandered in exile in the desert, so too the New Israel, as it wanders in search of a future and abiding city, is called the Church of Christ. And this is only right, for Christ has bought it with his blood, has filled it with his Spirit, and distinguished it with the attributes of a visible and social unity. God has gathered together as one all those who in faith look upon Jesus as the author of salvation and the source of unity and peace, and established them as the Church, so that for each and all it may be the visible sacrament of this saving unity. While the Church transcends all limits of time and place, its mission is to extend itself to all regions of the earth and so enter into the history of mankind. Moving through trial and tribulation, the Church is strengthened by God's grace promised her by Christ—so that in the weakness of the flesh she may not waver from perfect fidelity but may remain a bride worthy of her Lord; that, moved by the Holy Spirit, she may never cease to renew herself until through the cross she arrives at the light that knows no setting.

Christ the Lord, chosen as high priest from among mankind, made of new people 'a kingdom, and priests to God the Father' (Apoc. 1: 6; 5: 9—10). Through regeneration and the anointing of the Holy Spirit, the baptized are consecrated into a spiritual household and a holy priesthood, so that in all works befitting a Christian, they can offer spiritual sacrifices and proclaim the power of him who has called them out of darkness into his marvelous light. Therefore, the disciples of Christ, persevering in prayer and jointly praising God, should present themselves as a living sacrifice, holy and pleasing to God. Everywhere on earth they bear witness for Christ and answer those who seek to understand that hope of eternal life that is in them.

The common priesthood of the faithful and the ministerial or hierarchical priesthood however differ from each other in essence and not only in degree; still they are related: each in its own way is a participation in Christ's priesthood. The ministerial priest, by the sacred power he has, teaches and rules the priestly people. Acting in the person of Christ he performs the Eucharistic sacrifice and offers it to God in the name of all the people. And the faithful, in virtue of their royal priesthood, join in the offering of the Eucharist, exercising their priesthood by receiving the sacraments, by prayer and in giving thanks to God, by the witness of a holy life, by self-denial and active charity.

The Eschatological Nature of the Pilgrim Church and its Union with the Church in Heaven

(from the Constitution on the Church, Chapter 7, section 18)

The Church, to which we are all called in Christ Jesus, and in which we acquire holiness through the grace of God, will attain its full perfection only in the glory of heaven, when all things will be restored. At that time the human race, as well as the entire world, which is intimately related to man and attains to its end through him, will be perfectly reestablished in Christ.

Christ, having been lifted up from the earth, has drawn all to himself. Rising from the dead, he sent his life-giving Spirit upon his disciples;

and through the Spirit he has established his body, the Church, as the universal sacrament of salvation. Sitting at the right hand of the Father, he is continually active in the world to lead men to the Church, and through it to join them closer to himself and make them partakers of his glorious life by nourishing them with his own body and blood. Therefore the promised restoration we wait for has already begun in Christ and continues through the work of the Holy Spirit in the Church. In it we learn the meaning of our earthly life through faith performing our Father's work in this world, with hope in the future, thus working out our salvation.

The end of time is already approaching; and the promised renewal of the world is already expected in some very real way. The Church on earth is already marked by a real though imperfect holiness. However, until there shall be a new heaven and a new earth filled with justice, the pilgrim Church with her present sacraments and institutions has a worldly and temporary appearance. She herself lives among creatures who still groan and travail in pain while awaiting the revelation of the sons of God.

Since we are united with Christ in the Church and signed with the Holy Spirit 'who is the pledge of our inheritance' (Eph. 1: 14), we are truly called; and we are the sons of God although we have not yet appeared with Christ in glory, when we shall be like God, and see him as he is. Therefore 'while we are in the body, we are exiled from the Lord' (2 Cor. 5: 6) and having the first-fruits of the Spirit, we groan within ourselves and long to be with Christ. By that same charity, however, we are urged to live more for him who died for us and rose again. And so we strive to please God in all things and we put on the armor of God, that we may be able to withstand the wiles of the devil and resist in the day of evil. Since, however, we know not the day nor the hour, we must be constantly vigilant as our Lord advised, so that, having finished the single course of our earthly life, we may deserve to enter into the marriage feast with him and to be numbered among the blessed; and that we may not be condemned to eternal fire like wicked and slothful servants, or to the exterior darkness where 'there will be the weeping and the gnashing of teeth' (Mt. 22: 13 and 25: 30). Before we reign with Christ in glory, all of us must appear 'before the judgment of Christ, so that each one may receive what he has won through the body, according to his works, whether good or evil' (2 Cor. 5:10). At the end of the world 'they who have done good shall come forth unto resurrection of life; but those who have done evil unto resurrection of judgment' (Jn. 5: 29). Considering therefore that 'the sufferings of the present time are not worth comparing with the glory that is to be revealed in us' (Rom. 8: 18), strong in faith we 'await our blessed hope and the glorious coming of our great God and Savior, Jesus Christ' (Tit. 2: 13) 'who will refashion the body of our lowliness, conforming it to the body of his glory' (Phil. 3: 21); and who will 'be glorified in his saints and be marveled at in all those who have believed' (2 Thess. 1: 10).

Inner Renewal

In the Age of Atheism

A Transcendent God
becomes a God who acts

Revelation
becomes Saving Event

Drawing: In the Council hall

On my way home from the Council, I encountered—especially among theologians and contemporary writers—a certain sense of disappointment about the Council's results. Their criticism was not based on the usual superficial objections—that there was no decision on the birth control question or on the problem of mixed marriages; or that nothing or almost nothing had been done about the reform of the Roman Curia. There is certainly some justification for all these complaints. But that was not what perceptive theologians were referring to. Their objections were focused on something at the very center, the very core of Christianity: on God. They admitted that the Council had issued statements on many practical things: on schools, seminaries, priestly life, religious orders, on relationships of Catholics to non-Catholic Christians, as well as to Jews and non-Christians. It warded off many theological quarrels, at least temporarily. All these achievements centered, more or less, around the Council's statement about the Church. 'What do you have to say for yourself?' is one of contemporary man's questions that was answered by the Council in a new key. So far, so good. But, after all, the crisis of contemporary man taps far more profound depths. It does not enter on the legitimization of the Catholic Church—how it compares, for example, with other Christians Churches or world religions. The burning issue for contemporary man—including the Christian and Catholic— is his quest for God. Without this, any 'church' forsakes its right to exist.

So then: Do we still need a God? Is he not merely a need of bygone days—in the times when people were confronted at almost every instant with the realm of mystery? There was but one answer for everything mysterious: God. That was how it was in days gone by. And perhaps it always was that way.

But our own era is something else again. For the first time in human history we no longer need God to help us cope with life. In fact, he is a downright obstacle. It is true that many cling onto him—due to habit, or even a degree of lazy-mindedness. For some, he is the anchor of salvation in crises or despair; but these are marginal cases. There may also be social reasons, such as respectability. After all, even today it is still 'in' to believe in a God. But why not face facts: This God has been dead for a long time. It has gradually become obvious that the God whom nobody hates or loves anymore—because it no longer makes any difference whether he exists or not—was only a sort of expedient hypothesis. He made it possible for men to live a morally decent life together. Unquestionably the world of today is swept along on these waves of alienation from God. So the Council had the responsibility of dealing with the question: 'What is the meaning of God today?' This is why the above-mentioned theologians were disappointed; the Council did not discuss God. Not a single Council decree bears the title, 'Concerning God'. The objection deserves a hearing. Pope Paul VI in his speech on December 7, 1965, revealed his awareness of this complaint (probably received via the Curia). 'Men will say', he remarks, 'that the Council devoted itself less to divine truths than to discussion of the Church—her nature and make-up, her ecumenical vocation, her apostolic and missionary activities. . . . True enough.'

Now, we could content ourselves with the two dry words and say: True enough; we would misjudge the Council if we insisted that it speak on all important issues of the day; we ought to be satisfied that it has dealt with the issues where change is most imperative. Yet such a response would be unsatisfactory. After all, is anything of greater concern to the Church than the problem of God? And could anything be more imperative for the Church than to improve the way it presents God, since the old style of presentation is no longer effective? The objection is a most valid one.

The Age of Atheism

Nor is the problem solved by asserting that the Council, in both the third and the fourth sessions, dealt with the problem of atheism. Some of the most important speakers asked for a statement on this—for instance, Cardinals Meyer of the USA, Silva Henriquez of Chile, König of Austria, Seper of Yugoslavia, Archbishop Wojtyla of Cracow, and Bishop Spülbeck of Meissen, Germany. They did not want new anathemas pronounced against atheism. It is obvious that the Church rejects atheism. They were far more concerned with how the Church might speak to men about God today, so that God would not appear to them as an embellishment that can be easily put aside. They asked whether the Church's witness in its life today was not defective, whether the Church itself bears at least some share of guilt for the fact that contemporary man does not often find his way to God. 'Let us not forget', the bishop of Metz ex-claimed, 'that we have to preach the message of God in an age of atheism.'

For this reason the pastoral Constitution on the Church in the Contemporary World includes three paragraphs on this theme, paragraphs not originally contained in the text. It may safely be said that they are perhaps the finest in the entire document. They were developed by a specially appointed commission whose co-presidents were Cardinals König and Seper. In addition to Bishops Aufderbeck (Fulda), Kominek (Breslau) and the Czech Hnilica, really expert theologians attended for the first time—men like the Jesuits de Lubac and Daniélou and the Salesian Miano, of the Secretariat for Non-Believers. The bright theologians at home who were complaining as they wrote about the transcendental way to God, together with the 'anonymous' theologians who were busy hunting for some kind of launching pad for a set of contemporary apologetics, were wrong if they thought that their 'major issues' were taboo at the Council. They were not.

But what do these three little paragraphs signify in a Council four sessions long? What do they mean, these three small paragraphs which barely touch the main problem—alongside a hundred other paragraphs which sometimes seem overblown? The three paragraphs don't really resolve the question, yet there is a deeper and better answer. I am not trying to apologize here. It would be quite possible for a Council to bypass one question—even the most important question facing it. That would be a human and understandable short-coming. In fact, it would be a failure, and we would simply have to admit afterward that it was a failure.

Nobody makes the serious claim that this was the best of all possible Councils. Yet it seems to me that the problem of God and 'divine things', as Pope Paul VI puts it, was not shunted aside, as we might think from a superficial glance. Of course, God was included almost despite the 'program', and only thanks to the fact that certain circles were, in a sense, rendered helpless. This is precisely why the result seems so much more worthwhile; for neither calculating strategy nor power politics explains what happened.

There is nothing wrong with pastoral strategy, of course, so long as it is backed by solid theology. We need plenty of planning, particularly in these days when every bishop and every parish priest is trying to carry on as best he can. We have barely begun to plan and this is certainly unfortunate. Such human failure can help us to recognize more effectively the hand of God when, despite obviously defective planning, something happens that only an ingenious planner could have envisioned. But this is exactly what did happen in the very first text of the Council.

The Constitution on Liturgy

This was one of seven draft texts—number five—given to all the bishops before the start of the Council. No less than four important texts preceded it. It would have been better if it had been placed at the beginning: it and the last two texts looked like pawns in a chess game. Naturally the people around Cardinal Ottaviani clamored for this arrangement. All the concerns dearest to the heart of the 'highest' congregation for the preservation of the faith were first set forth systematically point by point. All the dangers were eagerly tabulated and a persistently negative tone was already evident in such titles as 'Maintaining Purity', 'The Moral Order', 'Chastity', followed by catalogues of condemnations defined in terms which were at once lucid and abstract. The bishops were not happy with these texts for they seemed to contain the Council's death sentence. Not that all the statements were false; not at all, except for a few points—though rather important ones—which were still completely open to discussion. The thinking represented in these documents viewed everything only legally or analytically. Where practical matters were concerned, the statements were mostly negative. Later, Patriarch Maximos IV of Antioch expressed his opinion in these words: 'I believe everything that is said here, while it is correct, does not have the truth in it.'

Pope John XXIII had read the texts but he, too, was unhappy with them. Yet he had no intention of interfering directly in the matter. His silence was not a tacit declaration, however, that the Council was to be a kind of 'fools' paradise', as some periodicals suggested. The Council was not meant to be a Mardi Gras; no more than it was meant to be a dictatorial procedure complete with party-line indoctrination and censorship. This is why Pope John took an indirect tack and made his famous introductory address, which insisted that the present time is not geared to condemnations and a reiteration of past doctrine. He warned the Council in general not to get involved in the minutiae of theological questions. The positive central message of Christian life needed proclamation, in a manner best adapted to contemporary man.

This last point has received too little attention in analyses of the Pope's talk. Yet it was in fact the most important point. It implied two things. First, that God in his revelation is not just a God who speaks; he is also and above all, the God who acts. This is the sense in which Jews speak of the 'living God'. So he is more than the 'God of the Philosophers', deduced by reflection on the essence of things and with attributes of eternity, immutability and infinity. The Christian God is a God who is forever toiling with men. This culminates in the incarnation of God in Jesus Christ. This is primarily an event—an event which persists in the life of the Church. The Church is the community of the 'living', of all those who bear the life of Christ within themselves. The Church, too, is an event—the continuation of God's life within mankind.

It seems to me that this view of God provides contemporary man—so largely oriented toward 'happening'—with an authentic starting point. But where is this 'happening'—this activity of God with man—most overt, tangible and public except in the liturgy, the Church's worship of God? It is inspiring to read in the Constitution on the Liturgy itself that liturgy is not primarily seen as divine worship; what is emphasized is God's dealing with man. He transformes men; his Church is being continually constructed through the liturgy; through history he brings the Church 'to the ripeness of man's maturity'. Thus history is being forged here.

The Honest God

In 1962 the Anglican suffragan bishop of Woolwich, England, John A. T. Robinson, wrote a book called *Honest to God*. It was a phenomenally successful bestseller, precisely because the bishop said that the God preached about today in the Christian Churches is a God 'above' and 'outside' man. He really has no hand in real events. He changes nothing in human life which could not proceed just as well without him. The bishop wants to argue that this is not what God is. Yet the Church, with its liturgy, earns no small share of the blame for this impression. There is no point merely in alleging that God acts with men, that men aren't able to experience this because the gestures and ritual are incomprehensible or, at any rate, do not speak to them in a living and spontaneous fashion. Robinson's book concerns itself precisely with the upsurge of atheism which we have just discussed, apart altogether from his lopsided viewpoint and tendency toward exaggeration.

It is precisely this atheism which is the target of the Constitution on the Liturgy: 'God is different' from what you believe him to be; 'God is with us'; God is 'happening'—not only something that happened once upon a time, but something that is happening today, right here and now. This is precisely what the Church wants today's men to be aware of in a dynamic way. How can people say that the Council did not speak of God?

Thus this constitution really becomes a highly dogmatic statement, although it was never labeled 'dogmatic'. It was not so labeled because it put its message, not in conceptual terms, but in an explanatory and descriptive way. True, the constitution contains a first chapter giving general principles about the nature of sacred liturgy and its importance for the Church's life. It's mentioned there—God's dealing with men, the effect of this action of God on daily living, the people of God, and the general priesthood (so long and shamefully neglected) which is the source of the specialized priestly office. In short, it gives us the view of God which is natural and appropriate to Christianity, a view which corresponds to today, yet was so difficult to recognize in the liturgical forms of yesterday. But it is very significant that these theoretical statements were not originally in the schema at all. They were worked out by a special commission only at the end of the preparatory period in order to elucidate the meaning and purpose of all the individual changes and suggestions.

History of the Liturgical Movement

But where did the specific improvements come from? They have a very long history reaching back to the time of the pastoral pope, Pius X. Like the ecumenical movement, the liturgical movement came from within the Church and originally grew out of pastoral practice. It passed through periods of trial and error. It threatened to become a pet theme of the elite. It was endangered by an aesthetic mentality which wanted a one-sided 'pure praise of God', highly artistic in form and at the same time divorced from real life and almost in conscious revolt against the mundane affairs of daily

life. But eventually—particularly after World War II— the liturgical movement managed to find its way back into the mainstream and became a worldwide force. It may have been unpalatable to Pius XII personally, but he was far too intelligent and religious not to see the working of the Holy Spirit in it. Through his encyclicals on the liturgy—MYSTICI CORPORIS (1943) and MEDIATOR DEI (1947)—he officially and solemnly recognized this spiritual quality. In fact, he proved this through a revision of certain liturgical regulations, such as rules for the celebration of the Easter Vigil in the liturgy of Holy Week, permissions for evening masses, relaxation of the Eucharistic fast, revision of the ritual with greater provision for the use of the vernacular, a fresh translation of the psalms, and the initiating of breviary reform.

It was no surprise that his approach here was strongly formalistic. The members of the Congregation of Rites had zealously and lovingly woven the fabric of the rubrics. The idea was to work it out harmoniously and with exquisitely eternal taste, down to the most minute detail. But what escaped these rubricists was that no human being could possibly remember all the rules. These regulations were in fact so numerous that they tended to block rather than sponsor man's efforts to lift his heart to God. Here was a masterpiece which seemed totally remote from contemporary humanity, apart from its appeal to a small, rarified cultural elite. It had increasingly lost its missionary appeal. The superb tapestry of the rubrics was regarded as God's unique vestment, wrought with timeless perfection. More and more God was viewed exclusively as a God to be adored and less and less as the God dynamically acting in the history of salvation. This stiff and rigid vestment seemed to imply that he himself was entirely immobile—present, of course, but also inactive. Naturally the rubricists were not entirely wrong. But they begin to lose their usefulness when they do nothing else but drum up new details. Moreover, the idea of a completely changeless God is only one side of the Christian image of God. This view insufficiently reflects the fact of the incarnation.

It now had to be ensured that the other side would not go off as blindly and onesidedly. Fortunately, the leadership of the liturgical movement was divided equally between the pastors and scholars. Cardinal Lercaro and Father Jungmann are two examples of the pastoral and scholarly groups respectively. The cooperation of these two groups was completely harmonious. Liturgical centers sprang up on every continent all the way to Manila. The scholars provided an organic connection with history and especially with the origins of Christianity. The main idea was: the nearer to the spring, the clearer the water. Early Christianity provided the indispensible and most fertile elements for the liturgy, while later ingredients, though justified, represented adjustments to temporal conditions—which change. Granted the need for enriching the liturgy, yet this process of enrichment could still be onesided, depending on the circumstances of a given time. In different situations, modifications were not only permissible but necessary. This is what the scholars had to figure out. The pastors, on the other hand, contributed elements drawn from their present-day practical experiences.

The Only Acceptable Draft

All this was going on even before the Council began. It is not surprising, therefore, that the preparatory Liturgical Commission was able to submit a text acceptable to the bishops at first sight. There was only one such text, and it was the only one which retained its original basic form. The only fathers to oppose it were certain groups of bishops from countries where the liturgical movement had not yet really taken root—for example, the United States. Cardinal Spellman discribed the idea of liturgical centers as 'romantic fantasies of ivory tower scholars'. Another opponent referred to them as half-wits. The resistance centered in the Roman Curia, or more precisely, in a part of the Roman Curia—namely the people to whom liturgy and rubrics meant the same thing. They felt threatened by an impending catastrophe. Accordingly, the Congregation of Rites, moving 'with a rapidity entirely unusual for Rome', issued on July 25, 1960, a new codex of rubrics for breviary and missal; they published, on October 5, 1960, guidelines for the publishers of liturgical books; on February 14, 1961, they issued special regulations for the calendar of feasts for dioceses and religious orders. All this was intended to be a purely technical framework. Mention was certainly made of the 'great principles of liturgical reform' upon which the Council was supposed to pass judgment. But the 'framework', into which these principles were supposed to be squeezed, was already set up in the 230 articles prepared in advance. This was ridiculous. The Council has since swept away all this. Pope Paul VI set up the so-called liturgical commission under Cardinal Lercaro, archbishop of Bologna, to work out a step-by-step process of reform in line with the great principles of liturgy.

I have said almost nothing about the use of the vernacular which was one of the most hotly debated issues of the Council and which is still being contested in certain circles everywhere. It seemed more important to me to emphasize the main outlines and purpose of liturgical reform. For this, the use of the vernacular is only one means, and one means among others. If we dwell on the means as though they were ends, we can find ourselves in interminable arguments. And liturgical reform has most certainly sacrificed some very real values. They were abandoned in favor of more important values. These losses should not alarm anyone who appreciates the nature of the central issue. Even today, liturgical reform is still a matter of unfinished business. Most of the changes to date concern the trappings and the frills of such change, but this is not all that has to be done. The more difficult and positive work still lies ahead, and we cannot judge the whole until we see the final result. All the accusations of 'chaos breaking out', of wild 'anarchy', of godless 'iconoclasm', of a 'relapse into barbarism' ignore the total perspective; they lack insight into the religious renewal which is the Council's intention. Actually, we should welcome these wails of anguish, not because somebody has been hurt, but because they prove at least that a live nerve has been touched.

The Dogmatic Constitution on Revelation

Renewal through liturgical reform, *per se,* could not accomplish enough. But this concrete and genuine inner renewal was complemented by a second declaration of the Council which, in its present form, points in the very same direction. The very title of this statement shows that it has even greater force: It is the Dogmatic Constitution on Divine Revelation. It is well known that the original formulation presented during the first session carried the title, 'On the Sources of Revelation', and this title itself immediately precipitated a battle. What was at stake was the relationship between scripture and tradition—a relationship which had not been completely clarified by the Council of Trent. Also at stake was the question of modern methods of exegesis which Pope Pius XII had already defended within certain limits—i. e., insofar as they were genuinely scientific. He had done this in his encyclical, *Divino Afflante Spiritu* ('With the Inspiration of the Divine Spirit'); but the encyclical did not break down the resistance of certain circles, especially in Rome.

Fogs Out of the North

Before the Council began, Rome was still ringing with the battle between two papal institutions, the Lateran University and the Gregorian University, or more precisely, its Biblical Institute. The first was staffed by secular clergy, the second by Jesuits. The function of the first was primarily to educate Roman clergy, while the second had a more international flavor to it. Until shortly before he became a Cardinal, Augustin Bea, a German, was the head of the Pontifical Biblical Institute. He is said to have had a decisive influence on Pius XII's encyclical on scripture. But it would be false to attribute this quarrel between the universities to international rivalry alone. It cannot be denied that nationalism played some part in the dispute. For example, Spadafora, in an attack on two German and French exegetes teaching at the Biblical Institute, asserted that people in Rome were not prepared to have their faith clouded by 'ideas from the foglands of the North'. Both professors were removed from their academic positions, on orders from the Pontifical Biblical Commission, shortly before the Council opened.

It became evident at the Council that the great majority were displeased with the schema, which reflected the spirit of the Lateran University. Nevertheless, more than a third of the fathers were opposed to rejecting the schema. It was only due to the intervention of Pope John XXIII that the discussion was broken off anyway, and the text handed over to a mixed commission composed of members of the theological commission and the Secretariat for Christian Unity under the joint presidency of Cardinals Bea and Ottaviani.

I won't go into the disputed points now because they were deliberately left open in the revised version. Paul VI, in an address at the Lateran University during the second session, made it unmistakably evident that he wanted an end to all unscientific and grotesque polemics. The two men were restored to their professorships at the Biblical Institute, and the Pontifical Biblical Commission was granted a more balanced membership.

The extent to which some people were disturbed and the emotional intensity engendered as a result was clear from a letter signed by 19 cardinals and sent to Pope John XXIII at the end of the first session. It was dated November 24, and was dispatched on December 4, 1962, by the Cardinal Secretary of State to the president of the mixed commission, Cardinal Ottaviani. In the letter the cardinals expressed their fears that these innovators would cast a false light on the tradition of the Church. They especially emphasized such criteria as the 'sense of the Church', and universal uniformity in matters of faith. Five cardinals later withdrew their signatures once they realized that there was no substance to this fear. This fact only serves to show how deep the confusion was at that time.

Just when the quarrel was approaching its climax, John XXIII lost his patience and declared (in a general audience and therefore intending the entire world to hear): 'We cannot believe that the whole problem can be settled with a few words. What is needed is mutual good will, listening to one another, and a precise formulation of one's own thoughts on these important questions. And these people have to reach the kind of agreement that will result in a teaching which is also an encouragement and a praise of Christ in his grace and his power.' (November 14, 1962.) Startled by the critical sharpness of this statement, Osservatore Romano cut these words from the text of the speech. Such censorship of a Pope was not uncommon. But the Pope had hit the nail on the head, as the present text on Divine Revelation has since proved. So this text is by no means merely a compromise. It actually does offer something new.

What was the ultimate reason for the difference of opinion? The first party had increasingly seen revelation as a summation of articles of faith. These statements were contained in scripture in an obscure and disorderly way or else in the unrecorded oral teaching of the Apostles. They were guarded by the teaching office of the Church and faithfully handed on from generation to generation. The task of the theologians was to arrange them in a systematic and orderly sequence. All this took place on a purely intellectual plane. The result was a dogmatic edifice that was most impressive in its consistency. In fact, it was so grandiose and easily grasped that it was really better to keep the Bible away from those less educated. It could only bring confusion to theologically untutored minds. Naturally, the ordinary believers were to honor the Bible as the word of God; but since it was difficult to understand and not systematically arranged, it was better for them to read the catechism which met with ecclesiastical approval. The Church was guaranteed the assistance of the Holy Spirit. Therefore, she could never make a mistake in proclaiming an article of faith. The faithful had no fear, then, of being led into error, so there really wasn't much point in their reading the Bible.

This attitude, which I have sketched in an oversimplified but essentially precise fashion, was opposed by the others—the majority. They preferred to think of revelation as no mere system of articles of faith, but rather as a simultaneous doing-and-teaching. Christ not only says what is true about God; he is the truth. Beyond that, he is also the way and the life. Thus God's revelation, which reaches its fullness in the Christ beyond whom there is no further revelation, is something that is given. It is something of living value. It was entrusted to the apostles by Christ. In itself it does not grow. But since it has been implanted in history, it does grow, and must grow, inasmuch as mankind will receive increasingly more from it and will never completely exhaust it even to the end of time. True, it does have an inner consistency which reveals itself to the believer. But it is not some kind of philosophical system. The Holy Spirit does not strut around the Church like a kind of State policeman, preventing the ecclesiastical teaching authorities from denying revealed truth or from adding to the revelation. The Holy Spirit acts rather as a teacher and friend, introducing believers to what is revealed, and doing this in line with the necessities of the times. Here scripture and tradition cannot be separated. In a very true sense scripture can, in itself, be called tradition, and tradition can never do without scripture. Together the two form a living whole which is neither a dead letter nor merely articles of faith to be handed down.

Each of these two contrasting opinions can be carried to an extreme. In one case, revelation becomes a rationalism of faith—a closed system which very easily reaches the point where it no longer measures itself against the sources. After all, certain scriptural texts, certain results of exegesis can become very uncomfortable for the system. Or else the system shuns concrete realities, and then human problems and facts can become even more inconvenient. A good example of this is the case of

Galileo. In the other instance, however, there is the danger of underestimating the value of concepts and doctrinal formulations. This approach can easily be headed straight for a relativization of truth itself. Actually both tendencies contain some value. But the progress of this council lies in the fact that the first opinion can no longer claim to be the official and dominant one after Vatican II. Before this Council, anybody who spoke of an evolution in dogma and denied that knowledge of revelation grows only through a logical combination of truths, was seen as a destroyer of faith, and was threatened by having his writings put on the Index. Now all this is a thing of the past.

In the very first chapter we read: 'This plan of revelation is realized by act and words that have an inner unity.' The text, speaking of apostolic tradition, says: 'It progresses with the help of the Holy Spirit within the Church.' Father Schillebeeckx correctly remarks: 'Texts of previous councils stressed continuously the unchangeability of dogma. For the first time, it is acknowledged that dogma develops. For knowledge of revelation grows in the course of history.' Even during the Council, a pastoral letter by the Dutch bishops on revelation was practically banned. It was not permitted to be published in Italy. Yet its essential concepts are now incorporated into the text of the constitution: 'Revelation is primarily a reality, a salvation history, and not just a handing down of things known.'

And finally on scripture itself: it is emphasized that the 'teaching office of the Church is not above the word of God, but rather serves it.' And even more in the sixth chapter, which concerns scripture as a factor in the life of the Church, we find the statement that the entire Christian religion must be nourished and guided by scripture. Therefore scripture constitutes the 'rule' or norm for faith. Moreover, 'in the sacred books the Father in heaven meets his children; he is full of love, and has a conversation with them.' From this it is clear that every believer should be admitted to this dialogue and that everyone should read scripture. While definitions also contain revelation and give it conceptual formulation, they do not constitute the direct speech of God. This is why scripture can never be 'replaced' by the statements of teaching authority. Such statements serve merely to explain scripture. So Christian revelation means primarily proclamation, not systematization. All of scripture is, after all, practical proclamation—kerygma. But in fact, our teaching, including our sermons, has been reduced to systematic lectures.

So, during the first session, it was rumored that theologians and pastors lived in opposite camps. This was not true. Two kinds of theology stood in opposition to each other: two theologies rooted in two different conceptions of divine revelation and, therefore, two different conceptions of God himself. For we know God only in the way he speaks to us. So it may be said, once again, that the Council *did* speak of God; and the inner renewal of the Church springs to life at exactly this point.

Aggiornamento or Renewal?

Pope John's approach—he wanted a 'pastoral Council'—was from the very first day highly controversial. Actually it was not so easy to grasp what this phrase meant. In the first phase—immediately after the Pope's opening address—the question was asked: Was this a council of technocrats or of theologians? 'Why do I sit here listening to the bishops thinking up new ways to sell their fixed dogmas?' a Protestant asked somewhat irritably. 'I could be at home writing a book on Catholicism.' This was their first reaction and ours too. At first even many Roman canonists saw the Council this way; they regretted, they said, having lost so much time and spent so much money for nothing. Then it gradually became clear how profound the changes promised to be. This came as a shock to many. In this history of the Church, purely disciplinary councils—worried about little changes in ecclesiastical law—never have stirred up much excitement. The word 'aggiornamento' began to sound like 'adjustment at any price'. A famous Protestant theologian wrote, 'Isn't it the Church's task to adjust the world to the gospel, and not the other way around?' Of course external reform, even in Rome, even in the Church, presupposed a certain attitude toward life, and an attitude toward life presupposed a theology. The Council threatened to become a debate among theologians—'essentialists' who think in terms of fixed essences, and 'existentialists' who look to concrete reality. This is how Father Edward Schillebeeckx characterized the situation. The solution lay deeper. Pope Paul VI indicated it: 'Christ alone in his praying Church'—the reform flows from gospel and liturgy.

Before every general congregation (working session), after the celebration of the eucharist, the gospel book was 'enthroned'. For this an especially valuable old tome was selected. The enthronement consisted in putting it on the altar between two lighted candles. This rather formless ceremony displeased many bishops. The rite was changed on October 23, 1962: now a bishop would carry the gospel book in solemn procession down the nave, while all present sang the psalm, 'Praise to the Lord', with the refrain 'Christ conquers, Christ rules, Christ commands' after each verse. At the fourth session the book of gospels was enthroned before mass.

Following page: The Constitution on the Liturgy permitted wider use of concelebration to indicate the oneness of the priesthood. This had not been applied even once during the first and second sessions. It was only toward the end of the first session (December 6, 1962) that the bishops succeeded in getting 'permission' for a simple sung mass. During the second session permission was obtained for lay people, who had been present since October 2, to receive Holy Communion beginning October 11. But when the Pope himself said mass on October 28, the masters of ceremonies were 'speechless' when he went to give communion to the congregation. With the beginning of the third session, concelebration on special occasions became the rule, especially at the beginning and the end of the session, when the Pope himself celebrated the eucharist together with twenty-five bishops. The road from a decree on paper to the reality in practice is a hard one.

A very special kind of bishop at the Council was Msgr. Péssoa Helder Câmara. Until the third session he was still a titular archbishop, an auxiliary to Cardinal Câmara of Rio de Janeiro who was in charge of the *favelas*—the slums on the outer fringes of the metropolis with their poor inhabitants crowding in from the Brazilian interior. He was given on March 12, 1964, as archbishop of Olinda e Recife, one of the most difficult dioceses in Brazil, in the country's northeast. He now had eight suffragans plus one auxiliary bishop. His own diocese numbered more than one million faithful, served by fewer than 300 priests. The transition to industrialization brings with it all the difficulties of early capitalism. The bishop is trying to cope with these problems by courageously taking the side of the impoverished and uneducated population. He never spoke in a public general congregation at the Council. But through personal contact and the openness of his ecumenical and social ideas, his influence grew from year to year, so that a newspaper at the end of the fourth session was able to say that he was perhaps the most influential of the Council fathers. An idealist as well as a realist, he promoted above all the idea of the Church as servant of man, caring for his every need. At the end of the Council he was one of the bishops who committed themselves radically to a simple personal life, with no triumphalism whatever. Pope Paul VI is a personal friend of Archbishop Helder Câmara, and many of the Pope's speeches show the unmistakable influence of the Brazilian archbishop, who repeatedly and very graphically pleaded before the press and the public for intensive post-conciliar work.

The Role of the Theologians

In sharp contrast with former councils, at which theologians often addressed the fathers in plenary congregations, none of them was so honored during the Second Vatican Council. Why not? To underline the Council's pastoral character? Or would such an attempt have been embarrassing to the minority which was hardly in a position to provide any eminent theologian? Whatever the reason, the influence of the theologians was nevertheless undeniable. Sometimes they became so influential that many Council fathers turned harshly against them. They were also officially restrained from voicing particular doctrinal views and were cautioned not to criticize the Council (September 15 and 16, 1964). The sting was taken out of most such censuring motions by Cardinal Tisserant or Msgr. Felici, when they prefaced their reproofs with remarks like, 'What would we do without the experts?' In fact the more it became clear that even purely pastoral problems have their theological background, the more eagerly the Council theologians were called upon to lecture at bishops' conferences. Never had the bishops had the opportunity of getting to know the progress and work of theologians so thoroughly as at this Council. 'There were theologically underdeveloped countries before this Council; there will be none left after it,' one American remarked. Actually the theologians were the 'Council's cooks'. They did the job they were asked to do. They did not choose the topics, but they had decisive influence on the bishops' opinions and the actual work of the commissions was in their hands. Few bishops measured up to Cardinal Lercaro's standard, when he said that the bishops themselves should again be great theologians.

Left: A pre-eminent contributor was Father Henri de Lubac, S. J. Under Pius XII, he had been accused of being a protagonist of the so-called 'new theology'. He lost his professorship in Lyons, although Cardinal Gerlier tried to support him. He was allowed to publish only such books as were approved by the Jesuit general's office in Rome. This largely restricted his activity to purely scholarly works dealing with the history of religion. Due to a fortunate oversight on the part of the Roman censors, he came into public view again as theological interpreter for Father Pierre Teilhard de Chardin. John XXIII appointed him a member of the preparatory theological commission (1961). He did, after all, owe his reputation to his books about the Church. His influence grew when the composition of the commission changed through elections at the Council. The Africans especially liked to call him in on their deliberations. He was also an indispensible help to Cardinal König's secretariat (on dialogue with non-believers), since he had written a well-known book on *The Drama of Atheist Humanism*. He became important at the Council for the very thing that earlier had led to his condemnation.

Right: There were also theologians who were not 'Council theologians', in other words, who were not officially listed as theologians whom the various commissions might call on for help. But they nevertheless exercised enormous influence, through lectures held at bishops' conferences and through their help in preparing suggestions for the improvement of various texts. They were present in Rome throughout the Council. Bishops, aware of their value, had taken them along as their theological aides. The most important among them, and at the same time the most modest, was the Dominican Father Marie-Dominique Chenu. A famous generation of modern French Dominicans had gone to school to him: we need mention only Congar, Feret, and Schillebeeckx. From 1932 to 1942, Chenu was rector of the graduate theological school of Saulchoir. He was a systhematic thinker in the grand style. In 1937 he wrote a book entitled *A School of Theology*. It was never published for its language was very personal. But it spread via private channels far beyond French borders. In 1942 it was put on the index of forbidden books. This did not paralyze Father Chenu. Besides medieval theology, he was deeply interested in the link between theology and history. The French 'Social Weeks', the Jocist movement, the worker priests, the Christian Family Movement, the Mission de France, all were decisively influenced by Chenu. So he was the logical man for the schema on the Church in the Modern World. What is best in it shows his influence, although he was able to supply only the starting points.

The name of John Courtney Murray, S. J., was not found among the Council experts until 1964. But it is to him that the Council owes its declaration on religious liberty, especially in its three last versions. In its two earlier versions, he had been excluded by the Secretariat for Christian Unity even though he was famous as the great American expert in this field. His writings and articles had been known and studied during the 50's in Europe as well, especially in Germany. He attended the Council as an advisor to Cardinal Spellman. All the conferences of bishops invited him to lecture; so did the press. The more ground the Secretariat lost due to its unhistorical presentation of the problem, the more decisive Murray's influence became. Thus he saved the declaration. At the end of the third session he suffered a heart attack, but at the fourth session he was back, working tirelessly.

Father Sebastian Tromp, S. J., had a leading position even during the Council's preparatory period. He was Cardinal Ottaviani's theological brain; Ottaviani himself was a jurist and pastor. During the Council Tromp acted as secretary of the theological commission. A Dutchman, he had a notable past. Pope Pius XI's encyclical on the Mystical Body of Christ (1946) is thought to be his work. Though the document showed an alarming narrowness in regard to ecumenism, it was nevertheless a landmark on the way that led beyond purely juridical thinking. If there can be said to be a Tromp card, it was certainly played in all those dogmatic drafts prepared for the beginning of the Council. Tromp remarked at that time, 'For the present we are still in control', thus hinting his clear awareness of what lay ahead. Actually none of the proposed schemata satisfied the Council. Yet Tromp went on working untiringly, selflessly and without intrigue. This won him high respect even from his opponents.

Probably the most widely read of all French theologians during the post-war era was Father Yves Congar, O. P. Historical studies were his field. But wherever there was a live issue to be discussed, the witty professor from Saulchoir was invited to speak, especially by the students of Paris. Subjects like the Church, lay people, true and false reform in the Church, separated Christians, Jews, and the last things, made him a 'prophet' in Germany too during the post-1945 period of intellectual starvation. Then he was undercut, along with the worker-priest movement, by the reactionary wing of French Catholicism, which was favored and even supported by the Holy Office. None of his writings was put on the Index, but new editions were forbidden. He himself was banned from Paris. He was afterwards seen in Jerusalem, London, and finally at Strasbourg, busy with new studies. He was also called by John XXIII to be a member of the preparatory theological commission (formed in 1961). There is probably no Council father who did not meet this indefatigable theologian in Rome. In Paris, however, when he explained the new liturgy, conservatives pelted him with rotten eggs.

Father Karl Rahner, S. J. (left) seen here in intensive discussion with Father Hans Küng of Tübingen (at right) was certainly one of the foremost advisors of German bishops. Rahner had gone through a period of persecution or 'muzzling' during the frigid years before the Council. He was also appointed by John XXIII to one of the preparatory commissions—not the theological commission but the commission on sacraments, which never consulted him. Hans Küng was not honored by being made a papal theologian at the Council until the second session, under Paul VI. Rahner's great hour came during the first session, when a counter-schema, written for the most part by him, on 'The Revelation of God and Man in Jesus Christ' circulated unofficially through the Council hall as a possible alternative to the schema on 'The Two Sources of Revelation'. The presidents of the bishops' conferences of Austria, Belgium, France, and Holland intended to submit this text to the Council. But the unfortunate vote on November 20, 1962, which forced Pope John to intervene, prevented this. Yet the four bishops' conferences were not themselves in unanimous agreement about Rahner's text. Only one of the French bishops unqualifiedly accepted it, thirty asked for basic changes, and eighty were opposed to it.

Upper left: The Yugoslav Franciscan, Karl Balic, was a member of the preparatory theological commission. A noted Mariologist, he is a special admirer of Cardinal Ottaviani. At the Mariological Institute in Rome, which he directs, there is a portrait of Ottaviani which he shows to every visitor. Balic fought passionately at the Council for a special decree on Mary. He wanted the Council to at least indirectly approve the idea that Mary is 'Mediatrix of all graces' and 'co-redemptrix'. It was during the Council that Protestants saw his institute for the first time.

Upper right: Even before the Council began, the young Canadian Augustinian Gregory Baum was advisor to the Secretariat for Christian Unity. He had become famous for his 400-page book on *The Jews and the Gospel*, which he dedicated to his mother, who died in Berlin in 1943 'when the annihilation of all Jews was ordered'. The fate of the declaration on the Jews was naturally of special concern to Father Baum. On the whole, he was satisfied with the end result, though the experts on the American press panel were not a little stunned by his sharp attacks.

Lower left: A brilliant theologian, but at no time a papal *peritus* (theological expert), was the Dutch Dominican, Edward Schillebeeckx, O. P. He influenced the bishops' conferences through his many lectures on profound theological issues, like faith and history, the eucharist, the Church and the world. Thus he saw to it that the Council was never satisfied with what had been accomplished. So unofficial Council theologians like Schillebeeckx, Chenu, and at first also Küng, had because of their greater freedom the responsibility of keeping the Council alert. As Archbishop Péssoa Helder Câmara put it: 'They could say what the Council was unable to say.'

Lower right: The role of prudent mediator was played by the Salesian, Hubert Jedin, now 66 years old, author of *The History of the Council of Trent*, on which he is supposed to be the foremost authority. Since 1949 he has been professor at the University of Bonn. Men like him, extraordinarily and incontestably knowledgeable and balanced in their judgment, kept their historical perspective amid all the events of the Council and thus formed a bridge between conservatives and progressives. Without them and their quiet and tireless work, the Council might easily have broken up.

From the Constitution on the Sacred Liturgy

Introduction

The purpose of the Constitution

It is the goal of this sacred Council to intensify the daily growth of Catholics in Christian living; to make more responsive to the requirements of our times those Church observances which are open to adaptation; to nurture whatever can contribute to the unity of all who believe in Christ and to strengthen those aspects of the Church which can help summon all mankind to her embrace. Hence the Council has special reasons for judging it a duty to provide for the renewal and fostering of the liturgy.

In the liturgy the work of the redemption is carried out

Through the liturgy, especially the divine eucharistic sacrifice, the work of our redemption is carried out. The liturgy is thus the outstanding means by which the faithful can express in their lives and manifest to others the mystery of Christ and the real nature of the true Church. It is of the essence of the Church that she be both human and divine, visible and yet invisibly endowed, eager to act and yet devoted to contemplation, present in this world and yet not at home in it. She is all these things in such a way that in her the human is directed and subordinated to the divine, the visible likewise to the invisible, action to contemplation, and this present world to that city yet to come which we seek. Day by day the liturgy builds up those within the Church into the Lord's holy temple, into a spiritual dwelling for God—an enterprise which will continue until Christ's full stature is achieved. At the same time the liturgy marvelously fortifies the faithful in their capacity to preach Christ. To outsiders the liturgy thereby reveals the Church as a sign raised above the nations. Under this sign the scattered sons of God are being gathered into one, until there is one fold and one shepherd.

Chapter 1

The nature of sacred liturgy and its importance for the life of the Church

God, who 'wishes all men to be saved and come to the knowledge of the truth' (1 Tim. 2:4), 'in many and various ways . . . spoke of old to our fathers by the prophets' (Heb. 1:1). When the fullness of time had come he sent his Son the Word made flesh, anointed by the Holy Spirit, to preach the gospel to the poor, to heal the contrite of heart, to be a 'bodily and spiritual medicine', the mediator between God and man. For his humanity, united with the person of the Word, was the instrument of our salvation. Thus in Christ 'there came forth the perfect satisfaction needed for our reconciliation, and we received the means for giving worthy worship to God'.

The wonders wrought by God among the people of the Old Testament were but a prelude to the work of Christ the Lord in redeeming mankind and giving perfect glory to God. He achieved his task principally by the paschal mystery of his blessed passion, resurrection from the dead, and glorious ascension, whereby 'dying he destroyed our death; rising, he restored our life'. For it was from the side of Christ as he slept the sleep of death upon the cross that there came forth the wondrous sacrament which is the whole Church.

In the power of the Holy Spirit

Just as Christ was sent by the Father, so he also sent the apostles, filled with the Holy Spirit. This he did so that by preaching the gospel to every creature they might proclaim that the Son of God, by his death and resurrection, had freed us from the power of Satan and from death, and brought us into the kingdom of his Father. His purpose was also so that they might carry out the work of salvation which they were proclaiming, by means of sacrifice and sacraments, around which the entire liturgical life revolves. Thus, by baptism, men are plunged into the paschal mystery of Christ: they die with him, are buried with him, and rise with him. They receive the spirit of adoption as sons 'by virtue of which we cry, "Abba, Father"' (Rom. 8:15), and thus become those true adorers whom the Father seeks. In like manner as often as they eat the supper of the Lord, they proclaim the death of the Lord until he comes. For that reason, on the very day of Pentecost, when the Church appeared before the world, 'those who received the word' of Peter 'were baptized'. And 'they continued steadfastly in the teaching of the apostles, in the communion of the breaking of the bread, and in prayers ... praising God and being in favor with all the people' (Acts 2:41—47).

From that time onward the Church has never failed to come together to celebrate the paschal mystery, reading 'in all the scriptures the things referring to himself' (Lk. 24:27), celebrating the Eucharist in which 'the victory of his triumph and his death are again made present', and at the same time giving thanks 'to God for his unspeakable gift' (2 Cor. 9:15) in Jesus Christ, 'to the praise of his glory' (Eph. 1:12), through the power of the Holy Spirit.

The active presence of Christ

To accomplish so great a work, Christ is always present in his Church, especially in her liturgical celebration. He is present in the sacrifice of the Mass, not only in the person of his minister, 'the same one now offering, through the ministry of priests, who formerly offered himself on the cross', but especially under the eucharistic species. By his power he is present in the sacraments, so that when a man baptizes, it is really Christ himself who baptizes. He is present in his word, since it is he himself who speaks when the scriptures are read in the Church. He is present, finally, when the Church prays and sings, for he promised that 'where two or three are gathered together for my sake, there am I in the midst of them' (Mt. 18:20). Christ indeed always associates the Church with himself in the truly great work of giving perfect praise to God and making men holy. The Church is his dearly beloved bride who calls to her Lord, and through him offers worship to the eternal Father.

Rightly, then, the liturgy is considered an exercise of the priestly office of Jesus Christ. In the liturgy the sanctification of man is manifested by signs perceptible to the senses, and is effected in a way proper to each of these signs; in the liturgy full public worship is performed by the mystical body of Jesus Christ, that is, by the head and his members.

From this it follows that every liturgical celebration, because it is an action of Christ the priest and of his body the Church, is a sacred action surpassing all others. No other action of the Church can match its claim to efficacy, nor equal the degree of it.

Chapter II

The sacred mystery of the eucharist

At the last supper, on the night on which he was betrayed, our Savior instituted the eucharistic sacrifice of his body and blood. He did this in order to perpetuate the sacrifice of the cross throughout the centuries until he should come again, and so to entrust to his beloved spouse, the Church, a memorial of his death and resurrection: a sacrament of love, a sign of unity, a bond of charity, a paschal banquet in which Christ is consumed, the mind is filled with grace, and a pledge of future glory is given to us.

The Church, therefore, earnestly desires that Christ's faithful, when present at the mystery of faith, should not be there as strangers or silent spectators. On the contrary, through a proper appreciation of the rites and prayers, they should participate knowingly, devoutly, and actively. They should be instructed by God's word and be refreshed at the table of the Lord's body; they should give thanks to God; by offering the immaculate victim, not only through the hands of the priest, but also with him, they should learn to offer themselves too. Through Christ, the mediator, they should be drawn day by day into ever closer union with God and with each other, so that finally God may be all in all.

From the Dogmatic Constitution on Divine Revelation
(Chapter 6: Sacred Scripture in the Life of the Church)

Sacred scripture as the supreme rule of faith

The Church has always venerated the divine scriptures just as she venerates the body of the Lord, since from the table of both the word of God and of the body of Christ she unceasingly receives and offers to the faithful the bread of life, especially in the sacred liturgy. She has always regarded the scriptures together with sacred tradition as the supreme rule of faith, and will ever do so. For, inspired by God and committed once and for all to writing, they impart the word of God himself without change, and make the voice of the Holy Spirit resound in the words of the prophets and apostles. Therefore, like the Christian religion itself, all the preaching of the Church must be nourished and ruled by sacred scripture. For in the sacred books, the Father who is in heaven meets his children with great love and speaks with them; and the force and power in the word of God is so great that it remains the support and energy of the Church, the strength of faith for her sons, the food of the soul, the pure and perennial source of spiritual life. Consequently, these words are perfectly applicable to sacred scripture: 'For the word of God is living and effective' (Heb. 4:12) and is 'able to build up and give the inheritance among all the sanctified' (Acts 20:32).

Ecumenical translations also recommended

Easy access to sacred scripture should be provided for all the Christian faithful. That is why the Church from the very beginning accepted as her own that very ancient Greek translation of the Old Testament, the Septuagint. And she has always given a place of honor to other translations, Eastern and Latin, especially the one known as the Vulgate. But since the word of God should be available at all times, the Church with maternal concern sees to it that suitable and correct translations are made into different languages, especially from the original texts of the sacred books. And if, given the opportunity and the approval of Church authority, these translations are produced in cooperation with the separated brethren as well, all Christians will be able to use them.

The pastoral importance of scripture study

As Bride of the incarnate Word, and student of the Holy Spirit, the Church is concerned to move ahead daily toward deeper understanding of the sacred scriptures so that she may unceasingly feed her sons with the divine words. Therefore, she also rightly encourages the study of the holy Fathers of both East and West and of sacred liturgies. Catholic exegetes, then, and other students of sacred theology, working diligently together and using appropriate means, should devote their energies, under the watchful care of the sacred teaching office of the Church, to an exploration and exposition of the divine writings. This task should be done in such a way that as many ministers of the divine word as possible will be able effectively to provide the nourishment of the scriptures for the people of God, thereby enlightening their minds, strengthening their wills, and setting men's hearts on fire with the love of God. This sacred Synod encourages the sons of the Church who are biblical scholars to continue energetically with the work they have so well begun, with a constant renewal of vigor and with loyalty to the mind of the Church.

Scripture study as the soul of theology

Sacred theology rests on the written word of God, together with sacred tradition, as its primary and perpetual foundation. By scrutinizing in the light of faith all truth stored up in the mystery of Christ, theology is most powerfully strengthened and constantly rejuvenated by that word. For the sacred scriptures contain the word of God and, since they are inspired, really are the word of God; and so the study of the sacred page is, as it were, the soul of sacred theology. By the same word of Scripture the ministry of the word also takes wholesome nourishment and

yields fruits of holiness. This ministry includes pastoral preaching, catechetics, and all other Christian instruction, among which the liturgical homily should have a preeminent place.

Diligent and prayerful reading of scripture

Therefore, all the clergy must hold fast to the sacred scriptures through diligent sacred reading and careful study, especially the priests of Christ and others, such as deacons and catechists, who are legitimately active in the ministry of the word. This cultivation of scripture is required lest any of them become 'an empty preacher of the word of God outwardly, who is not a listener to it inwardly' since they must share the abundant wealth of the divine word with the faithful committed to them, especially in the sacred liturgy. This sacred Synod earnestly and specifically urges all the Christian faithful, too, especially religious, to learn by frequent reading of the divine scriptures the 'excelling knowledge of Jesus Christ' (Phil. 3:8). 'For ignorance of the scriptures is ignorance of Christ.' Therefore, they should gladly put themselves in touch with the sacred text itself, whether it be through the liturgy, rich in the divine word, or through devotional reading, or through instructions suitable for the purpose and other aids which, in our time, are commendably available everywhere, thanks to the approval and active support of the shepherds of the Church. And let them remember that prayer should accompany the reading of sacred scripture, so that God and man may talk together; for 'we speak to him when we pray; we hear him when we read the divine sayings.'

It is the responsibility of the bishops, 'who have the apostolic teaching', to give the faithful entrusted to them suitable instruction in the right use of the divine books, especially the New Testament and above all the gospels, through translations of the sacred texts. Such versions are to be provided with necessary and fully adequate explanations so that the sons of the Church can safely and profitably grow familiar with the sacred scriptures and be penetrated with their spirit.

Furthermore, editions of the sacred scriptures, provided with suitable commentary, should be prepared also for the use of non-Christians and adapted to their situation. Both pastors of souls and Christians generally should see to the wise distribution of these in one way or another.

Ecumenism does not mean conversion
but
Without conversion Ecumenism is impossible

The Church reaches beyond itself
and
The State must respect Religious Liberty

Ecumenism is a sign of Salvation history
and
Religious Liberty is a sign of the times

Drawing: The Milvian Bridge

'Wherever we are to blame for the division, we humbly beg God's forgiveness; at the same time we beg forgiveness from our brothers should they feel they have been offended by us.'   (Paul VI)

Ecumenism—A Dream Become Reality

The Council stirred worldwide interest by its ecumenical initiative. Neither the Pope nor the bishops nor the heads of the important communications media (television, radio, press) had expected such a vivid response from the world. Interest grew from week to week, despite inadequate initial reporting and the apparent inconclusiveness of the first session. The attention of the world persisted even later when the first Council crises and setbacks appeared, when what happened at the Council was sensationalized in pocketbooks written in the style of late Renaissance intrigue, and when many an illusion vanished like a cloud, yielding to a more sober view that disappointed many people.

We need to ask why this interest in the Council developed. Many explain the worldwide response in terms of the personality of Pope John XXIII. There is undoubtedly much truth in this. He was a rare and extraordinary man who, like John F. Kennedy, had an overwhelming personal appeal. Both were succeeded by men, who, despite their proficiency and expertise, lacked this gift for stirring masses of people. But I truly feel that I am right in saying that the real basis of world interest was and is the Council's ecumenical initiative. This answered a mysterious wish of many diverse people. I dare not call this wish a hope, and certainly not an expectation. These words would go too far, because everybody thought that such a wish could not be fulfilled.

This is why the appearance of an ecumenical initiative was surprising: the unexpected happened; a kind of utopian dream came true. I have no intention of saying that the Council brought the churches close to reunion. This is not true; and it is difficult to see how reunion could be achieved, even in a few hundred years. Honesty requires that we admit this. After all, the Reformation happened a good four hundred years ago. Nor will the Reformation churches find their way back to unity with Catholicism during the next four hundred years unless something truly extraordinary happens to both the Reformation churches and the Catholic Church, out of the present ecumenical movement. Nor can we say that the astonishment produced by the Council fell like a bolt from the blue without any historical preparation —like a *deus ex machina*. This also would be an unsupported exaggeration.

As is well-known, the ecumenical movement began with the Protestant missions who set themselves the goal of 'planting in every non-Christian nation a non-divided Church of Christ' (Edinburgh Conference, 1910). The ecumenical movement began almost in opposition to the various Church establishments, but it inspired the development of two great movements, known as 'Faith and Order' and 'Life and Work'. The Faith and Order movement, at first strongly influenced by Anglicanism, sought to clarify areas of common agreement and areas of disagreement in doctrine; that was of primary necessity for a serious dialogue. The second bypassed the question of doctrine and church discipline and sought community through common action. Today these first steps are a matter of past history. Essentially Protestant, the World Council of Churches has existed since 1938. It is neither a 'super-Church' nor a movement like the Catholic Una Sancta;

nor does it want to be. Rather, it is only a framework serving the divided churches in their efforts to perform a common task, seen as commanded by Christ. The Churches which form this Council therefore remain completely independent. The basis for their cooperation is faith in 'Christ as God and Redeemer according to the scriptures' and they seek 'to correspond to their common vocation, to the honor of the one God—Father, Son and Holy Spirit'. Since the convocation of the assembly at New Delhi (1961), almost 200 churches have been members of the World Council. The former International Missionary Council, within the framework of the World Council, has come to be called the 'Commission for World Missions'; 'Faith and Order' is also now a commission of the World Council.

Fifty years ago, no one would have thought this mutual searching and discovery possible. But the road leads further. There was talk at New Delhi of 'the unity we seek'.

The official Catholic attitude toward this Protestant movement was very reserved, even negative. The Catholic Church sees itself as a visible institution, founded by Christ, which has never lost its unity. The Catholic Church does not see the one Church of Christ as something synthetic, as a reunification of parts that today are scattered. Rather, Catholicism is already this unity. The Ecumenical Council was based on the view that this unity has simply been lost, and all that is now left is something residual, inasmuch as all baptized persons and all believers form one community which must 'manifest' itself as such.

The cool attitude of official Catholicism can be under-stood as a result of the different way in which the two bodies look at themselves. The World Council invited Rome to send observers, but all such overtures were at first rejected. Even so open-minded and pro-Catholic a man as the Swedish Lutheran, Nathan Söderblom, felt offended at this rebuff. There were, nevertheless, private Catholic initiatives which in a sense went rather far. But the Holy Office soon put a stop to this. One could only pray that the erring non-Catholics (and this was the only way to look at them) would come to their senses and be converted. They were simply heretics, not always in the formal sense, but heretics as a matter of fact, with whom there is no real possibility of genuine dialogue; and the Catholic faithful had to be kept from too close a contact with such people. This attitude was still evident in 1950 in Pope Pius XII's encyclical HUMANI GENERIS. But then pressure from below increased. The emphasis was still on extreme caution, and although an instruction issued by Rome in 1949 recognized that the ecumenical movement owed its existence to the 'inspiration of the Holy Spirit', there was still no official relationship between this movement and the Catholic Church.

The situation did not change until Pope John XXIII established the Secretariat for Christian Unity in preparation for the Council and put Cardinal Bea in charge (1960). Even this did not mean an immediate change in the whole atmosphere. As late as 1961 Cardinal Ottaviani warned me, in a private audience, of the 'euphoria' which tends to pervade contemporary ecumenism: 'Euphoria is always dangerous', he said, 'even if one has to admit that one should not resist the Holy Spirit where his activity is unequivocally clear.' Nevertheless, for the first time in the history of the Church an *official* connection with the separated churches had been established: Cardinal Bea's secretariat.

Subsequent events are today generally known. Through the World Council of Churches the separated churches were invited to send observers to the Council. Many did so, and according to the official list, their numbers increased from an initial 39 to 64, exclusive of 27 substitutes. The influence of the observers was responsible not only for the considerate language of all the speeches; they were also directly responsible for some of the speeches.

Was this mere 'euphoria'? Ecumenism does not mean merely that members of various confessions are friendly toward one another. This at best is only a first step. A certain mutual fear which could sometimes be observed during the first session later gradually disappeared. The suspicion that the development of this ecumenical relationship with the observers was only a tactical move soon disappeared. But the doctrinal question remained: in the final analysis, what was *Catholic* ecumenism? As late as October 23, 1963, Dr. Edmund Schlink, the delegate from the Evangelical Church in Germany, put it this way: 'The way the Catholic Church understands itself judging from the schema on the Church [when he was speaking the text was still in its second draft; it had not been finished] forces the question: What is the meaning of this new custom of addressing non-Catholic Christians as "separated brothers" rather than, as heretofore, heretics and schismatics? What does the text's praise of spiritual fruits in non-Catholic churches mean? Does this really serve as any-

thing more than an effort at absorption? Is this ecumenism something more than some Protestants think it is, a continuation of the counter-Reformation using other methods? In other words, a more attractive approach?' The question was pointed but necessary if euphoria was not to cloud up the real, ultimate issues. And what answer did the Council give to this?

The Church reaches beyond itself

The Council did not becloud or deny the fact that this was a serious problem. According to the Constitution on the Church, 'Only they are fully incorporated into the . . . Church who . . . accept her entire system and all the means of salvation given to her, and through union with her visible structures are joined to Christ who rules her through the pope and bishops. This union is affected by the bonds of profession of faith, of sacraments, of ecclesiastical government and of community.' This sentence comes almost word for word from Pius XII's encyclical on the Mystical Body of Christ. In this, then, nothing is changed. The necessity of the Church for salvation is emphasized as it always had been.

But then the door opens, and it is said that the Church is 'as it were, the sacrament, meaning, sign and cause of innermost union with God and of the unity of the whole of mankind', and so also for those who, in good faith, are outside the visibly organized Church. If the sign were not there, there would be no union with God and no unity for mankind as a whole. This is true for all men. Thus the statement that 'outside the Church there is no salvation' is given a deeper meaning here. It no longer receives the very narrow and negative interpretation so often given to it—an interpretation which disregards the universal, salvific will of God who has redeemed all men. All the artificial and awkward theories about membership in the Church 'by baptism of desire' had been eliminated by the Council along with the idea of a mysterious primeval revelation passed on for millions of years.

But this is still not ecumenism. Ecumenism is an affair of Christians who believe and are baptized in Jesus Christ. The Council not only teaches that Christians are, in the words of Pius XII, 'correlated' somehow with the Catholic Church; it also says that they have 'a certain, though not perfect, community with the Catholic Church', that they are 'justified and incorporated into the body of Christ', that they belong 'in some way to the people of God'. In the Council's view, therefore, the Church of Christ is broader than the Catholic Church. It has many 'layers'.

So there is a genuine unity of all Christians, and this unity is by no means something merely external, because Jesus Christ lives in the others too. The Holy Spirit works in them; they have faith, hope and love; they have revelation; they celebrate the eucharist, which also symbolizes to them a living community with Christ despite all the disparity of interpretation. Thus the 'sacrament of unity' is also at work in them. All this applies, not only to individual, separated Christians, but also to those communities which contain genuine ecclesiastical elements. This is why the Council no longer denies them the designation, 'churches'.

A symbol of salvation history

What all this means is that in the Catholic view, as set down by the Council, divided Christians are also part of that sign necessary for the salvation of all mankind. It said: 'The separated Churches . . . are not without significance and importance in the mystery of salvation. For the spirit of Christ has chosen to use them as a means of salvation.' This means that a new moment in the history of salvation has arrived. The separation involved sin 'on both sides', as the decree on ecumenism says. This is not to say 'that the guilt for the division should be imputed to those who had been born into such communities and have received *from them* their faith in Jesus Christ'. Such a statement cannot be made about heretics. The decree says, answering Dr. Schlink, 'The Catholic Church considers [non-Catholic Christians] brothers in respect and love.' It is even said that these separated churches may have a contribution to make 'to the upbuilding' of the Catholic Church. So a Catholic might learn from them, because they have developed some Christian values better than the Catholic Church.

Obviously this is a considerably deepened view of the Catholic Church. Without repudiating tradition, a traditional and evil, narrow and closed interpretation of the Church has been eliminated. As we have said elsewhere, the Church saw itself at this Council as a Church 'in progress', aware that it is always in need of reform; as fundamentally a Church of sinners and therefore itself sinful until it arrives at its final destiny. So the way is now open for a genuine participation in contemporary ecumenism. There is no Catholic ecumenism in contradistinction to the ecumenism of other churches, as though Catholic ecumenism were only another way of talking about conversion to the Catholic Church; while the others instead seek through common 'conversion to the Lord' to open up to one another. This begins, as Dr. Schlink put it, by 'diminishing as far as possible the causes of hostility such as proselytism, restrictions on religious freedom and missionary work, intolerance in the handling of mixed marriages'.

The Council did not hesitate to discuss this problem of the central meaning of ecumenism. It confessed, in the second chapter of the ecumenism schema, that 'there is no genuine ecumenism without inner conversion', meaning, as in other passages, 'conversion' of *Catholics* —conversion from their 'sins against unity', from that pride which refuses to beg forgiveness, from that obduracy which refuses to forgive, from that weakness which refuses to see one's own moral shortcomings, one's own lack of discipline, and defectiveness in the way one preaches doctrine. Furthermore the Council produced a special declaration on religious liberty. The decree on the missions speaks of avoiding proselytism and hostility in the mission field: Missionary activity must become a common effort of witness. The problem of mixed marriages was at least tackled courageously. It was no surprise to the well-informed that this did not reach a satisfactory solution in the Council itself. But the Council saw to it that something would be done by handing the question over to the Pope as 'an urgent matter requiring immediate attention'.

Meanwhile, in the Instruction on Mixed Marriages (of March 18, 1966), a first step has been taken to solve this problem. True, this is no more than a first step. Although the Council asked the Pope for a papal directive, the instruction was issued on the authority of the Congregation for Faith. Secondly, the instruction describes itself as 'an attempt', an experimental effort. Third, the text on almost all points falls short of the recommendations made by the Council. Bishops have not *yet* received all the powers they requested. The non-Catholic party is not *yet* accorded the respect for his conscience to the extent recommended by the Council. And the restrictions placed on the Catholic party concerning the religious education of children remain more stringent than the Council wished. This caution is understandable because nobody would benefit if the new regulation gave aid and comfort to indifferentism. But if this attempt succeeds, then a second and even a third step (perhaps going beyond the Council's recommendations), could be made without apprehension.

The present instruction provides the basis for such a hope when, for example, it recognizes the law of the land as a legitimate reason for relaxing the absoluteness of the Church's requirement for parents to raise their children as Catholics. At this point there suddenly re-emerges the formulation ('as far as the Catholic party can') which had been stricken from the Council's recommendations.

It would be regrettable were we to focus too closely on the details. The bishops were urged at the Council 'to stimulate participation of the Catholic faithful in ecumenical work'; it is 'permissible' and even 'desirable' for Catholics to pray together with other Christians on special occasions; seminary students are to be given a theology 'which has not been polemically formulated'. The constitution on Revelation speaks of joint scriptural studies. If we focused only on the great number of ecumenically-colored passages in almost all of the 16 Council documents, we might well be wary, along with Cardinal Ottaviani, of a dangerous 'euphoria'. This could vanish as quickly as the tides. But it will not disappear. This is shown by the new self-awareness manifest in the Church and now formulated and sanctioned by this Council.

Religious Liberty

Originally the schema on ecumenism contained five chapters—the last two dealing with the Jews and religious liberty. While these topics were connected with ecumenism, they really went beyond this particular problem. Ecumenism is a Christian matter. The Jews cannot be designated Christians, even though they hail as their own one part of the message of salvation recognized by Christians, namely the Old Testament. Religious freedom, though of prime importance to ecumenism, really concerns all religions.

Both chapters could have been inserted elsewhere in the Council text. For example, the declaration on the Jews could have been treated in the second chapter of the Constitution on the Church which concerns the People of God, and moves in ever-widening concentric circles, embracing first Catholics, then all Christians and finally all mankind. The Jews, 'this people so beloved because of its election for the sake of the Fathers', were mentioned first. Even today Jewish critics still complain that not even one special paragraph about the Jews was included. Then the declaration on religious liberty could have been inserted in the schema dealing with the Pastoral Constitution on the Church in the Contemporary World. Actually, the next to last version of this text contained a short passage which was finally omitted only because an independent declaration had been already assured by that time. The question of where to insert these two themes arose as early as the first session, was discussed rather exhaustively in the second, and hung like the sword of Damocles over the text right to the conclusion of the third session. Surely within the framework of a larger text, neither of the declarations would have obtained such detailed and penetrating treatment as they actually did receive. Morever, it should be noted that both were handled much more effectively by the Secretariat for Christian Unity—however little they may seem to fall within the jurisdiction of such a body—than they would have been, for example, by the theological commission presided over by Cardinal Ottaviani or the committee dealing with the so-called Schema 13 (on the Church in the contemporary world)—a committee composed of men whose theological backgrounds were not impressive.

Thus in retrospect we can say that it seems providential the two chapters were detached from the schema on ecumenism during the second session. The reason for this, alleged or real, was that at least the first three chapters would be saved and there was insufficient time to deal with them during the final days of that session. Thus, at any rate, they became independent declarations.

Both topics were of special interest to Pope John XXIII. As concerned as he was about not submitting a program of his own to the Council, he felt that whatever was really necessary would come from the dialogue, from an interplay of ideas and opinions among the bishops. Yet his native intuition and historical sense—for he was a historian—told him that certain issues were of unique value and would constitute landmarks of paramount importance. He felt that the declaration on the Jews was essential in order to stamp out once and for all the accusation of insidious anti-Semitism leveled at the Church. He did not have at his disposal opinion polls, like those produced at a later date by the Anti-Defamation League of B'nai B'rith, to show how far the Church unwittingly assisted and condoned the evil of anti-Semitism. He had a grasp of history, he knew the East and he was aware of the background. This was enough for him. There was a black blot on the scroll of ecclesiastical history, pointing to the Church's apparently helpless and ineffectual stance when faced time and time again with anti-Semitic outbursts—sometimes even on an official level. All this must go. It was much the same with religious freedom. John was acutely aware that the concept of individual human dignity holds an increasingly important place in contemporary thinking; and with a mind ever prone to astonishment at God's workings in history, he applauded this step toward progress. He was probably well aware, too, of the tortuous and artful explanations of Catholic moral theologians and jurists: the distinction they made between thesis and hypothesis, according to which the thesis means the ideal Catholic situation when the Catholic state grants complete liberty to the Catholic Church and suppresses any other religion; and by which the hypothesis means a permissible 'adjustment' to a pluralistic society, allowing the Catholic to 'tolerate' the erring religion as a minor evil. He knew, too, that the 'classical' doctrine, passionately defended by Cardinal Ottaviani, had already been revised tentatively by Pius XII, who tactfully emphasized personal dignity without totally disavowing the 'classical' doctrine. So John felt that a clear and simple statement had to be made. He also realized that unless this statement was universally comprehensible and free of theological and juristic crutches designed to prop up an idealistic but anachronistic image, the Church would continue to appear a hopelessly antiquated institution. In his encyclical, PACEM IN TERRIS, he had garnered almost all the necessary ingredients—or had them gathered together by 'bright young men', to mention only Msgr. Cardinale (now 50 years old), the apostolic delegate to Great Britain, whom Pope Paul himself consecrated bishop. The special statement by the Council itself was bound to have a totally different impact on the world at large. And what was even more important, the frozen stream of classical thinking could be thawed only through vital interflow of communication with the progressive groups from which the 'classicists' were geographically separated.

Pope John intended the declaration on religious liberty

to be an exemplary statement on the Church's historical nature and its growing awareness of the truth of the heritage called 'the deposit of faith'. He also meant the declaration to be a witness to the fact the Church was learning from the 'signs of the times' without abandoning its essential sense of tradition. All this had to be demonstrated by concrete example rather than in a long abstract discussion of doctrinal growth and historicity: only through such example could abstract and intellectual ideas become living experience.

This was a daring enterprise, and only in the hands of a man like Cardinal Bea, head of the Secretariat for Christian Unity, was it likely to succeed. Bea was an eminently skillful warrior who respected the courtly procedures of the Roman Curia and even appropriated them himself, but without adopting the Curia's inflexible modes of thought.

Now, once again, it would be erroneous to envision the Council as consisting merely of two solidly entrenched viewpoints at loggerheads with each other. Of course there were groups, composed of Italians, Spaniards, Portuguese (and other individuals including Germans), which represented the 'classical' position. Their argument was the thesis that error has no claim to rights, and that since the Catholic Church alone possesses full truth, it has the exclusive right to promulgate the same. 'Outside of the Church there is no right', is the way Fr. John Courtney Murray characterized their way of thinking. In line with this view, a heterodox community, especially if it has an erroneous conscience (even though that conscience is upright), can expect at best a certain personal esteem and tolera-

tion. Wherever Catholicism is in the minority, it may as well tolerate everyone else in order to avoid any greater disaster. But the primary idea is for Catholics to gain a majority, and then to place the fetters on other religions as much as possible. This position has earned the Catholic Church the stigma that it plays both sides of the table at once. And behind this attitude usually stands a paternalistic concept of the state. The state is faced with immature and ignorant masses of people whom it must save from the pitfalls of error. This is quite simply the image that Leo XIII had in mind despite his clear distinction between Church and state. In his time, the problem was attuned to the facts, and Leo XIII was, after all, a realist. But what was a realistic policy in his time was elevated to the status of an eternal truth in ours.

The opposite school argued the case for religious liberty considered as a civil right. This has nothing to do with the Pauline idea of the 'freedom of the sons of God' which is on a completely different level. Nor is it the idea that moral conscience is something based on pure subjectivism without reference to objective truth—the so-called 'ex lex' conscience. Nor does the kind of argument for religious liberty we are discussing have anything to do with the Church's claim to religious authority and religious obedience. All that is meant is that neither the state nor any temporal power has the right to interfere forcefully, either directly or indirectly, with the religious relationship between man and God. The state cannot, for example, discriminate against adherents of certain religions in the matter of appointment to public office. Since human religion has by its very nature a social aspect, social adherence to and profession of religion must be permitted, and the Church has no right to inject itself into the inner anatomy of the religious community or interfere with its freedom to relate to external communities.

The basis of this civil and juridical kind of argument can be traced to and found on the ethical level. The ultimate norm of morality for every human being is his conscience. God speaks to an individual through the conscience. Man is obligated by his conscience to seek truth and ultimately God. He is not morally free in this case. He is also bound to pay fealty to the dictates of his conscience even if in a given case his conscience should be in error. Within each human being there is this domain in which the person speaks to God; this constitutes the unique dignity attributed to man. Whether or not an individual's action corresponds to this objective dignity within him, it is in this inner dignity that his right to religious liberty is rooted. The state has no right to enter this territory. Can it be said, then, that the state should not concern itself with religion? By no means, say those who express the above viewpoint. Rather the state must pave the way for this liberty. The state must preserve it and also provide the necessary equipment for the free exercise of religion. That is the state's contribution. In this way the state shows its respect for religion. Yet the state does not sit in judgment on religion. Now, obviously, such a theory of the state differs considerably from the idea mentioned above. The new conception is appropriate for our times. Its basis is the distinction between society and state, as Cardinal Shehan (Balti-more) pointed out at the Council. According to this view, the state is but an organization within society. It is a public body which is furnished with governmental power and charged by society with the execution of certain limited functions aimed at the common good. It must be added—and this made the situation even more complex—that the proponents of religious liberty by no means spoke with one voice when it came to the method of presenting their point of view. Some proponents wanted to present freedom in terms of theological concepts, which would necessarily have juridical consequences. American proponents wanted to present religious liberty in terms of a juridical or constitutional conception; one rooted, however, in theology, ethics, political philosophy and law. Thus the approaches were diametrically opposed. The French school began with an awareness of the need for religious liberty on the part of the free human being. Here the constitutional question was of secondary and subsequent importance. But the American school began with a comprehensive analysis of the free human person under a government whose powers were limited. Here the constitutional issue and the theological and moral issues were parallel and of equal importance.

At first the schema was influenced almost exclusively by the French school. This meant that once again there was a kind of ideal image (thesis) to be adapted to the historical reality (hypothesis). This was so directly opposed to the 'classical' conception that as a result two ideal conceptions stood in violent opposition to each other. This also prompted aimless discussion about the rights of the sincere but erring conscience—aimless in this instance because civil authority is utterly incapable of judging on such questions. As one version of the schema gave place to another, however, the American school became increasingly influential. There was no problem of an ideal concept for the American school because its thinking focused wholly on the concrete. Moreover, the real crux of the issue became much clearer at this juncture. There was much discussion. The declaration was reviewed three times—in the second, third and fourth sessions. Moreover, there were four different versions of the statements, excluding the improvements that were made to them. Yet the Council disputants for and against religious liberty never really understood one another. It could hardly be called a genuine discussion as a result. Father Murray was probably right in saying, 'The differences between the two viewpoints lay so deep that it would hardly be possible to go deeper. They represented the contemporary collision between the classical mentality and historical consciousness.'

The first viewpoint accused the second of doctrinaire errors—of liberalism, subjectivism, relativism, indifferentism, Rousseauism, laicism, social and political modernism, humanistic personalism, existentialism, ethical situationism and false irenicism. But it is easy to point out how untenable these accusations were.

The second point of view accused the first, not of errors in doctrine, but only of false conclusions based on an incredible 'fixedness'. What is meant by fixedness? Any development of doctrine involves many phases. But some insist on 'freezing' at a certain stage in their growth; they refuse to distinguish the permanent from the time-bound. They also refuse to come to grips realistically with the permanent. This fixedness is rooted in an invalid generalization. What Leo XIII thought in his particular time, for example, cannot be transformed into an abstract thesis, in which a theory called 'the state' is supposedly bound in principle to an abstraction modelled on political formula.

This was the central issue and also the intensely painful one. The armor of a purely abstract, archaic, rigid mentality had to be pierced, and then replaced by a mentality conscious of history and also by an awareness of historical salvation. This is precisely what happened. It might not have happened if Paul VI had not quietly hinted here and there that he wanted this declaration. Thus, for example, on April 19, 1964, in the course of an audience for the United Nations seminar on freedom of communications, he said: 'The Church is busy now with a problem related to yours—the problem of religious liberty. The significance and scope of the problem are so great that the Council is almost spellbound by it. But there is well-founded hope that a text on this issue will be published—a text of great consequence, not only for the Church, but for all those who feel the importance of such an authoritative statement in this area.' For the moment, of course, it was a purely domestic controversy—a Catholic affair. Many observers were a little confused and nonplussed, and really did not understand what it was all about. But they may (finally) have realized that a gap was being filled here—a gap which otherwise would have allowed the flow of poisonous water to continue polluting the mainstream of ecumenism.

The Community of non-Catholic Christians

It sometimes seemed as if two Councils were in progress simultaneously. There was the official Catholic Council gathered in all its splendor—we might perhaps call it the 'violet' council, exposed to public view each day when the fathers left St. Peter's. (Violet is a color entirely suited to mystical flight. Anthropologists have proved this fact.) Then there was the unofficial Council of non-Catholic Christians. We might speak of this one as the 'multi-colored' council, despite the fact that the prevalent color was somber black. But of course on ceremonial occasions it was not only the Eastern bishops who knew how to dress in solemn splendor: there was the dazzling white habit of the Protestant Brothers of Taizé, and again the glittering golden chains of university presidents or deans. The headgear, too, was as multi-plumed as birds of the skies. Billowing, pleated robes were frequently in evidence. This all blended very well into the baroque atmosphere of the Vatican—in much the same way as the Waldensian Church rivalled the trappings of the 'pious' in the Catholic realm. There were obviously mutual problems that had to be tackled!

Quite a few observers maintained that the problems occupying the World Council of Churches—problems within each Church or problems about the relation between Church and world—are indeed similar to those of Vatican Council II. Their Churches are also confronted with questions about the 'anonymous Christian' and about such matters as ecclesiastical office, eschatology, history of form, and salvation history. To find a common solution is much more difficult for them than for the Catholic Church. While the observers stimulated the Council, the Council also stimulated dialogue among the observers. Could this possibly be a harbinger of common witness?

Augustin Cardinal Bea, head of the Secretariat for Christian Unity (founded in 1960 in preparation for the Council) probably traveled as much throughout the different countries of Europe and America as all the other cardinals of the Roman Curia combined. As a former professor of exegesis and head of the Pontifical Biblical Institute in Rome, his specialized knowledge afforded him many points of contact with Protestant scholars. This alone gave the Secretariat international publicity. Cardinal Bea's courage showed itself when the Spanish and Portuguese feared that Council ecumenists would adopt a minimalist stance on the Marian issue. Bea immediately traveled to their countries to enlighten them. In the picture we find him talking to Dr. Oscar Cullmann who, as a guest of the secretariat, was an observer at all four sessions. A native Alsatian, he is professor at the Universities of Basel and Paris. He also lectured frequently to the Waldensian Institute in Rome. The initiative he showed in ecumenical matters was praised by many Council fathers. Pope Paul VI respects Dr. Cullmann especially for his books on salvation history. The most recent of them was dedicated to the Secretariat for Christian Unity, 'in the belief that even what separates will contribute toward the progress of salvation history, which includes many byways.'

It was from this tribune that the observers watched the daily activities of the Council. They had a better vantage point, and were closer to the altar and the praesidium than the bishops. At left front is the table of the Council secretaries, and at the right, the place for the choir at mass. The Council theologians had an inferior vantage point in the tribune located above the heads of the bishops. A journalist was admitted only occasionally to a general congregation, and never to the places of honor designated by the Swiss guard except in order to assist there. Father Dupré, for example, assisted as an interpreter for the observers. Actually, the visitors were rarely in need of such help, for they assisted one another.

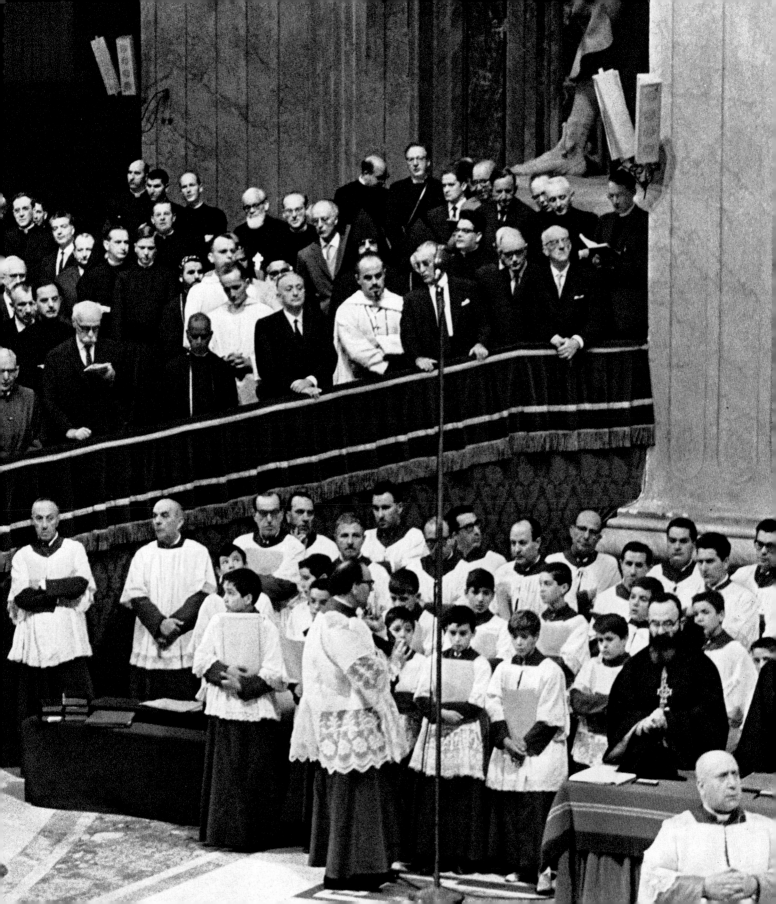

Once a week the members of the Secretariat for Christian Unity, led by Msgr. Willibrands (whom Paul VI rewarded by consecrating him bishop on June 28, 1964) and the observers would meet for dialogue on some issue currently facing the Council. It was said, at first, that the Secretariat wanted to 'tell the observers about the theological background'. Very soon this proved unnecessary, however. It soon became clear that among the observers themselves there was great divergence of opinion, and at times the debate among them was no less lively than the debate in the Council Hall. The meetings, at first somewhat stiff and formal, loosened up a little when the meeting place was transferred to the Foyer Unitas on the Piazza Navona. There the meetings were preceded by coffee, and a warm, human atmosphere was evident. The

Danish theologian, Kristen Skydsgaard is pictured here (left front) talking with Warren Quanbeck, an American theologian (center), and Dr. Vilmos Vayta (right), a Frenchman who is a member of the Institute for Ecumenical Research at Strasbourg. All three represented the Lutheran World Federation at the Council. Dr. Skydsgaard scored the highest number of points in a popularity contest among Council journalists. His press talks will survive the Council: He knew how to appeal to the heart.

Scarcely noticed by the public at the Council was a gathering of less than sixty people at the French center in Rome (St. Louis des Français). The first ones to speak there were Cardinal Martin (Rouen), president of the French National Secretariat for Christian Unity, and Pastor Marc Boegner, honorary president of the French Protestant Federation (both in left foreground). Martin declared that this was only a modest affair in comparison with the great events at the Council. Boegner, however, could not agree with this, for he felt that the hopes of the Council were being translated here into reality. What was the occasion? Professor Casalis of the Protestant Theological Faculty at Paris and the fiery young Dominican, Refoulé, explained the enterprise: A truly ecumenical Bible for everyone's use was in preparation. In this venture, every text was being translated jointly by both confessions and then revised by the Orthodox. The Letter to the Romans was chosen as a text, and double footnotes (one for Catholics and one for Protestants) proved to be necessary. This is to be a mass circulation Bible produced on a strictly scientific basis. The International Federation of Biblical Societies, a powerful organization on all continents, is to handle the distribution—in itself a most astonishing phenomenon, since this is a rather conservative organization. The work is supposed to be completed in ten years and will provide all Christians with a common Bible.

Today the Brothers of Taizé are known the world over. Two of them (Prior Roger Schütz and Max Thurian, the monastery's theologian) were guests of the Secretariat for Christian Unity at the Council. Pope John said to them, alluding to their white robes: 'I don't consider you competitors.' At Rome they rented an apartment in the heart of the city and set up an improvised monastery. Their main interest is South America. No one can say how many hours of consultation, prayer and meals they spent in common here with South American bishops and the Dominican sociologist, Father Lebret (with pipe). Not all South American bishops are considered open to the problems of the changing times. Yet in this instance, it is a matter of life and death. The Pope emphasized this in a speech he made at the end of the fourth session:

Which was more marvellous—the brothers' Christian readiness to be of assistance, or the bishops' grateful acceptance of this offer? A mere ten years ago they would have been described as 'intruders' and 'narrow-minded'. What changes have taken place on both sides!

Twice during each session, on one of the Council holidays, the observers would make a day-long excursion together. Among the most popular destinations were the ancient Benedictine monasteries of Monte Cassino and Subiaco which date from the founding of the order. They went not merely out of historical interest; the Benedictines are extremely hospitable people. The people, the cells, the praying, living and eating, provide a relaxed atmosphere. The visitor finds genuine pleasure in conversation with the monks. Here we find ourselves in Subiaco, where Benedict developed his order's rules from personal experience. St. Benedict's thorn bush stands in the monastery garden. Near it we see the observer from the Syrian Orthodox Church of India, Corepiscopus Abraham, conversing with one of the learned monks.

On December 4, 1965, near the end of the Council, something happened which for the holy city of Rome had a touch of the improbable. It happened 'outside the walls' because it went completely beyond the ordinary turn of events. The observers no longer conducted themselves like quiet and silent spectators, 'supposed to inform their Churches what the Roman Catholic Church in the Council is undertaking', as was stated in their statute. This time they were active. With the bishops, the Council fathers and the Pope, they held a joint prayer service in what is probably the most beautiful of Rome's basilicas, St. Paul's, in charge of the Benedictines. It was not supposed to be a spectacle, a public demonstration. People from television and radio, photographers and journalists were therefore excluded. Yet occasionally there was such a guest, as our picture testifies; for in Rome every rule has its exception, no matter how much we may talk of taboos. This, then, was to be an intimate occasion of common prayer. Protestant and Catholic representatives alternately read passages from scripture, in various languages. English hymns were sung. The Pope gave an address in which he cited Solowiew, an ecumenical theologian, who once spent a whole night in the corridor of the monastery because in the darkness he could not distinguish his cell door from the others. 'This is what often happens to those', says Solowiew, 'who are looking for truth. They often sleeplessly pass it by. They do not find the truth until finally a ray of the sun of divine wisdom brings the consoling discovery with great ease and joy.' The Pope added: 'And so, brothers, may this ray of the divine light make us all recognize the blessed door.' Such joint prayer services are, according to the Decree on Ecumenism, not only occasionally permissible, but also desirable.

With a long train, his eminence, Metropolitan Meliton of Heliopolis, delegate of Patriarch Athenagoras I of Constantinople, solemnly approaches the throne of Pope Paul on December 7, 1965. The Pope has at hand the brief he is about to deliver to Metropolitan Meliton, together with the kiss of peace. The brief says: 'We [the Pope] most deeply regret the unfounded words and actions' [of the year 1054, when the papal legate, Cardinal Humberto di Silva Candida and Patriarch Michael Caerularius of Constantinople insulted each other]. 'The excommunication imposed at that time, we delete from the memory of the Church and declare it null and void. It shall be forgotten and buried. . . .' To the left, next to the Pope, Cardinal Bea is reading a declaration jointly written by Paul VI and Athenagoras I which says the same thing as the brief. Meanwhile, in Constantinople, Patriarch Athenagoras I is receiving a delegation from the Pope, to whom he gives a *tomos* (the Greek equivalent for a brief) abrogating the excommunication of the papal legate while the same joint declaration is read. These acts do not yet constitute a reunion between the Catholic and Orthodox Church. Rather they serve to clear the atmosphere of its poison. There can be no rapprochement if distrust and bitterness still linger in people's hearts. In this sense, this solemn act at the conclusion of the Council was an impressive milestone on the way to a beginning of ecumenism.

Have Expectations Been Fulfilled?
(Response of a Protestant Observer)

Oscar Cullmann, professor of New Testament in Basel and Paris. Excerpts from a lecture given in Rome on December 2, 1965.

Have our expectation been fulfilled? The question, put this way, is perhaps premature. For this Council, to a much greater degree than earlier councils, can only be judged in terms of its effects....

Legitimate expectations

What did we expect? Only Pope John's definition of the Council's goal, given in his opening address on October 11, 1962, can tell us what expectations may be considered legitimate. This is the inevitable point of departure: 'The authentic teaching of the Church is to be studied and presented according to the methods of research employed by modern thought. The substance of the ancient doctrine contained in the body of faith must be distinguished from the formulation which has clothed it.' John XXIII then specified that such formulation must take into consideration the pastoral and ecumenical aspects. Negatively he had specified that no heresies should be condemned, no new dogmas formulated and no previous dogma repeated, for 'a Council would not be necessary for this'. This, then, is the framework within which our legitimate expectations must be considered....

I would especially like to emphasize the fact that the renewal of the Christian Church has to mean more than mere adjustment to the modern world; consequently, *aggiornamento* can never be the sole motive for renewal. This was also John XXIII's position, when he spoke of the difference between unchangeable substance and formulation. Now the problem of the borderline between unchangeable substance and formulation is most difficult and complex. Yet neither Pope John XXIII nor the Council have dealt with this problem. Given the framework of the Council, perhaps it was impossible to do so. Yet the Council seems to me to suffer from the fact that this question—the line between unchangeable substance and changeable form—was considered already answered. I do not overlook the fact that many Protestant theologians, too, in their effort to make the biblical message acceptable to the present world, give this problem no attention at all. Paul VI's address on November 18, 1965, did try, quite rightly, to reject a false conception of *aggiornamento*. Yet this address did not contribute any clarification to our question. It must be admitted that the idea of *aggiornamento* is in itself insufficient. It doesn't help to say that the substance and formulation must be distinguished, if we neglect to show what the core is and what is formulation.

The value of the unchangeable substance

But the problem lies deeper. Not only must we admit the problem about the line between substance and formulation; we must above all be concerned to see that reformulation is not a purely external affair; it must proceed from the substance itself. I must discuss this fundamental question, because the answer to our question about the fulfillment of expectations is closely dependent upon it.

The Protestant Reformation was able to produce its very important effects because its basic principle was *not* the removal of contemporary deficiencies, as is often alleged; in other words, it was no mere *aggiornamento*, because the attack upon deficiencies came primarily from a motive of faith. So too, the Council's *aggiornamento* should only come as a consequence of an impulse from the core. *Aggiornamento* should be a consequence, not a starting point.

Fortunately this *has* been the case, in both the text of the Council and its outcome. The overall impulse behind this Council would be unthinkable were the desire for renewal not grounded in faith and theology. Yet it is still regrettable that an overarching principle did not control what the Council did. We Protestants did expect something more than mere devising of formulation: we expected that these reformulations would proceed from a certain rearrangement of values within the unchangeable substance. This is possible without surrendering any of the substance. It may be that certain elements belonging essentially to the core were at length wrongly removed to the periphery and peripheral elements shifted to the center. A renewal can aim at a rearrangement which refocuses on the original situation without surrendering any element of substance.

This is what to a great extent actually did happen. Our expectations have been partially fulfilled, not in regard to an explicit overall principle, but in regard to what actually happened. They were fulfilled insofar as the *aggiornamento* was no mere *aggiornamento*, but rather the result of a rearrangement within the core itself. If in many texts biblical concepts which view things in terms of salvation history have replaced static scholastic ideas, then this willy-nilly somehow touches the substance. And so those sections where a dynamic and biblical thinking has replaced static thinking best fulfill the expectations of the observers. And these are precisely the texts where the Council's desire for renewal comes through most clearly. For here the connection between present, past and future is most clearly seen in a perspective of salvation history; here is seen the stream within which the Church moves, and here the problems begin to find solution.

Specific texts

The *liturgy* schema, which filled us with joy from the very beginning, not only makes suggestions for liturgical reform which are entirely in line with our own suggestions, but it is inspired throughout by the Bible. This is clear not only from the language used, but in the fundamental treatment of Christian worship of God. Here my expectations were not only fulfilled; they were entirely surpassed. . . .

The schema on the *Church* not only uses a new vocabulary but also, where it speaks of the People of God, speaks in language which brings the Catholic concept of the Church very close to our Protestant concept. The schema on the *lay apostolate* is orientated toward the Bible and toward salvation history. The same is true of the schema on the *missions*, which is set in an eschatological framework, and also of certain parts of the theologically very important schema on *divine revelation*, to which we will return later. Everywhere we find ourselves on common ground, despite the fact that some very profound differences do remain. Many sections of these texts we can accept without any alteration.

One text especially, and one which is not sufficiently appreciated by those who are not Catholics, deserves special attention—the schema on *priestly training*. I believe it is one of the best and most important. Here the study of scripture has moved entirely into the foreground. This text is concerned more than any other with bringing the Council's influence to bear on the future. If the future training of priests follows these principles, the orientation of Catholic thought in terms of scripture and salvation history is assured. The real work of *aggiornamento* will then be carried on through a deepened reflection on the substance of Christian belief. Here we can say without reservation that our expectations have been surpassed.

In the schema on *revelation* we find some real gems among the statements on scripture. We are indeed very far removed from previous Catholic statements regarding scripture as a dead letter, when we read today in the liturgy schema that God speaks in his word and in his sacraments; and in the schema on revelation when we read that God comes through scripture to meet his children and engage in dialogue with them. We are unreservedly happy with statements to the effect that the study of scripture is the soul of theology, that preaching must go to the Bible for nourishment; and in general with most of the statements in the last chapter of the schema on revelation on the place of the Bible in the life of the Church. As an exegete, I am completely in agreement with the principles of exegesis employed in the fifth chapter dealing with the New Testament in general. For all practical purposes I also agree with statements regarding textual exposition.

Did we expect more in the schema than we found there? *Could* we expect more in a Catholic text on this subject? I hardly think so. But I would like to warn those Catholic friends who stand theologically closest to us that they should not think that because so many of our expectations have been fulfilled we are in agreement with the statement on the relationship of scripture, tradition and the teaching office. On the contrary, it is precisely in areas like this, in which the Catholic position is so close to the Protestant position, that the fundamental difference between these two positions becomes most clear. Even though we also admit that scripture is to be expounded in the Church—and I mean *in*—and that tradition may help us uncover its positive values, I insist that scripture must be a criterion. By this I mean that in post-apostolic tradition we must distinguish legitimate elements from distorting elements; and that in these cases, scripture must be viewed, in comparison to the Church, as a higher authority and a critical norm. In view of the dogmatically established view of tradition and the infallability of the teaching office, I believe, as I have said, that we should not have expected much more. Nevertheless it is regrettable that even the word 'norm' has disappeared from the text. . . .

You will hardly be surprised that the schema on *ecumenism*, in its quality as an ecumenical statement, far surpasses our boldest expectations. At the beginning of the Council we hardly hoped that, in an official statement of the Council, non-Catholic Churches as such would be recognized to such a degree; and that their individual characteristics would be evaluated positively as charisms. An entirely new conception of ecumenism has been presented here; and along with it an entirely new Catholic conception of the Church: the Roman Church is no longer viewed as the one Church which is to absorb all others. According to the original intention, this new ecumenical orientation was supposed to be manifest in all the texts. This orientation is generally in evidence, and it is especially marked in the text on the missions and in that on divine revelation (where in biblical translation cooperation with the separated brethren is recommended); we find the ecumenical stress especially in the schema on the lay apostolate, which explicitly states that through cooperation with other Churches the laity bear witness to Christ as redeemer of the world and to the unity of the human family.

In this connection I would like now to point out a passage in section 11 of the schema on ecumenism. This passage, considered in all its consequences, offers the most far-reaching hope for the future; it seems to me to be the Council statement which offers most promise for the furthering of renewal and facilitating of dialogue. Yet, strangely enough, very little has been said about it. Here we read that 'in Catholic teaching there exists an order or hierarchy of truths, since they vary in their truths of the Catholic relationship to the foundation of Christian faith'. This hierarchy makes possible a rearrangement of the very substance of Catholic teaching. . . .

The texts alone not sufficient

In addition, I would like to add this general remark: it is not right to consider only the texts of this Council. To do this would be to approach the Council without a sense of history. Here, more than in any other Council, the *Council event* as a whole will have as much effect on the future as the texts themselves. For this reason we are grateful we were permitted to be present as observers. Even the most severe critic will have to admit that a desire for renewal has animated this Council. This desire has not been completely stifled even in texts which underwent many changes. Often the first rather than the later texts more clearly show this prophetic spirit. However, the reverse is true of other texts, especially the schema on revelation. . . .

The enthusiasm of the first session has, of course, disappeared. This is the fate of every movement of reform; the sixteenth century Reformation was no different. We have, however, been able to establish that even without this enthusiasm, there was greater depth in the discussions of the following sessions. We all too readily forget that much which was considered revolutionary in the first session and was contested as such, was in the second considered self-evident. The reaction to certain regrettable incidents also showed that renewal was at work.

Above all we must not forget that all votes proved that a clear majority of the Council fathers, from the beginning to the end of the Council, desired this renewal. While we did hope for this from the Council, we were not entirely certain that we should expect it. That the majority of Council fathers wanted renewal must be remembered in the future. The Council fathers witnessed even more than the texts to this desire for renewal. Anyone who heard their speeches, inspired by very profound biblical faith, will not forget them. It was above all in the brief testimonies which so often seemed to us prophetic statements, that we experienced something of that prophetic spirit of which John XXIII had spoken. . . .

Outlook for post-conciliar times

How will the Council take effect? Precisely here must we keep in mind not only the texts (although they are important too), but especially the spirit of renewal present in them, even if often only haltingly. . . . The theological motif given expression by this Council should become the model for post-conciliar renewal, and this motif was the thorough penetration of Catholic belief with the spirit of the Bible and salvation history. Deeper reflection upon the boundaries between external formulation and substance of belief seems to me to be necessary.

Finally, let me touch on what concerns us Protestants most of all: namely, the ecumenism of the post-conciliar period. There is today a sort of fashionable ecumenism. Ecumenism has become a slogan. Today there is actually an *ecumenical triumphalism* which, like all Church triumphalism, is not good because it overlooks what I call the tension between the 'already' fulfilled and the still distant 'not yet'. . . .

Another danger is *ecumenical sentimentalism*. Because we have, in the course of this Council, come extraordinarily close to one another, we are in danger of minimizing for the sake of friendship the divergencies which remain. In doing this we only injure the cause of further rapprochement. . . .

If I say in retrospect at the conclusion of the Council that, seen as a whole, the expectations, insofar as they were not illusions and disregarding individual small points, have been fulfilled and in many respects even surpassed; and if, looking ahead toward its effect in the future, I express the conviction that the Catholic Church, while preserving her identity, will further change her appearance and that reunion will make further progress, it is because I am convinced that, in addition to all other influences and despite diplomacy and discord, *the Holy Spirit also* was at work.

Structures of the Church

The Pope is Nothing without the Church

The Horizon Broadens
and the Bonds are Strengthened

Many Together are Stronger
than One Spread Thin

The Proof of True Unity is Multiplicity

Drawing: The Square of St. Peter's at night

The bishops, who are successors to the college of apostles in their teaching and pastoral office, and in whom the apostolic body continues to exist, are, together with their head, the Bishop of Rome, equally endowed with supreme and full power over the entire Church.

(The Constitution on the Church)

A Condition Often Neglected

To obtain some idea of where the Church is headed in the future, it is essential to examine what lines the Council pursued. These ramifications can be traced to best advantage by finding out which proposals were most vigorously debated and demanded the longest time for the Council's consideration. These items may not necessarily be the most profound and important, for seldom is a decisive battle fought in a nation's capital. Yet the most controversial issues can provide a strategic vantage point from which inroads can be made into more profound themes. The problem of why these themes were debated so vehemently and extensively, and why they were 'strategically important' are questions that have been ignored in many assessments of the Council. The overall picture has been tilted out of perspective as a result. We mentioned earlier the importance of realizing that at this Council the 'classical' theological mode of thinking retreated before the methods of 'historical' theology. This was obvious, for instance, during the discussion on religious liberty and revelation. But why were these two issues so bitterly contested while the text on ecumenism was passed with hardly a dissenting murmur? And why did this text actually become more positive instead of being weighed down with compromising modifications? The decree on ecumenism was assuredly an example of theology based on historical theology. Why then was it welcomed so readily, while the texts on religious liberty and revelation were so hotly contested? Wherein lay the difference? It is perhaps hard to appreciate the fact that the ecu-menical movement is a relatively modern phenomenon. Ecumenism has not been opposed as yet (not even in the Catholic Church) by a counter-movement, nor has it become embroiled in polemics, apologetics or controversies. These latter methods of dialogue have gradually become the blunt weapons of theology. They are still with us, still in operation, and we must attempt to explore the reasons for their continuing existence. Let us remember that Father Sebastian Tromp, S. J., secretary of Cardinal Ottaviani's Theological Commission and certainly a typical 'classical' theologian, said at the beginning of the Council: 'We still have firm control of the wheel.' Note that the use of the word 'still' implies a position of increasing weakness.

Since ecumenism did not collide with a counter-movement 'still' bitterly struggling for mastery, it fared much better than issues like religious liberty and revelation which carry with them a prolonged history of heated controversy. When argument sprang up in the Council, it was not simply a question of mobility against rigidity; the conflict was rather between two contending historical movements. A pointed example of this is the 'two-source' theory of revelation. Ecclesiastical records show that the Council of Trent not only failed to resolve the issue, but even deliberately chose to leave the question open. But the 'classical' theologians of Vatican Council II deemed it an opportune time to proclaim this theory as universal Catholic doctrine. In terms of 'classical' Church thinking this meant that theology was on the march!

Much the same can be said about the question of religious liberty. The statements of Pope Leo XIII

(1878—1903) spelled out doctrinal progress; after years of confusion, he had quite definitely separated Church and State. But it was not clear whether his concept of the state represented timeless doctrine or embodied a unique kind of political stance. Now the champions of classical theology felt that the experts had completed all the doctrinal homework that was necessary, and therefore wanted Leo XIII's conception of the state declared one of the eternal truths of the Church. So we find that here, too, the classicists are trying to do something more than defend a position 'still' held.

The battles were not fought in those areas where the new movement met with customary immobility, but in an arena where flexibility already existed. The movement of the majority did not merely want to halt the minority (or 'classical') movement; they wanted to reverse it. It is not surprising therefore that on this issue alone controversy reached its zenith. Yet it is essential to note that neither of the two currents of opinion intended to make any 'inorganic' or extrinsic assault upon the mainstream of Church tradition. Was there to be revolution or evolution? Revolution obliterates what has burgeoned historically; it shackles continuity and seeks to replace the old with something entirely new. But evolution is an organically constructive process, by which stone is planted upon stone until the edifice is completed.

There is, of course, a kind of evolution in which certain original values are swamped and replaced by some other value which temporarily flourishes in the normal way. Catholic teaching itself takes into account the fact that even the Church is sometimes subject to this kind of evolution, a fact which is not necessarily something to be deplored. It should be regarded more as a transitional, provisional process. A perfectly sound value may blossom and grow, but to excessive proportions. Yet other values, temporarily suppressed for the sake of this growth, must have *their* right to expansion and development. When this happens, the swollen value must be deflated to make room for values that have long slumbered under the dust of neglect.

The Council majority borrowed from past tradition. It did not herald something revolutionary, nor did it unravel from scripture something hitherto unknown. The majority did demonstrate values which, seeking their origins in scripture, had flourished in a long drawn out dawn but had subsequently faded into the twilight of obscurity. The majority insisted that the time had now arrived to examine and restitute certain neglected aspects of the Church, and that these resurrected items be given their rightful place in the sun where they could flower again. Yet members of the minority wanted to continue watering the doctrinal plants of 'recent times'—sometimes interpreted in their eyes as 50 years, sometimes even a century or more. The minority was at no time prepared to concede the possibility that *any* values had been neglected, obscured or banished from the light of day.

Pope and Council

The most pungent example of a fundamental controversy in the Church was the issue of the structures of the Church. In this respect, it should be made clear that ecclesiastical functions are not more important than the real work of the Church. Official functions are services, and services are subordinate to the person or the human reality being served. These services are like scaffolding, and scaffolding is functionless without a building; while a building devoid of scaffolding does serve a purpose. It was not an obsession with the scaffolding of ecclesiastical functions that prompted the Council to examine this question. It was but attempting to determine the nature of the structure of service. For example, what was the function of a council in relation to a pope?

At the Council of Constance (1414—1418), when three popes reigned simultaneously, the prevalent view seemed to be that a council outweighed the pope in authority. This conception had its strongest advocates at the Council of Basel (1431). But nothing was definitely decided there, and the question smoldered on. Nor did the Council of Trent solve the problem. At Vatican I (1869—1870) the twin definition of papal primacy of jurisdiction and papal infallibility in matters of faith seemed to swing the pendulum once and for all toward the idea that all power was exclusively vested in the papacy. But this was not the case. During Vatican I, for example, Cardinal Rauscher of Vienna pointed out that, while the issue was clearly the nature of the relationship between the pope and the bishops, a relationship can be correctly understood only when we keep our sights focused simultaneously on both points of reference. This valid point was ignored as long as discussion itself separated the two main points of reference involved; that is, when dialogue dealt exclusively with the pope first and foremost, and only

with the bishops as an afterthought. On this issue the function of the papacy alone was discussed at Vatican I. The chaos that existed at the time prevented discussion of the other point of reference, and the Council adjourned without having considered the juxtaposition of the bishops. Vatican I provided not only an incomplete but also a lopsided answer to the question of the relationship between pope and bishops. This answer would be completely erroneous if the Council had not announced explicitly that the pope cannot be examined alone, in isolation from the bishops or from the Church as a whole. He cannot be viewed as someone enthroned before the Church, like a monarch surveying his vassals. Vatican I's schema on the Church, prepared prior to the Council, said: 'What was given to Peter alone—supreme power of binding and loosing—was obviously given also to the apostolic college united with its head.' Yet this schema never reached the discussion stage. Consequently, although the currents of thought which had led to the definition of papal supremacy exerted great influence on doctrine as well as practice after Vatican I, there was no corresponding influence from the currents of opinion that converged on the question of the bishop's power.

The Evolution of the Papacy

In the first centuries of Christianity, the role of the papacy was of minimal importance. Bishops dominated the early councils. Rome certainly held the prime position of special privilege. But there was no explicit theory concerning Rome's preeminence. Nor was there any centralization, since the dominant concept was that of community. Rome acted as supreme arbiter in conflicts which were otherwise insoluble, and even then it wielded power as an exception rather than as a rule. Considering the consciousness of the Church in those centuries, it would be easier to prove episcopal collegiality than point to papal primacy. But gradually the legal primacy of the pope emerged. This preeminence could be vindicated by scripture and it already existed in a rudimentary way within the Church's consciousness. Conflict with secular power played an important role in this development, since the pope was a powerful guardian of the office of bishop. The idea of a straight, clear-cut evolutionary line thus continued to dominate.

Distrust and Anxiety: The Roots of Over-development

But then feuds between popes and powerful groups of bishops sprang up, while political motives came into play. The Christianity of East and West was sundered by the great schism. In short, confidence decreased as distrust increased. Rome solidified its juridical approach and made an increasingly intense and anxious effort to centralize Church government in order to ward off any future rifts. Conciliarism, Gallicanism, Febronianism in Germany, and finally the Reformation prompted Rome to tighten its reins and centralize ecclesiastical life.

Meanwhile the Church began to widen its horizons with the discovery of the New World, an event which led to missionary activities on a worldwide scale. These developments were followed in turn by easier and swifter communications, while in the political sphere the power wielded by absolute monarchs assumed new dimensions. With the declining influence of theological speculation came the more acceptable norm of juridical thinking. All these factors were gradually fused together to create an ecclesiastical edifice which differed from an absolute monarchy as drastically as one egg differs from another. Court customs were carefully aped in every detail, from gardens, thrones, crowns, and glittering ceremonials right down to the very buckles on shoes. An otherwordly atmosphere of remoteness and aloofness was emphasized above all. The pope had to eat alone, for example; he could be approached only after a ritualistic display of genuflections; while in his august presence people had to remain kneeling. On public appearances he had to be exalted above the rabble. After all this, could there by any justification for regarding the pope as the 'servant of the servants of God'? Was there anything left of the 'fraternal community' ideal except mere abstract theory? Could anything be found in the Church corresponding to the idea that bishops possess power 'by divine right'?

It is hardly surprising that there were men at Vatican II who wanted to see this autocratic line of development carried to its ultimate: namely the recognition of the pope as the sole source of any right in the Church; the pope as the only guarantor of truth; the council as a concession granted by the absolute monarch, the pope, who would provide the guiding light and be the source of unity not only on a social level but also on the plane of human existence itself. And this concept was supposed to be the fruit of a century-long development toward enlightenment.

Such a trend toward papal supremacy went hand in hand with another tendency—toward uniformity. The Uniate Eastern Churches, which still had to be gradually brought into line, possessed diversities and anomalies which in the eyes of the Roman uniformists seemed a kind of residue from the schism. These diversities in liturgical language, in canon law, in spiritual matters and in theological thinking would all have to be flattened out to a uniform pattern, so that total harmony could be attained down to the last individual. The Church of Christ throughout the world would then talk with one single voice and would be seen in its identical trappings everywhere. As a result, any member of this Church would automatically feel at home anywhere. This was the idea. An idyllic idea indeed—and one which is totally unrealistic.

While nurtured in the realm of abstraction, this was certainly a noble ideal. Meanwhile, back in the world of reality, it was feared that a modern Catholic would feel as little 'at home' everywhere as he felt when he actually *was* at home. The alienation created by this uniformity would make it increasingly impossible for the Church to find roots anywhere. The Church, alienated from the world all over the world, proclaimed herself to be the source of unity that men craved. From this claim arose the danger of its being considered an unbelievable institution, and the mounting suspicion that the Church seemed uncannily like a totalitarian state.

Moreover in its own sphere of activity, the Church had begun to function more like a piece of machinery than a living organism. From top to bottom everything seemed to operate smoothly and without tension, while fewer and fewer sounds of dissent were being heard from the bottom. Up at the top, all that was heard were reports that commands had been obeyed, together with incessantly urgent pleas for new directives. Individual personal responsibility seemed increasingly paralyzed. Pius XII was already aware of this—and it terrified him.

The Counter-Movement

But at Vatican II a breakthrough came when this lopsided development was met by a powerful counter-movement which enjoyed the blessing of Pope John XXIII. Neglected lay people, 'underdeveloped' bishops, priests forever doomed to cringing servitude—they all were now insisting on their right to live. True, there was already an international lay movement; here and there conferences of bishops existed, sometimes covering entire continents. The central administrative offices were ready to make at least temporary concessions in view of special situations in various countries. The Curia did delegate power when speedy action was necessary and empowered its emissaries to act on their own responsibility, albeit temporarily and within defined limits. But this did not change the principle that required everything to flow from top to bottom—all power, all initiative, all wisdom, grace and truth. And from bottom to top nothing came but petitions and cries for help. So, as in the past, the horizontal bonds fell in shreds. The Church now seemed a vertical monolith.

Without doubt the Roman congregations were ready for some measure of reform. The technical need for some kind of decentralization was even admitted. (On several later occasions Paul VI praised the Curia's willingness to reform.) But a distinction must be made between merely technical adjustments which reorganize but leave the system essentially unchanged, and those changes that sprout from a radically different theology of the Church. While institutions may more or less resemble one another in externals, their inner meaning can differ quite fundamentally. The new vision of structure has been described as representing a tendency toward democracy. The parallel cannot be denied entirely, even though profound differences between political and ecclesiastical structure tend to make such terminology inaccurate. A democratic government obtains its power from the people; it is they who determine its concrete form. This is not so in the Catholic Church. Popes and bishops derive their office from Christ. Christ left no doubt that this office is one of service, but the nature of this service is immutable. This is what is meant when it is said that pope and bishops exist by 'divine right'. Consequently the pope cannot abolish the episcopacy (and nobody has ever tried to claim that he can) any more than the bishops can abolish the papacy. This is not the matter under discussion, however.

The Bishops' Independence

What we must ask here is whether or not a bishop, by virtue of the fact that he is placed in charge of a given region, is invested also with the powers necessary for governing that region or that community. The question also arises whether the pope may temporarily *limit* those powers only if this becomes necessary for the general well-being of the Church. This is one of those highly controversial questions. In the press of centralization many powers had been removed from the individual bishops. In the first draft of Vatican II's schema on the bishops, it was suggested that the bishops' powers again be broadened by way of papal *grant*. But the bishops refused. They did not want their powers broadened by gift; they wanted their own rights back. This explains why the decree on the pastoral office of bishops now reads: 'As successors to the apostles, the bishops have in the dioceses entrusted to them every ordinary, independent and immediate power necessary for the discharge of their pastoral function.'

The Pope in the Church

The other aspect of the problem is far more important. René Laurentin correctly says in his commentary on the second session that it would be inaccurate to say that Vatican II had given us, in its statement on the bishops, a kind of addition to the statements on the pope made by Vatican I. The statements of Vatican I on the papacy were not meant to be the opening chapter of a theology of the Church. In its definition of papal prerogatives Vatican I did not intend to convey a deeper grasp of the Church, but rather to establish an unconditional authority in a time of crisis between reason and faith. In fact, this temporary anxiety sidetracked the schema on the Church originally planned for Vatican I. Vatican II, however, expressly intended to produce a theology of the Church.

And so Vatican II was not supposed to repeat endlessly Vatican I's definitions on the papacy; it was supposed to show how these definitions fit into a total view of the Church. Some bishops made an effort in this direction, notably Bishop Descuffi of Turkey. He attempted to show that the pope, although not legally bound to get the other bishop's formal approval when he issues an infallible pronouncement, can nevertheless only express the faith of the Church as a whole. This appropriate postscript was not included, however, because some bishops misunderstood it and were so agitated that it was thought better not to insist upon it.

Collegiality by Divine Right

The doctrine of episcopal collegiality was even more important. Collegiality means that the bishops as a body enjoy as supreme an authority in the Church as does the pope alone. This applies to questions of faith as well as matters of discipline. Obviously this college also includes the pope since he is its head. Thus the false opposition of bishops to pope, for centuries such a painful fact of Church life, was in principle eliminated. So also was the mechanistic and simplistic notion of a vertical, authoritarian regime. This was surrendered in favor of the horizontal unity that so far had been neglected. It was even maintained that episcopal ordination alone (as long as it was validly and licitly conferred within the community of the Church) makes the ordained a mem-ber of the college of bishops and gives him authority over the entire Church. This collegial power is solemnly exercised at any council and also whenever any collegial act is performed. The pope may call for collegial acts; and for such actions to be legally valid it is necessary that the pope 'approve them or accept them freely' because if he did object, collegiality would be incomplete.

No New Theory

This means a completely new concept of the Church, a highly unlikely concept considering the previous development toward centralization. But the concept is not revolutionary: It comes from the gospel and the early centuries of the Church. More than this, the Council fathers who defended this position proved that collegiality had never been extinct; it had only been neglected in practice. It was most astonishing to hear the young auxiliary of Bologna, Bishop Betazzi, point out that the strongest defenders of the papacy at the turn of the 18th century—Christianopoulos, Bolgeni, Capellari (who later became Gregory XIV)—were equally energetic defenders of collegiality. The view that all jurisdiction is solely papal in origin dates back no further than the middle of the 19th century.

Paralysis in the Council

We see then that a rather recent tendency has passed itself off as the result of a long doctrinal growth. But it is the opposite view—collegiality—that represents genuine development. Yet this conflict paralyzed the second session of the Council for weeks. When the moderators wanted to pose five questions to clarify the majority's position, the motion was stalled for two weeks due to the objection of some of the presidents and the head of the Council's coordinating commission, Secretary of State Cicognani. Superficially, this was a question of jurisdiction, but the deeper motive was the minority's desire to hide its numerical inadequacy. On October 29, 1963, the five questions *were* posed and the minority which opposed collegiality was unable to muster more than a fifth as many votes as the collegialists. Now came a minority campaign to invalidate this vote, a campaign led by Curia cardinals—Browne and Ottaviani—and by Bishop Carli, the minority's theological spokesman. This lasted until November 13, and during this time there was no decision on whether the theological commission or the bishops had the right to say the final word. This was most certainly an unparalleled calamity!

Even Bishop Charrière of Fribourg in Switzerland and a man who in no sense identified himself with the 'progressives', said in a public lecture after the second session: 'The Holy See will always need an agency to supervise everything connected with faith and morals. If, however, the responsible heads of this agency opposed the decision of papally-appointed moderators as openly as they did at the Council, then the inevitable conclusion is that their attack is an attack on the pope himself. And if heads of an agency representing the pope behave that way, then it is impossible to see how they can any longer impose decisions on others in the name of the pope—or for that matter how they can ever expect obedience. What this amounts to is the self-destruction of the Council minority. The entire Church has [had] to suffer from their opposition to the moderators. It is precisely because I do think it indispensable to have a strong and flexible agency empowered to act in the name of the Holy See, that I regret the attitude of those who presume to defend the pope against Council moderators whom the pope himself has appointed. This is an evil which can no longer be tolerated.'

Actually Paul VI settled the whole affair in that indirect and quiet way so typical of his noble yet wholly independent approach—an approach which has been widely misunderstood. First, he altered the makeup of the theological commission through new elections held at the end of the second session (on November 21, 1963); he saw to it that the minority no longer dominated this commission. Second, he quietly made it clear to Ottaviani that the commissions were the Council's executive agencies and not its judges. Third, he emphasized in his opening address at the third session that he was well aware of what the situation was when he continued the Council, and that therefore any attempt to remove collegiality from the Council agenda was completely out of line. A great deal of needless public excitement and confusion would have been avoided had the address been analyzed in this perspective.

The Consequences

But let us return to our problem. Even in the weakened form in which episcopal collegiality was eventually incorporated into the text (as a fact of faith, not as a definition) it shows that the recent practice of one-sided emphasis on papal authority is out of harmony with the Church's structure. This is not to say that popes abused their prerogatives, but that powers instituted for emergencies were pushed to the limit and made out to be the norm. And so now efforts will have to be made to restore normal operations in keeping with the Church's true structure. Here the pope has primary responsibility. He must no longer act as an absolute ruler but as the head of a college. Paul VI gave up his tiara during the third session; at the Council he appeared before the bishops on foot and with only a small entourage; frequently he went unnoticed and alone. He had already reduced the number of guards, simplified their equipment, and took away the rifles of the palatine guards. These were all small steps, but the eventual result will no doubt be a dignified ceremonial in no way reminiscent of a court.

More essential is the issue of Curial reform. There is no denying that the pope needs the Curia. But the bishops criticized three things: (1) They objected to the Curia's methods, particularly those of the Holy Office. Cardinal Frings emphasized the prime need for distinguishing administrative and judicial procedure in all congregations, including the Holy Office. 'The procedures employed by the Holy Office', he said, 'are often out of harmony with modern times; they damage the Church and are a scandal to non-Catholics. The work of those who have labored for years in the Holy Office in defense of revealed truth is difficult and arduous. Yet even this authority must refrain from condemning or judging any person accused of deviation in faith without a hearing in the presence of his bishop, and without knowing the charges adduced against him and his writings, and without his being given a chance to improve his work.' Cardinal Ottaviani indignantly refuted these accusations —accusations, he said in a quivering voice, which could only have come 'from ignorance, not to say something worse'. He described the care with which the Holy Office proceeded in order to form an 'objective' judgment. True as these explanations may have been, they did not answer Cardinal Frings' criticism. Actually the reform of the Holy Office effected by Paul VI at the end of the fourth session followed point by point the suggestions of the Cardinal Archbishop of Cologne.

(2) The bishops, particularly Cardinal Lercaro, criticized the structure of the Roman Curia. It lacked, he said, a suitable coordinating agency. This function was in practice discharged by two of the extant congregations, both of them unsuited to the task—the Holy Office and the Secretariat of State. The Holy Office had a merely negative function—the preservation of purity of faith—whereas the Church's mission is to preach the gospel in a positive fashion. The secretariat is a relic of the time when the Church was still a state, and is therefore political in viewpoint. This makes it even less acceptable to the universal Church than the Holy Office. Lercaro therefore suggested (Cardinal Rugambwa of Africa concurring) that the entire structure of papal offices be revaluated, and that a coordinating agency oriented toward pastoral goals be put in charge. The pope complied with this wish by giving the Holy Office a positive goal—the promotion of

faith—and changing its name to fit this new purpose. It is now the Doctrinal Congregation. It has been distinctly deprived of its claim to primacy among the offices, since it is no longer called 'holy' and is no longer 'first'. So far nothing has been done about the Secretariat of State, but some kind of change is expected. (3) The most far-reaching change was proposed by Maximos IV Saigh, the Melchite patriarch of Antioch. Not only should papal offices be forced to accept non-Roman membership—and thus become international-ized—and to hear the opinions of local bishops on their decisions; a kind of synod or council of bishops is also needed. The synod would be above the Curia, and would assist the pope in governing the Church. For Roman bureaus to be ranked (even in the name of the pope) above the episcopate instituted by Christ is contrary to the divinely constituted structure of the Church. The pope's natural auxiliaries are the bishops. They represent the manifold shape and diversity of the Church of Christ, and so a far-reaching autonomy should be restored to them through patriarchates set up in modern form, each with its own liturgy, its own canon law, and its own theology. This of course went far beyond mere Curial reform. The pope complied with these wishes in a way. He appointed Archbishop Garrone of Toulouse, the sharpest critic of the Con-gregation of Seminaries, as head of this congregation. Into the former Holy Office, now the Doctrinal Congregation, he put—as third ranking member—the Belgian Moeller, who for years had been professor of modern literature. He placed the Congregation of Rites under the newly formed Liturgical Commission, headed by Cardinal Lercaro, and staffed by local bishops. The Council itself had decided to subordinate the Congregation for the Propagation of the Faith to a missionary commission whose members are drawn from candidates proposed by local bishops' conferences. Finally Pope Paul established three different kinds of synods—international synods, territorial synods and synods for special problems. The members, elected by bishops' conferences, are themselves bishops. The synods are not yet what Patriarch Maximos envisioned, but they can be considered a step in the right direction. Their statutes specify that they are temporary.

Beyond this the bishops and pope have decided to establish national and supra-national episcopal confer-ences throughout the world. Individual bishops are to set up diocesan councils to govern their dioceses in a more collegial fashion. Even the local parishes are to have councils formed from lay parishoners. Without doubt this will give the whole structure of the Church an entirely new character. Except for the sphere of liturgical renewal, it is here that the consequences of the Council will be most distinctly visible. Yet these changes have only begun. Whether they will be changes inspired by the Spirit, whether they will advance the two-way dialogue between leadership and members, whether a non-totalitarian, living diversity will make the Church attractive (especially to Eastern Christianity) —all this depends not on external forms alone, but on whether or not collegiality and all that we call interior renewal is actually put into effect.

Structural Reform in Externals

'We said: critics. Yes, because it is known that the Roman Curia, while praised and appreciated for its incontestable merits, is also criticized. . . . We never do what we ought to do when it is a question of service to the cause of Christ and of souls. It is therefore understandable, and in line with Divine Providence, that such a phenomenon should recur again and again in the course of the history of the Church.'

(Paul VI on Reform of the Curia)

Structural reform of the Church was given long and detailed discussion during the Council. This was discussion in depth; it tried to measure the shape and form of Church government today against the Gospel, and against the earliest times of Christian history when the will of the founder was still a vital force. The idea was to try to distinguish between historical accretions and the wishes of Christ, Lord of the Church, and to find guidelines for action in line with present-day requirements. The fathers found a surprising similarity between the will of Christ and the needs of the hour: among the guideposts for reform were simplicity, detachment from politics and diversity, along with the preservation of unity. Simplicity was the chief necessity in a time without princes and kings or elaborate courts; a time in which two-thirds of humanity went hungry, and in which truth produced conviction only when it spoke and manifested itself in simplicity rather than in ceremonial pomp. That is why Pope John XXIII, in his message of September 11, 1962, proclaimed the Church 'Church of the Poor'. This expression never lost its hold on the bishops. 'The poor have the Gospel preached to them,' the Lord said in proclaiming the arrival of the Kingdom of God. Did the Vatican measure up to this standard? The difference was striking. 'If your eye is the source of scandal, put it out.' These, too, are the words of the Lord.

At the opening of the Council, and at every solemn session thereafter, the Swiss Guard assembled in battle formation. This was surely more of a spectacle than a serious affair. Today, halberds and cuirasses are no longer useful in war. The Guard was established in 1506 by Julius II for the personal protection of the pope. In 1527, at the sack of Rome, 147 of them were killed. Pope John XXIII reduced their number from 200 to 100 and gave them a raise in pay. But since Vatican City is only symbolically a State, the Guard is only symbolically a guard. The question is whether they could not be given some kind of work in the service of the poor, like the Volunteer Corps planned by President Kennedy. There are many poor in Rome who still live in caves.

Left : Rome still stubbornly maintains the fiction that Vatican City is a sovereign State. At its 'border', Italian carabinieri wait for the Cardinal Secretary of State to come to reciprocate the visit of a diplomat. The streets are blocked off and traffic is detoured. At the end of the Council OSSERVATORE ROMANO gave an accurate name-by-name listing of all the statesmen who were present. Over 80 sovereignties were represented. This semi-official Vatican paper speaks of the 'august Pontiff', the 'grandeur' of ritual, of 'imposing' hymns, of an 'elect company' and of the 'immaculate' performance of the papal guard. Yet the Council has renounced all triumphalism.

Right : On February 24, 1966, Cardinal Amleto Cicognani, Secretary of State, celebrated his eighty-third birthday. At the Council, Cardinal Suenens had energetically advocated limiting the age of residential bishops to 75. It became more and more evident from session to session that the Secretary of State of Vatican City, who was also president of the Council's coordinating commission, had much more power than the moderators, who were 'legates' of the Pope. Even the secretaries of the Council were really Cicognani's secretaries. Now once again he is the first president of the post-conciliar commission entrusted with implementation of the Council's resolutions. Cicognani is a prudent statesman. He has never had a post as pastor.

Left: A cosmopolitan air blows through all the rooms of the State secretariat. No doubt about it: everything tastes of sophistication. Here, for example, is a waiting room or parlor where vignettes done by Raphael greet less important visitors. 'I would will all of it to the State, because we must detach ourselves from ancient cultures,' a South American bishop commented. A bishop's first task is to teach people how to be human beings. Perhaps he would succeed in this, were the highest agency in the Curia a 'Secretariat for Pastoral Care'. But the Secretariat of State is still number one.

Right: Msgr. Dell'Acqua, 'Substitute Secretary for Ordinary Affairs', is a kind of Catholic Secretary of the Interior. The Church has no territorial boundaries. The whole world is the realm in which it serves.

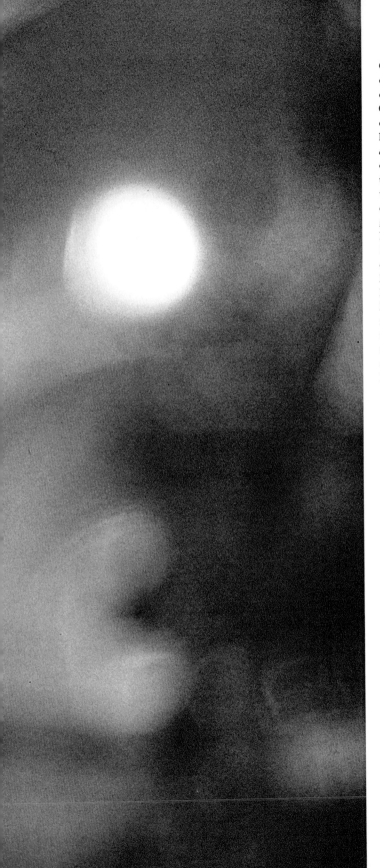

On October 29, 1965, when the fourth Council session was almost half over, Alfredo Cardinal Ottaviani was 75 years old. There were no big celebrations, because the nearly blind secretary of the 'Supreme Sacred Congregation of the Holy Office', as its former title read (it is now called the Congregation for the Faith), is personally very modest, and has no love for display. A correspondent for the liberal *Corriere della Sera* got an interview. Ottaviani abhors the 'opening to the left' of the Italian Democratic Party, but he showed himself sympathetic to the Italian Liberal Party. The journalist asked the controversial cardinal what stand he intended to take on the innovations which are obviously coming, due to the Council. Ottaviani replied: 'I am an old policeman guarding the gold reserves. Do you think I would do my duty if I started to sell out, if I left my post, if I just winked at these things? My dear boy, 75 years are 75 years. I have lived them in defense of certain principles and certain laws. If you tell an old policeman that the laws are going to change, he will realize that he is an old policeman, and he will do everything possible to prevent them from changing. If the laws change anyway, God will surely give him strength to defend the new treasure, in which he believes. Once the new laws have become the Church's treasure, an enrichment of her gold reserves, then there is still only one principle: loyalty in the Church's service. But this service means loyalty to her laws—like a blind man. Like the blind man that I am.'

The papal police do their work very discreetly. They date back to the year 1816, when the Benedictine Pope Pius VII, just back from prison, established the corps. He did not want to be again hauled out of bed and abducted, as he was by Napoleon in 1809. The energy of this pope, moderated by Benedictine discretion, is still alive in the Vatican police, who are considered part of the 'papal family'.

It was only with difficulty that a photographer was able to worm his way into this august assembly. Here are represented the so-called 'three heads' of the Council, who met whenever there were difficulties or decisive turning points. We see the presidium, with the bearded Cardinal Tisserant, center, as chairman. The second group, formed during the second session, was the Council coordinating commission, whose president was Secretary of State Cardinal Cicognani and which included five other cardinals as well as the four Council moderators. Finally there was the general secretariat of the Council: Msgr. Felici and five undersecretaries, bishops from various countries. In the picture the secretaries are at left. At rear right are the presidents and coordinators together. The microphone in the middle makes it possible for the pope to follow the deliberations and to get a word in any time he wants. The coordinating commission and the general secretariat now comprise the post-conciliar 'central commission'. Of the presidents, only Cardinal Tisserant continues on the commission; he is its number two chairman.

Among the most important post-conciliar innovations are the national and supranational bishops' conferences to be set up everywhere. There were only a few of these at the Council's opening, and even these few were very often loosely organized. Now they are mandatory everywhere, with fixed statutes, a permanent secretariat and regular meetings. Auxiliary bishops, hitherto excluded, are now admitted, and in certain cases the conferences can pass binding resolutions. The conferences elect most representatives of the 'synods' to be convoked by the pope. During the Council, these conferences formed quite spontaneously. Here an animated discussion is in progress at an African bishops' conference.

More important than all the legal apparatus of collegiality is the spirit and attitude of fraternal co-operation. Such legal arrangements as the exchange of priests, transfer of excess funds; as the establishment of reasonable diocesan boundaries, of joint central seminaries, and of unified supra-diocesan care of refugees and migrant workers, and the co-operation between the various rites—all these will be successful only if they are the expression of a genuine spirit of unity, which in the early ages was already a treasured possession of Christianity. The photograph shows two Latin Americans from Argentina. The problems to be solved there are as numerous as the solutions which have been offered.

On the Reform of the Curia

Patriarch Maximos IV Saigh of Antioch, in an address given on November 6, 1963.

The first chapter of the schema on the bishops and the governing of dioceses has in view the congregations, tribunals and offices collectively called the 'Roman Curia', when it speaks of those around the Pope who help him in the exercise of his primacy over the entire Church. In section five we find timid mention of a slight reform in regard to this group, namely, that bishops from all over the world be invited as members or advisors to the offices of the Roman Curia.

To limit the cooperation of the Catholic episcopacy in the central government of the Church to the Roman Curia seems to me to correspond neither to the actual needs of the contemporary Church nor to the collegial responsibilities of the bishops toward the Church. I would like to take the liberty, then, to propose a new solution which corresponds better to the needs of our time and to theological principles. The pope and the bishops are what Peter and the apostles were. The pope is also bishop of Rome, primate of Italy and Patriarch of the West. Compared to this universal primacy, these titles are secondary, though real. From this supposition it follows that the pope must share responsibility in his government of the universal Church with the college of bishops which is the successor of the apostolic college and not merely with the priests, deacons and other clergy of Rome. One particular Roman office, which is an institution of the Roman diocese, must not replace the apostolic college that continues in the bishops.

This is why the Council must make certain that this truth is clearly set forth. For this truth has been obscured by centuries-old practice. This obscuring has gone so far that many of us thought that the situation was quite in order. This is certainly not the case. The curia of the bishops of Rome and the apostolic college are two entirely different things. People outside the Catholic Church, and even many within it, are able to recognize only with difficulty in the papal curia of today the ecumenicity of the Church. What they see in this curia is rather the parochial, local church which has gained, through the favorable circumstances of human history, considerable scope, power and wealth. Even the fact that cardinals are given titles related to the Roman Church shows clearly that the cardinals are part of the local church of Rome and not of the universal Church of Christ.

It is easy to see that not all the bishops of the world can be regularly assembled in Rome for a Council. The practical task of helping the Pope in his universal governing of the Church must be limited to a group of bishops who represent their brother bishops. Such a group could make up the *true sacred college* of the universal Church. It would comprise the most important bishops of the Church: first of all, local patriarchs, incumbents of apostolic sees which were recognized by the ecumenical councils of the first centuries. Next should be included the cardinal archbishops, who have their dignity as cardinals from their cathedrals and not through a Roman parish church. And finally, the bishops elected by the conferences of the bishops of each individual country. This last suggestion is in need of a more thorough study. This universal sacred college could be convoked by the pope at fixed times, as well as whenever the need arises, to deliberate on the general affairs of the Church.

This, of course, would not be enough. Some of the members of this apostolic and universal college would have to be present in Rome. The Eastern church calls this the 'Synodus endimousa'. They would take turns joining in work with their head, the pope, who on the basis of his primacy always would have the final word.

All Roman offices would have to be subordinate to this governing body. This body would have its own rules of action, in line with its own constitution. It would project Christ throughout the entire world, especially the pagan world. Because it would not be limited to a circle closed in upon itself, it would never face the temptation of drawing all things to itself, of ruling all things by itself, or regimenting everything in a narrow fashion. It would recognize that the problems of nations would have to be solved by these nations themselves, or together with them, but never without them.

Summing up, we might say that the Holy Father is no more able than any other man in the world to govern and direct so large an institution as the Church universal with the members of his household, especially when Christianity is at stake throughout the world. Moreover, such a collegial arrangement is more in line with the gospel. But if the Church was entrusted especially to Peter and his successors, it was also entrusted to the apostles and their successors. If the government of the Church is entrusted to persons not designated for governance by Christ —persons such as the members of the papal household and the local Roman clergy—this is to the detriment of the common good, and the consequences can be really catastrophic, as history proves. These theological structures and practical truths have a special urgency and a special weight in our time.

In the Mediterranean area, things could go on as they have indefinitely, if we were to be content with giving to the bishops' conferences, which are basically a modern form of the ancient patriarchates, greater power. But in nations with a huge population concentration, such as China and India, nations of a higher and older culture which have nothing in common with the Mediterranean nations, something more must be done. And what this means will be discovered with the help of the Christian people. The same is true with regard to the African churches with all their dynamism. The work here is vast and reaches to the very fundamentals: These churches must feel at home in language, imagery, customs and *mores*. Christianity must not be something alien to them but rather a part of their very soul. These nations would enjoy an even greater autonomy, notwithstanding their necessary subordination to the Holy See. Only what is essential to the very nature of the Church can be insisted upon, just as in the case of the decision of the very first council of Jerusalem in regard to the gentiles. Can we, after so much work and so many sacrifices, say that Christianity has won the heart of these countries? And yet this must be achieved. It would be the responsibility of this new sacred college to clarify these problems, and to work out through prayer, study, and the necessary prudence, the best solution. If the members of this sacred college come from all parts of the world, they can give to the Church a governing body able to direct all nations in Catholic unity.

The Patriarchal Structure of the Catholic Church

Johannes Hoeck, abbot of Scheyern (Bavaria), on October 19, 1964. The central point in the whole issue of reunification with the Eastern churches is the patriarchal structure of the Church. From the earliest times, the structure of the entire Church was patriarchal. This was the constant structure throughout the entire first millennium of the Church's history, during which the Church remained one and undivided. Not the least of the causes of the deplorable schism was that the understanding of this structure gradually came to be lost in the West toward the end of the first millennium. And this happened under the influence of various ideas, some of them political—the orientation of the Holy See toward the Franks, the growth of the 'patrimony of Peter'—and also under the influence of an increasingly juridical thinking, and through the well-known forged documents, as for instance in the infamous 'Constantinian Donation', and the decretals of pseudo-Isidore....

It is true that the institution of the patriarchate has been restored for the small Eastern churches which have returned since the sixteenth century to reunion with the Roman Church; but the rights of these patriarchates were and are only a faint shadow of the rights they once possessed.... Today the legal status of these churches within the Catholic Church is the central object of interest for those large Eastern churches which are still separated from us. These churches rightly ask us what their place and status will be within the Church once the hour of the great reconciliation has come. Who of us could imagine a resolution that would dictate that they are to be subordinated to the Roman Curia, especially when we think of the Eastern congregations and their patriarchs being subordinated to the College of Cardinals?

The primacy and its exercise

Who would think that the autonomy they enjoyed during the millennium of unity with the Roman Church could now be refused to them? Certainly they would have to recognize the primacy of the successors of Peter, just as this was recognized in the former time of unity. But the way the powers of the primate are exercised today is entirely different from the way the primacy was then exercised. To understand this fact, we have only to read the book, *Rome and the Eastern Patriarchates*, in which this whole question is soberly and fairly treated on the basis of authentic documents. These documents establish as facts the following: 1. During the entire millennium of unity the Eastern churches freely elected their patriarchs and bishops, and they freely established and changed their dioceses. 2. On their own authority they handled their liturgy and canon law. 3. They were completely autonomous in regard to discipline of clergy and people. So there was a relative autonomy. Certainly no one denied the right of the Roman pontiff to intervene. But this happened very seldom—less than twelve times in the whole period. But how many interventions have there been, and how many are there these days? We have only to look in the acts and the archives of the Vatican, in the records of the congregations for propagation of the faith and for the Eastern churches. If the Catholic Church was able to exist for a thousand years and fulfill its mission without such an exercise of primacy, why cannot it do the same thing today? It is true that times have changed. The different parts of the world have drawn closer together and the individual churches can and must unite and co-operate today more closely than in those long-ago times. But they will be able to do this better in freedom than under coercion. A diversity maintained in love accomplishes more than a unity maintained by coercion.

Is it not only right and proper to invite the churches separated from us to a reunion under the same conditions which prevailed before separation? And did we not agree on ecumenism, in conformity with the apostles, that 'nothing should be imposed on them beyond what is necessary'?

We should not say that the whole question should be left to the pope to settle. What is at issue here is not the granting of privileges, but the very structure of the entire Church. And if the Council has been given the responsibility by the Pope of declaring to the whole world what the Church is, this is one characteristic which must not be ignored. To ignore it would be to be guilty of doing irreparable damage, and of committing a great error.

Certainly it is the Pope's responsibility to confirm or not confirm the Council's decrees. But it is our task to discuss this and vote on it. And for my part, I cannot see that the Pope would not accept such proposals. For he himself has set such a clear example for us by his fraternal meeting with, by his embrace of, Patriarch Athenagoras.

Are we ashamed to follow his example? Or are we unashamed to refuse to follow it? It is true that the patriarchal structure is confirmed in the Constitution on the Church—but anonymously and in so obscure a manner than even experts are almost unable to detect this. And no mention at all was made of this in the schema on the pastoral office of bishops. What was said on this question in the decree we are discussing shows little or no progress. Only in one of the amendments is mention made of this question—where we agreed that the rights of patriarchs should be restored as soon as possible to the condition in which they were during the era of unity. But even this statement seems vague and open to many interpretations.

Proposals for the reconstruction of the Church

I venture therefore to propose that this whole issue—which, as I said before, is the essential issue in the entire question of reunification with the Eastern churches—be again placed on the agenda, and not only for the debate on this decree, but also for debate on the Constitution on the Church and on the decree on the pastoral office of bishops.

But this issue should not be debated by this commission alone: since it is predominantly composed of Eastern fathers, it could be suspected of speaking in its own interest. Rather a new mixed commission should be formed, from members of our commission and of the theological commission, which deliberates on issues concerning the bishops and ecumenism. And Council fathers, with some experience in this matter yet not directly involved in it, should be included. This commission could deliberate the problem whether additional patriarchates should not be set up—for instance, for the Ukrainian Church, which today is by far the largest of the Uniate churches, which has had to suffer so much in the past, and which is in such danger because of its worldwide membership.

Another problem to discuss would be whether the Latin Church should not be subdivided into more patriarchates, and not merely titular patriarchates. Because, comparatively speaking, it is too large and always in danger of dominating and suppressing the other churches. This way it would also be easier to counteract the overcentralization so often complained of.

All in all, there is much to be said for this decree, with which we wholeheartedly agree, especially after the amendments proposed by other fathers have been made. But it can be questioned whether it is for an almost exclusively Roman Council to decide such questions for the Eastern churches. While the decree itself, like the decree on ecumenism, solemnly declares that the Eastern churches are permitted and encouraged to govern themselves, in accordance with their own laws, do we not contradict ourselves here? Should the Eastern churches themselves not be asked, before we take the overall vote, whether or not they agree with the idea that the entire Council should decide these questions?

This historic hour

Just about the only question really of concern to the entire Council is the question of the patriarchal structure of the Church as a whole. And this question, as we have said before, has been treated in a wholly inadequate fashion.

I entreat you therefore, Venerable Fathers, to direct your earnest and serious attention to the historic responsibility entrusted to us, and to give it appropriate consideration, so that we do not miss another opportunity, as has so often happened in the history of the Church, and so that we can say honestly and truly to our brothers in Christ: 'Look, the home of our common Father has been made ready! Our doors and our hearts are wide open! DIXI ET SALVAVI ANIMAM MEAM: I said this and saved my soul.'

Church, Laity and World

Lay people are not in the Church only to be saved, they are themselves part of the sign of salvation; they are the Church—and also the world

Church and World
are the Work of the divine Word

The world, searching for itself,
finds the Church
The Church, searching for the world,
finds itself

Drawing: View of St. Peter's Square

'Inspired by no earthly ambition, the Church seeks but a solitary goal: to carry forward the work of Christ, Who came into this world to liberate and not to judge, to serve and not to be served. To carry out such a task, the Church has always had the duty of scrutinizing the signs of the times and of interpreting in the light of the gospel.'

(Pastoral Constitution on the Church in the Contemporary World: Preface.)

The contribution of the non-Europeans

In the long series of ecumenical councils Vatican Council II was the first to which the word 'ecumenical', understood in its original meaning as the total inhabited earth, really applied. That this came about was not simply the result of scientific advances that enable even those from the remotest part of the world to gather in Rome without any great loss of time. It was also the result of a far-reaching renovation of the missions, begun by Pius XI and consistently carried forward by his successors. The provisional apostolic prefectures, usually under the control of the Congregation for the Missions, were replaced by indigenous episcopal sees whose bishops, as far as possible, were natives. Thus, among the bishops entitled to take part in the Council, there were 256 from Asia, 250 from Africa, 96 from the Arab world, 70 from Oceania, 601 from Latin America, and 332 from North America. Most of these actually attended. At Vatican Council I (1869—1870) the 800 participants came chiefly from the European countries. At the Council of Trent (1545—1563) delegates from Latin countries predominated.

This time the Europeans still clearly predominated theologically, although there were imposing individual figures from overseas—Léger from Montreal, Silva Henriquez from Chile, for example. These men, however, brought no theology indigenous to their own country. Moreover, opinion at the Council was divided along European lines. The few Eastern bishops were the only non-Europeans who tried occasionally to contribute something from their special perspective, yet usually they made no lasting mark. This will no longer be the case at future councils. In one or two generations, not only will non-Europeans be greater in number but they will be able to make their presence felt qualitatively as well.

On one issue, however, the non-Europeans were a decisive force even at this council—the problems of the contemporary world. I believe that the great Pastoral Constitution on the Church in the Contemporary World would have not been considered at all if it were not for the presence of all these fathers from the developing countries. The marks made by the so-called 'foreign' bishops is evident in the usual way in which the Council gave voice to their concerns. When did a council ever send 'messages' to the world? Here was such a message right at the beginning. To this very day no one is sure whether it should be counted among the official council promulgations.

Until now, pastoral statements of a council used to be called 'decrees', 'dogmatic statements', 'constitutions'. The new term, 'pastoral constitution', seems to many to be a contradiction. Such a thing had never existed in all twenty previous councils, covering a rather significant period of history. Now a new category of council statements was initiated which extended beyond the framework of classical council thinking. We may safely attribute such statements to the world, concerned with the world's problems, to pressure from non-Europeans. No matter how we may judge the style and solidity of the famous Schema 13, the fact is that the council did take a risk by issuing such a text. And its issuance was due precisely to the non-Europeans.

The Position of Lay People in the Church

Before discussing the specialized character of this pastoral constitution, we should consider the gradual development of Catholic doctrine on the one particular subject excluded from previous treatment of the meaning of the world: the subject of lay people. Primarily, lay people seemed to be the Church's link with the world. The decree on the lay apostolate says that lay people are simultaneously Christians and citizens of this world. They are specifically dealt with in the fourth chapter of the constitution on the Church as well as in 33 paragraphs of the above-mentioned decree. Moreover, there are important passages about them in the decree on the missions.

For thirty years before the Council there had been an ever-growing lay movement. Its prime motive, as was often repeated in papal documents, was the idea of relieving the over-worked clergy of part of their burden. This is the source of the expression, 'the participation of the laity in the work of the hierarchy'; and lay people who generously contributed their time in such work often received an explicit mandate for this. This was 'Catholic Action'. It was conceived by Pius XII as a kind of movement, but it developed in many countries into an organization of its own. Its purpose was first, the evangelization of men, and second, the formation of lay people's consciences within the secular vocations in which each of them was involved. Yet the fact that a special mandate was granted indicates that the layman was assuming here an additional responsibility which went beyond his own proper scope.

To no one's surprise, the lay person began to reflect more on his own proper position within the church. It cannot be denied that in the Church's history, lay people had been slowly but steadily downgraded, both intellectually and spiritually, in the course of centuries. More and more lay people frequently became passive *objects* in the Church; they were less and less active *subjects*. A rift opened between clergy and lay people. Even at this Council there were men among the bishops —for instance Cardinal Ruffini (Palermo)—who understood lay people as having really only one job: to obey instructions from the clergy. Laymen were regarded as the long arm of the clergy, reaching into politics, culture, economic and social life.

Soon, however, the overwhelming majority at the Council had adopted the new idea that meanwhile had been developing theologically and had been taking root among lay people—an idea coming from the new perspective of the Church and described in preceding sections of this book. In this view the lay person is a full-fledged member of the community of the People of God. He is not supposed to be a perpetual adolescent. This people as a whole has a mission in the world. All the baptized share in Christ's office as priest, prophet and king. The 'universal priesthood' spoken of in scripture, which since the Reformation had been only reluctantly discussed within the Catholic Church, was reinstated in its full meaning. The general priesthood gives its meaning to the ordained priesthood, rather than the reverse. Every layman must cooperate, through the witness of his life and through the service of his words, in building the body of Christ up to its full manhood—on his own responsibility. Every layman is called to holiness, but it is by no means inferior to some supposedly greater holiness required of clergy and people in religious orders.

This is why the title of the decree on religious orders, which originally read 'On the State of Those who Strive for Perfection', was radically changed—first into a text 'On Members of Religious Orders', and finally into 'The Contemporary Renewal of Religious Life'. There is only one way of Christian perfection: to love God and our fellow men. All Christians are called to it in the same manner but not along the same path. Then, too, despite Cardinal Ruffini's protest, it was acknowledged that the Holy Spirit, 'who blows where he wishes', bestows his special gifts of grace and charismata upon lay people. It was Cardinal Suenens of Belgium who, in a great Council address, had asked for this insertion. Lay people too have a sense of faith. So it is emphasized especially that 'they have, in line with their knowledge and competency and position, the opportunity and sometimes the duty, to express their opinion on issues involving the Church's welfare.' For this purpose consultative bodies are to be instituted in the dioceses 'on the parish level, on the intra-parish and intra-diocesan level, and also on the national and international level'. In addition, a special secretariat is to be created at Rome for the service of the lay apostolate in the broadest sense of this term. Representative of the most diverse movements working all over the world, as well as clergy and other lay people, are supposed to share responsibilities and work together. All of this might be called reevaluation of lay people within the Church.

If that had been all, the reproach of one bishop would have been justified when he said: 'The chapter has been conceived in the sin of clericalism.' What he meant was the hierarchical emphasis mentioned earlier. This approach gives insufficient attention to the proper task of lay people—the work which distinguishes them from the clergy and which gives them a spirituality of their own in a sphere where they are themselves responsible. Fortunately the Council went on to say much more—somewhat hesitantly at first, in chapter four of the Constitution of the Church, and then with much more emphasis and detail in the subsequent decree on the lay apostolate. What we are talking about here is the secular and worldly character ascribed to lay people: 'They live in the world—that is, in each and all of the secular professions and occupations. They live in the ordinary circumstances of family and society from which the very web of their existence is woven.' As a result of this, 'by virtue of their special vocation they seek the kingdom of God in the administration and God-centered ordering of temporal things.'

But is that simply their unfortunate lot in life? Or isn't 'the penetration and perfecting of the order of temporal things with the spirit of the gospel', spoken of in the decree on the lay apostolate, a completely essential mission of the Church? I say 'of the Church', not of the hierarchy. It isn't the hierarchy's responsibility to shape the temporal world. (The medieval mind made the mistake of thinking that the pope had received both 'swords' from Christ, secular as well as spiritual power. The Church could hand the secular sword to the emperor without giving up any direct control over it.)

Though Christ is undoubtedly Lord of the world as well as of the Church, the hierarchical Church has no control over the temporal order, not even an indirect control which might enable it arbitrarily to order lay people around in the secular sphere according to its whim. The hierarchy can inform the lay conscience, but this is, after all, nothing but a negative restriction. In his positive actions and decisions the lay person himself remains responsible. He acts as the Church. This understanding of the lay role is often spoken of as 'Christian responsibility'; but now the lay person is not merely obeying orders from the hierarchy.

The Council has not gone so far as to say this outright, but it is clearly emphasized that the ordering of the whole temporal sphere toward Christ is the lay person's proper task. This is the primary apostolate of the lay person as seen in the Decree on the Lay Apostolate and in decrees on the missions (there, in fact, the laymen is in community with other Christians). Here the Council has at least a starting point for establishing a meaningful relationship between the Church and the world. Yet the concrete references to contemporary themes—the position of woman, the social environment, social interrelationships, international solidarity, developing countries—have strangely not been treated with reference to lay people. Did the authors of Schema 13 (the Church in the Contemporary World) shy away from this? Did they feel that lay people alone build too flimsy a bridge between Church and world?

The Meaning of Schema 13

At first the significance of a Council text on the Church in the Contemporary World was scarcely clear to any group of bishops. Cardinal Suenens (Belgium), in his address at the end of the first session, termed the dialogue between Church and world as the third point in the overall plan of the Council.

What did he mean here by 'world'? The first point in his 'plan' was the inter-Christian dialogue, the dialogue within the Church, including dialogue with non-Catholic Christians. His second point concerned dialogue with non-Christian religions. It would have been consistent to introduce atheists at this point, as a third group—just as Paul VI later added, to the Secretariat for Christian Unity, a second secretariat for contact with non-Christian religions (under Cardinal Marella), and a third secretariat for dialogue with atheists (under Cardinal König).

But the dialogue with the world fellows a different line: 'World: this is where human history takes place', as the pastoral constitution says. This means the family of man today, inasmuch as it shapes its earthly life within this universe. The Church's proper mission is religious; Christ did not give it power to shape the earthly life of politics, economy and culture. Nevertheless, insofar as the shaping of earthly life is connected with the Church's religious objectives, it has to say something about this too. After all, the Church is made up of human beings.

Was the Council, then, supposed to write a doctrinal treatise on the relationship between Church and world?

I believe nobody had anything like this in mind. Or was it supposed to formulate the Church's principles regarding the ordering of social life, at first in a general and only abstract way, and then to apply these principles to present-day problems? There is no denying that, at first, some considered such a method of presentation appropriate—for example, Alfred Bengsch, the Bishop of Berlin, who proposed even as late as the fourth session that the entire text be reformulated along these lines. Yet the most bishops were not inclined to agree with his concept. Why not? At what point did the difference of opinion arise? Bishop Bengsch declared: 'It is merely a matter of a different method of presentation. The text, as it stands, follows the inductive method. My proposal chooses a deductive approach. The result in both cases is the same.' Undoubtedly the difference can be summarized in so simple a formula, but we can hardly say the end result would be the same in both cases. In the case of the deductive method—which moves from the general to the specific—the schema on the Church in the Contemporary World is seen as nothing but a practical implementation of a previously formulated doctrine. The schema is related to the major and central constitution on the Church of Christ, as are so many other decrees. Consider, for example, the decree on the pastoral office of bishops, or that on the renewal of religious orders, the one on the lay apostolate, or that on missionary activity. If this were true, it would be difficult to see why the text on Church and world should not simply have been called a 'decree'. Actually there was far more at stake. Let me try to express it by using the words with which the great French theologian and sociologist Dominique Chenu, concluded an address on Schema 13 during the fourth session: 'This text on the Church in the Contemporary World is not merely a moral and social application of the Christian commandments. It defines the Church itself as something planted in the world, by its very mission.' Chenu's opinion is confirmed by what Pope Paul VI, while still Cardinal Montini, said in an address to young priests (January 1963): 'The Church, in its effort to define and describe herself, goes to the world in order to be herself.' This means that the presence of the Church, being in the world, is no mere accidental or burdensome element. This does not mean mere co-existence between two alien societies that have reached some sort of agreement about their mutual boundaries. Rather, it means a mutual inclusiveness, a desire for co-existence despite the disparity of the purposes of each. In other words, being in the world makes the Church what it is. Otherwise it would make no sense. Thus the text on the Church in the Contemporary World does not stand in some vague relationship to the Constitution on the Church. Rather, we have one and the same constitution divided into two structurally homogeneous parts. In what the Church says to the world at the present time, there is no question of adjustment of eternal truth to present circumstances, but rather the presence of the gospel in the truest sense of the word.

Perhaps Pope John's reflection might clarify what is meant here. Every section of his encyclical, PACEM IN TERRIS, concludes with a sign of the times. The Pope is convinced that God is active in all man's doings, for

God is the creator who has not only brought the universe into existence, but continually preserves it, and more than that, he also works in all men through the grace of Christ even though they are unaware of it. Through evolution man makes the universe more human or appropriates the universe and shapes it according to its own dimensions. But through this very act, man himself grows, becomes increasingly human, becomes in a fuller sense a man. At the same time he opens up to grace; he becomes more capable of receiving grace within himself. The Church's responsibility is to watch this development of man attentively and to share in it. With this, her own understanding of the message of salvation deepens. The Church is called an extension of the incarnation of the Word of God, an increasing maturation, an immersion into full human existence. These two processes complement one another.

It is certainly not easy to recognize where and how the world actually grows toward a more complete humanity. Is it through the ever-growing socialization of our time, the increasing social interrelationship which even the most isolated mountain dweller does not escape? Or is it through the transition from manual work to mechanization, which has not only fundamentally changed man's patterns, but also his culture, his art, his religious attitudes as well? Or are we simply to consider the desacralization of the world connected with this progress? The world is no longer seen and experienced as a sacral place with all the attendant taboos.

In all this there is an element of a more completely developed humanity. But at the same time there is also a threat or a temptation for man here. The mystery of sin, after all, continues to be operative in the world. It is uncanny that this very process of movement into new dimensions tempts man to destroy himself, to misjudge himself, and thus become alienated from himself.

We have an example of this in contemporary atheism. One cannot apply here Pope John's idea of a 'sign of the times'. But the *causes* underlying this development, tempting man to accept atheism, can be considered 'signs of the times'. If the Church continues to proclaim her faith in God in the same way as heretofore, men will not hear her call. Her message will ricochet. Only when the Church has deepened its message to make it correspond to the contemporary human condition, so that it represents a response to the question about God —a question dormant in contemporary man—then the Church has the chance of having its word really accepted. But it can do this truly only if it has felt the full impact of the experience of man's temptation to atheism. The Church must grow with man. Its whole nature lies in missionary work; and it is part of this nature, part of being in the world, to always be bound up with the life of man. This not in order to rule the world—that is not its task—but rather to help the world. Dr. Skydsgaard expresses it in these words: 'In one corner of our hearts all of us are atheists, and only thus can we proclaim faith in God to contemporary man!' Anyone who has followed thus far sees immediately that Bishop Bengsch's view misjudges the real purpose of the Pastoral Constitution on the Church in the Contemporary World. It is not a question of applying an abstract system of ideas, a doctrine which is ever the same, to the burning issues of the present day. Rather, since our present world reaches open-handedly toward a more genuine humanity, this groping has to be supplemented by care and love; we must guard against mistakenly rejecting this outstretched hand into which the message of salvation must be placed.

Perhaps the Church may not always find a way to respond immediately to the world. Response may perhaps come only after long dialogue with the world, for only through dialogue will empathy with the problems of the world be possible. This is the process sought in the pastoral constitution. It makes an initial groping attempt to find the open hands of the world and place the Christian message in them in a way that such a need is truly met. The world on its part must find what it is really seeking, and even more.

Overcoming the dualism of matter versus spirit

Thus the first painstaking attempt of the Church aims to make clear that it does not scorn the material world and the human body. The view that sees material and bodily things as inferior gains no support from the Christian message. Actually, human civilization at present is largely characterized by exploration of the earth, development of technology, the subjugation of matter. Man creates his own world for himself. 'Nature becomes a child begotten by man,' Karl Marx said. For its part, the Church, influenced by Platonism more in practice than in theory, had almost detached the material existence of man from the spiritual sphere and had devaluated the material. Religious appreciation of economic and technical development was for a long time almost impossible. The very word 'spirituality' suggested that the Church was hostile to bodily things and to technology; its only message seemed to be 'save your soul'. In the Church's eyes, earthly activity and striving meant only opportunities for exercising virtue—patience, meekness, self-control. It is this more or less definite dualism, this artificial angelism in the idea of man which is now jettisoned by the pastoral constitution. The very first section, which deals with principles, corrects this defective, and in part absolutely false, Christian attitude. It seems to reflect a certain optimism, an optimism which is not traceable to Pope John's good disposition, his readiness to look for the positive everywhere. Rather it comes from deeper understanding of the faith. In other words, it takes seriously the teaching of the Constitution on the Church, according to which God and the grace of salvation are actually at work in all men, individuals as well as mankind as a whole.

The obvious question arises: Where is there evidence of this today? Until now the question was mainly and almost exclusively: Where does the world deviate from the right path? From this attitude came condemnations. Condemnations may have their place, but if they are not supported by faith in the positive, they remain ineffectual and ignore the historical dimension of salvation, of redemption, which began with the incarnation. This is not to say that the Council fully succeeded in working out this basic tendency. There was no theology of earthly realities. Not much good work had been done on the relationship between secular and salvation history. A theology of the mystery of sin was also lacking.

So the text of the first part of the constitution has all the earmarks of unfinished work. In part, it was rather opaque; later sections were rambling and filled with platitudes; the connection between the five chapters was not immediately obvious; it was too repetitive. Yet all these flaws did not prevent the basic idea, sketched here, from shining through.

Particular Issues: Marriage, Culture, Economics, International Unity

This is the light, too, in which the individual problems treated in the second part must be seen. These problems are not chosen at random; rather they constitute 'signs of the times'. This makes the text more valuable than it would be if it provided neat, practical 'solutions', expected by many but rarely treated. We can single out at least the more important of the 'signs'.

On the question of marriage and family, whoever reads paragraphs 47 to 52 of the Constitution must be astonished at the more profound idea of marriage presented there. Married love is given primary emphasis, and is understood as a genuine, personal and total meeting between man and woman. Here the text is indebted to modern psychological and biological research. The issue is not so much the physiological correctness of the marital act, but rather the full integration of sexuality into the individual's personality and into loving personal encounter with the partner. Nothing must deprive the meeting in marriage of its character as a genuinely personal encounter in love, nor interfere with

this. Cardinal Léger of Montreal and Bishop Reuss of Mainz, particularly, gave tireless emphasis to this aspect, so neglected in the past. Obviously the Church is now able to deepen this through its teaching on the sacrament of marriage, by pointing marriage to the relationship between Christ and his Church. But it must be conceded that in Christianity, viewed historically, the marriage act was largely considered something that left man unclean. Thus a morality too narrowly centered on the marital act had prevented sexuality from being seen in its total context. In this respect, recent moral discoveries have become 'signs of the times'.

A new attitude toward fertility in marriage is the result of all this. Marriage is not simply an instrument for the procreation and education of children; it is primarily a conjugal community. It is, however, intrinsically ordered to the child. An important distinction is made when the text says that the obligation to procreate applies, not to the individual act, but to marriage and married love as a whole. This can have considerable consequences. It can deliver married people from many anxieties of conscience. It is especially emphasized in this connection that the parents alone have the right to responsibly determine the number of their children. This obviously does not mean arbitrariness. Instead the married partners 'must decide on the basis of objective criteria which come from the nature of the human person and of their acts . . . how to join married love with the responsible transmission of life'.

The 'sign of the time', in this case, is not so much the present-day population explosion, which would compel people to limit the number of children, but rather the growing consciousness of human responsibility—man's position as a planner of the world created by him. The Church here acknowledges this responsible selfhood and no longer wants to view it in terms of a confessional box morality. Here the Church more properly and more profoundly follows the gospel than it did in former times, as Patriarch Maximos IV pointed out in a brief but clear intervention. It is well-known that the proponents of the traditional teaching tried, even at the last moment, to get the Pope to support the old formulations (about primary and secondary ends of marriage, with an explicit condemnation of contraceptives), through verbatim quotations of the statements of Pius XI and Pius XII. The Pope transmitted their petition to the commission which, by pointing to the special marriage study group instituted by Paul VI, refrained from taking a stand on 'immediately concrete solutions'. Cardinal Ottaviani would have preferred a different approach; so he sent the commission's version, with its 'correction of the corrections', back to the Pope. The tone of Ottaviani's covering letter is tinged with the hope that the Pope would not agree with the commission. Paul VI, however, wrote one sentence below the statement: 'The corrections are accepted in the form proposed by the mixed commission. P.'

A further 'sign of the times' would be contemporary science and culture, which more and more recognize and claim their autonomy. Here we have a sharp contrast to former times when the Church (or, more precisely, its clergy) functioned as sole sponsor of Western culture. So it is not surprising that the Church should find it difficult to acknowledge here that such an autonomy of the world, such secularization, is justified. The Church, in many of its representatives, is only too prone to keep the sciences, arts and higher life of mankind 'on a short rein', as Bishop Elchinger remarked.

It is, however, precisely by granting the right kind of freedom of research, of thinking, of expression of opinion, and by detaching itself from fixed systems of thinking, from proven methods of instruction, from concrete forms of art, that the Church, as Cardinal Lercaro said, will prove itself to be 'truly poor, committed to no particular age, embracing all nations, and knowing how to become involved with any form of culture without fossilizing within it.' The constitution hardly hints at all this. The dialogue here has obviously begun. Of much more immediate concern are new forms of economics and social life where everything is certainly still wholly in flux. But there can be no doubt that the new regard for the human person, which fascinated John XXIII so much, had its root precisely in this area of development, even though human dignity continues to be threatened by discrimination and servitude of all kinds, sometimes even in new forms. The Council's text repeats what is said in Pope John's encyclical, PACEM IN TERRIS, but in some instances it boldly goes beyond it, for example, in what it says about work and the sharing of all in the management and profits of business enterprise. (Representatives of German private enterprise vainly tried by every conceivable means to suppress this passage.) This development could have great repercussions for the Church itself—right down to seminary training and the involvement of all types of lay people in pastoral responsibilities.

Finally, there is the great problem of international peace. The 'sign of the times' here is in the predominant trend toward a single great family of nations, with limitation on the sovereignty of individual countries. The development inevitably points in this direction. The Council has clearly recognized this trend and given it its blessing.

Here, too, the part may not be detached from the whole. The 'whole' in this case is the development toward international unity. This, in turn, has its effect on the Church which, inspired by such a development, recognizes in a deep and living way her supranational unity, her Catholicity, and begins to act in line with this realization as never before in her history. The 'part' is the problem of war. The Council has made a noteworthy step forward in that it has, once and for all, buried the ancient classical distinction between just and unjust wars. Moreover, the Council took an unequivocal stand against war with 'technological' weapons and called the arms race 'an utterly treacherous trap for humanity, and an insufferable injury to the poor. Instead of doing away with the causes of war [nations] threaten to add to them.' Even more 'the unique hazard of modern warfare consists in this: it provides those who possess modern technological weapons with the occasion to commit crimes such as the destruction of whole cities; and it can drive mankind, through a certain inexorable chain of events or to the most abominable decisions.' Never has a Council spoken so sharply against war. A group of bishops, especially some from the United States, did try at the very last moment to collect signatures for a petition to reject this text in the course of the final voting. But in vain. If the Council did not strictly condemn all atomic defense, as some may have desired, it was precisely because the fathers probably realized that the problem would find its final solution, not through such a prohibition, but instead within a wider framework—the establishment of a genuine authority representing all nations.

Thus the Council came to an end with a pastoral constitution that is not at all grand and glorious—as the Council itself is well aware. Yet it does not retract this constitution, for in its humble and halting language, the text marks a path toward a new future of service of mankind.

Auditors and Journalists: Lay People at the Council

From the viewpoint of dogma, lay people were represented at the Council by bishops. This was the answer given to the questions of journalists. I have no intention of contradicting it, although it is not entirely clear, then, why superiors of religious orders participated in the Council. They are certainly not 'successors of the apostles', and yet their vote, according to present-day practice, even in questions of doctrine, was as weighty as that of a bishop. But there are other historical precedents for lay representation. Let's disregard the political machinations of the middle ages. In the earliest Christian centuries, the influence of lay people within councils was far stronger than today. Be this as it may, the bishops urged that lay people be represented. This was in line with the desire for 'dialogue'.

In the first session, however, only M. Jean Guitton of the Académie Française managed to get into the assembly. There was great embarrassment when good Pope John, pressured by certain Frenchmen, let him in. Where was he to sit? He wound up in the tribune reserved for the 'separated brethren'! But before the second session, on September 12, 1963, Paul VI announced that lay representatives of international Catholic organizations were to be admitted as 'auditors'. At first there were ten; later the number increased to thirteen. OSSER-VATORE ROMANO did not dare to publish their names because these gentlemen were for the most part as unknown to the public as the international organizations they represented. They were simply called 'professional laymen'. Then in the third session women were also admitted. In the fourth session the total increased to twenty-nine 'auditors' and twenty-three 'auditrices'. Unlike the observers, they even sat in as advisors on various commissions. Such a step must be considered simply a beginning, for the development is almost certain to continue.

Much more important for the Council was another group of lay people, also comprised of men and women—the journalists. Cardinal König said quite rightly, 'Public opinion played a determining factor in the Council's activities. Today journalists play the part of diplomats and ambassadors while public opinion itself plays the role formerly played by kings and princes.' One cannot say that this view was generally shared by Secretary General Pericle Felici, or even by the bishops' press committee set up during the second session under the direction of the rector of the North American College in Rome, Archbishop Martin O'Connor, who is also president of the papal commission for film, radio and television. In the eyes of these gentlemen, the publication media were the Council's instruments of propaganda. The ideal here was the Vatican daily newspaper, OSSERVATORE ROMANO. In line with this, only carefully tailored reports, often distorted beyond recognition, were officially released, especially at the beginning. The notion of the 'long arm' of the hierarchy was here still very much alive. Even in the fourth session, Archbishop O'Connor refused a press pass to Father Edward Duff, S. J., who was acting as an American journalist, because Father Duff had criticized him (very objectively) during the session.

Conversely it should also be said that the heads of the various communications media did not anticipate the vastness of the public response to the Council, and at first simply did not send their best men to Rome. Still this is true: that a real dialogue developed between hierarchy and public—both within the Church and without—and that credit must be given to the communications media for effecting precisely that which, in the Council texts, remains on paper.

Mr. and Mrs. Jose Alvarez Icaza, a wealthy Mexican couple, were named auditors at the fourth session of the Council. In Rome they rented an entire floor at 78A Via della Croce, a narrow street near the Spanish Steps. Here they set up an office and went to work on a study of the practical aspects of the problem of the population explosion in underdeveloped countries. They submitted thousands of letters from all over the world to the appropriate Council commissions. In the meantime they had left their four children with an aunt in Mexico. In the last draft of the chapter on marriage in the Pastoral Constitution on the Church in the Contemporary World, Mrs. Luz Icaza showed the commission that women can sometimes be more courageous than men.

By drying up the Pontine marshes, Mussolini succeeded in freeing the Eternal City of disease-bearing mosquitoes. But they were replaced by a new and comparable nuisance—shutterbugs. Only by strict regulation and the deployment of plenty of special police was the Council able to head them off. But the police were not inhuman; they were well aware that we live in a visual age. Toward the end of the fourth session there was even a photography contest, with prizes for the best pictures of the Council. Not one single photographer was on the jury. This was probably all for the best, since the aim was to find out which pictures the public preferred, not to conduct an artistic competition.

Here we see lay auditors receiving communion during mass at the beginning of a general congregation. This was not so easy to bring off, because the rubrics, over which Msgr. Enrico Dante, the principal papal master of ceremonies, watched so anxiously, made no provision for it. On September 29, 1963, the second session began. From then on, lay auditors were present every day. The Constitution on the Liturgy had provided that, at every mass, as many of the lay participants as possible should receive communion. But it was not until October 11 that the lay auditors were 'permitted' to receive their first Council communion. The bishops celebrated two masses each day—one by themselves, and the second (without receiving communion) at the Council. Did this make much sense? Few thought so.

Perhaps the most interesting journalistic event was the daily afternoon American press panel. Experts answered journalists' questions on issues discussed at the general congregation just concluded. The discussion was conducted with a frankness unknown in Europe (outside of Holland), without anybody becoming offended. One of the high points of excitement was after the Jesuit General, Pedro Arrupé, spoke of an international atheist conspiracy dominant even in the West: many Catholic journalists worked for non-Catholic papers.

In the picture is the former communist Dorothy Day, foundress of the Catholic worker movement, who has been amazingly selfless in her efforts against racial discrimination and in favor of pacifism.

Every Wednesday evening the German-speaking journalists gathered at the so-called 'Kampe Circus'. There Auxiliary Bishop Kampe (Limburg) introduced with great flourish the best theologians of the Council, and even notable bishops. The picture reminds us that non-Catholic theologians and journalists were regular guests in the crowded room. Here (center) is Gottfried Marron, who wrote very critical weekly reports for the Swiss Evangelical press service and for the papers of the German Evangelical Federation; these later appeared also in the *Bensheimer Hefte*. At the right is Hanno Helbling, author of the well-known reports, also valued very highly by Catholics, in the *Neue Zürcher Zeitung*.

Here are the French language journalists. These individualists, with all their deep feeling for 'community', were never able to get a regular press conference organized. Maybe there is too much of a split within French Catholicism between 'right' and 'left' wings. Yet they had a brilliant spokesman in Msgr. Pierre Haubtmann, who issued a daily press release. On all progressive issues 'left wing' journalists took the lead, unlike a considerable part of the French episcopate. In the picture the journalists are questioning the experiment-minded Mexican bishop, Mendez Arceo (left), who maintains in his diocese a monastery full of psychoanalyzed monks. At the right is Père Roquette; in the background is Mr. F. Major; M. Henri Fesquet has his back turned; at the far right is the Belgian Jan Grootaers.

The Council and the World

What was on the minds of the bishops that made them insist, despite all resistance and all the tradition of the Church, on a schema on the Church in the contemporary world? Father Gerald Mahon, an Englishman and the superior general of the missionary Mill Hill Fathers, remarked that in the First Vatican Council the Church offered the proletariat not a single word of encouragement. The definition of papal infallibility, as far as the workers were concerned, was, he said, a dubious consolation. For years, the Second Vatican Council had been discussing important questions of ecclesiastical life; but it had not issued a call for international social justice. And yet the proletarian nations, he went on, looked expectantly toward Rome, wondering whether the Church of Christ would act on their behalf. Every year 35,000,000 human beings die of hunger, 400,000,000 suffer from hunger and 1,500,000,000 are undernourished, Mahon pointed out.

We can quote the African Archbishop Lalula of Leopoldville: 'It seems very appropriate to me—yes, I would even say absolutely necessary—that the Council publicly condemn racism. I mean the suppression or persecution of a group on the ground of color or race. Any racial injustice, perpetrated anywhere in the world, is an injustice against every human being. It is true that our people in black Africa suffer from a certain complex in this respect . . . but the Church can help them to overcome it. African tribalism—feuding between tribes—is a bleeding wound, an attenuated form of racism. It affects even Christians, and yet it only results in hatred, terror, violence, vengeance and torture. The Council ought to condemn it as a mortal sin. It has often been said that the gospel has been an important contributing factor in emancipating women from slavery. But the attainment of complete freedom is a long-range undertaking. Why doesn't the Council raise its voice and declare the full human dignity of woman and her totally equal responsibility?'

Archbishop Athaide of Agra, India: 'Even in our days secret slavery still persists. Human beings are bought and sold. There are places even in the free world where some citizens are deprived of their full civil rights. It is a disgrace to us as Christians that this happens in areas which are proud of their Christian tradition. Mere words of sympathy are not enough. We must awaken the world's conscience. Let us praise a Mahatma Gandhi, let us praise a pastor like Martin Luther King, people whom Paul VI himself has praised. Let us not be afraid to be courageous . . .' As the South American Archbishop Pessôa Helder Câmara of Recife has said: 'The minimum we must achieve is this: In every diocese and in almost every parish we must be at home; we must be present in various worlds: the world of the poor and the world of the rich; the world of the worker and the world of the employer; in the world of scientists and in the world of artists; in the world of Christians, non-Christians and atheists. We must keep in mind our special responsibility to underdeveloped areas; their development must proceed harmoniously without interruption. Our special task is to improve the way of life of simple people. It is absurd to fear that this will lead to communism. We must speak up in favor of the masses whose living conditions are subhuman.'

These are a few examples to show why it was precisely the non-Europeans who demanded Schema 13. Does the text come up to their expectations?

Toward the end of the fourth session the Pope visited the Council press office. After a short discussion, the journalists crowded around him. Here a young German Protestant from Heidelberg (one of 13 students who wanted to make a firsthand study of the Council), approaches Paul VI and tells him that an Orthodox monk from a monastery in Asia Minor prays daily for the Pope and has asked this student to convey his cordial greetings to the Pope. The Pope listens, interested and amazed. A moment later, a woman journalist in the crowd fainted. The Pope came to her aid, gently reassuring her. In his closing address on December 7, four days later, the Pope said, 'We must be concerned for human beings as they are.'

The Pope's address to the United Nations was a perfect example of what the Council intended in the Pastoral Constitution on the Church in the Contemporary World: to recognize the 'signs of the times' and the activities of nations which, even if imperfect, still manifest the work of God; and to assist in their greater development. The Pope considers the United Nations such a sign. He wants to show the UN the way to be a true instrument of peace, making war impossible. On the motion of Cardinal Liénart, the address was later included in the acts of the Council.

In the meantime, a terrible war had been raging in Vietnam, where people who only wanted peace were in danger of being completely and hopelessly ground down between the millstones of large-scale international politics. This example forced the fathers of the Council to abandon age-old speculations about distinctions between just and unjust war. Cardinal Ottaviani made an impassioned plea in which he urged that 'all those things that in one way or another contribute to war also be condemned'. But the fathers of the Council were unable to offer any simple and immediate solution.

This is the way it was: This is what everyone felt on the opening night of the Council, when they stood with torches in hand in St. Peter's Square before the spectacularly lighted basilica. In former days the Church was the patron of culture. All Rome is filled with evidence of this. Every tenth house has a plaque telling which pope built it and which one rebuilt or renovated it. No one denies the greatness of the Council's achievements; no one has escaped its fascination. In former days there seemed to be no gap, not even a tension, between the message of the gospel and the achievements of culture. Perhaps many a historian has said to himself: 'These buildings were constructed with money gained from the sale of indulgences'; that was one of the reasons for the division of the Church.

And this is the way it is today: Rockefeller Center in New York City is a symbol of the forward movement of modern civilization. Civilization has become autonomous; it follows its own inner laws. In comparison, St. Patrick's Cathedral, across the street, is small and outmoded, like something unable to shake itself free of a former age. Have Church and world thus become enemies? Do Babylon and Jerusalem stand here as irreconcilable adversaries? The Council has tried to make the gap into a tension, a divinely-willed tension. Civilization has its own autonomy, and the Church is not the patron of cultural creativity. Its mission is something else. But the two should not stand side by side with no relation to each other as they do in this picture. St. Patrick's Cathedral is a symbol of anachronism. The Church must recognize whatever human creativity really makes man more human; the Church must reveal to the world its final eschatological meaning. This is the meaning of revelation.

The world of the rich

The Church must be present in both the world of the poor and the world of the rich. No bishop denied this. The Church is not a plant which flourishes only in a seedbed of misery, indigence and under-development. Of course, some have seen things this way; but they have been unfair. On the contrary, the Church must be one of the strongest contributors to the progressive development of mankind. But there still is the danger that she will suffocate in drawing rooms. 'Free us then', cried a bishop during the Council, 'from these glittering buttons, capes and sashes which we don't want anyway and which will lead no one to God.' What the Church needs is the inner freedom that will enable it to gladly shed these garments and to clothe itself in a fashion that will proclaim God's love more convincingly to men. But was this really demonstrated in the receptions given several times a week by the various delegations of the Council? Was this proof of the Church's sincerity about its servant function?

The world of the poor

Among the Council members there was a group of bishops who dedicated themselves in a special way to the problem of the 'Church of the Poor', as John XXIII had called it. They have seen the incredible misery which not only still exists in many places of the world, but which continues to spread anew, as this picture shows. Here we see one of the slums which surround the beautiful city of Rio de Janeiro. Here people, who have only recently arrived from the interior of the country, live in subhuman conditions in miserable, homemade shacks. These bishops did not want a special schema, but they made certain that almost every Council text included a few sentences insisting that concern for the poor should be a special mark of the Church, and pointing out the Church's neglect in this area. Among these bishops were Cardinals Montini and Lercaro of Italy, Bishop Ancel of France, Bishop Angerhausen of Germany and Bishop Helder Câmara of Brazil. Through their efforts the French priest-worker movement was reinstituted in a new form. Also there were various groups of bishops, formed at the close of the Council, who pledged themselves to eliminate everything superfluous from their personal style of living. They wanted to dedicate themselves in a special way to abandoned human beings, to give more time and attention to their problems than those of anyone else. They would forego luxury automobiles, would not decorate their residences elaborately, either in traditional or modern styles. How many bishops joined these groups was not publicly made known. But the very fact that they organized them—and did so very quietly—is certainly one of the noblest achievements of the Council.

It would be too easy to describe the changes made by the Council in terms of other-worldliness or worldliness. Rome stands second to no city in its appreciation of culture and worldly values; but it would be entirely the wrong place for such a pseudo-turning. Nevertheless, the Church has cut herself off, by and large, from this contemporary world —this world which has escaped from the Church's embrace, this world which is evil and seductive, which is sober, objective and 'profane'. This was nowhere so clear as in the case of the nuns who frequently have to live like dependent children. 'In this century of the emancipation of women, the women of religious orders must above all give a genuine and convincing example of adult womanhood and adult Christianity after centuries of feminine subjugation,' said an archbishop. But this is also true of priests, he said: 'The world today wants priests who do not have to think of woman as another word for sin in order to live chastely; priests who, to love heaven, do not have to feel obliged to hate the world; priests who discover in love for mankind, the most authentic way of loving God.'

227

During the Council period one cosmonaut after another was launched into outer space. Many narrow-minded individuals saw them as Promethean figures reaching for forbidden fire; and many an atheist rejoiced. No cosmonaut found God in the 'heavens'. This new concept of the universe seemed to obliterate the old image supplied by the Church; but the Council, recognizing the Church's mistake in the case of Galileo, was happy about the cosmonauts. The Pope himself did not hesitate to receive them, even when they happened to be Russians. 'We must show God to the world as he actually is—open, great and good. He is not afraid of man overtaking Him; like a good father, He is happy when He sees the victories and conquests of his adopted sons. We have to learn to understand Schema 13; it is the beginning of the dialogue with everybody.'

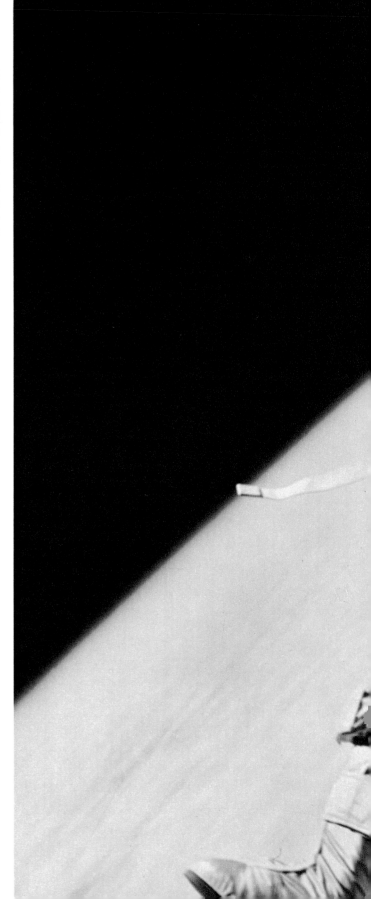

During the fourth session, a huge pilgrimage of gypsies came from all over the world to Rome. They wanted to see the great 'Shah', they said. The Pope came to visit them, and was almost swallowed up in the crowd. But he obviously enjoyed this. The gypsies are an ancient institution. The Church's open-mindedness toward modern man does not mean it should turn away from the old where it is still alive. Every culture tends to stand still—including that of the present time. The Church, however, is always on its way. Even if men were settled all over the universe, the Church would still have to remind them that the end was still to come. The Church's poverty means readiness to be continually reborn anew; it must never lose its sense of expectation of heaven!

Message of Pope Paul VI to the United Nations

(Address before the UN General Assembly, New York,
October 4, 1965)

. . . This encounter, as you all understand, marks a simple and at the same time a great moment. It is simple, because you have before you a humble man; your brother, and among you all, representatives of sovereign states, the least-invested, if you wish to think of him thus, with a minuscule, as it were symbolic, temporal sovereignty, only as much as is necessary to be free to exercise his spiritual mission, and to assure all those who deal with him that he is independent of every sovereignty of this world. But he, who now addresses you, has no temporal power, nor any ambition to compete with you. In fact, we have nothing to ask for, no question to raise; we have only a desire to express and a permission to request: namely, that of serving you in so far as we can, with disinterest, with humility, and love. . . .

We said also, however, and all here today feel it, that this moment is a uniquely great one. Great for us, great for you.

For us . . . whatever may be the opinion you have of the Pontiff of Rome, you know our mission. We are the bearer of a message for all mankind. . . .

Like a messenger who, after a long journey, finally succeeds in delivering the letter which has been entrusted to him, we appreciate the good fortune of this moment, however brief, which fulfills a desire nourished in the heart for nearly twenty centuries. For, as you will remember, we are very ancient; we here represent a long history; we here celebrate the epilogue of a wearying pilgrimage in search of a conversation with the entire world ever since the command was given to us: Go and bring the good news to all peoples. Now, you here represent all peoples. . . .

The UN as the mandatory way to world peace

We might call our message a ratification, a solemn moral ratification of this lofty institution. This message comes from our historical experience. As 'an expert in humanity', we bring to this organization the support of our recent predecessors, that of the entire Catholic episcopate and our own, convinced as we are that this organization represents the obligatory path of modern civilization and of world peace.

In saying this, we feel we are making our own the voice of the dead and of the living; of the dead, who fell in the terrible wars of the past; of the living who survived those wars, bearing in their hearts a condemnation of those who would try to renew wars; and also of those living who rise up fresh and confident, the youth of the present generation, who legitimately dream of a better human race. And we also make our own the voice of the poor, the disinherited, the suffering, of those who hunger and thirst for justice, for the dignity of life, for freedom, for well-being and progress. The peoples of the earth turn to the United Nations as the last hope of concord and peace; we presume to present here, with their tribute of honor and of hope, our own tribute also. That is why this moment is great for you, also.

We feel that you are already aware of this. Hear now the continuation of our message. It becomes a message of good wishes for the future. The edifice which you have constructed must never fail; it must be perfected, and made equal to the needs which world history will present. You mark a state in the development of mankind, from which retreat must never be admitted, but from which it is necessary that advance be made.

To the pluralism of states, which can no longer ignore one another, you offer an extremely simple and fruitful formula of coexistence. First of all, you recognize and distinguish the ones and the others. You do not confer existence upon states; but you qualify each single nation as fit to sit in the orderly congress of peoples. That is, you grant recognition, of the highest ethical and juridical value, to each single sovereign national community, guaranteeing it an honored international citizenship. This in itself is a great service to the cause of humanity, namely, to define clearly and to honor the national subjects of the world community, and to classify them in a juridical condition, worthy thereby of being recognized and respected by all, and from which there may derive an orderly and stable system of international life. You give sanction to the great principle that the relations between peoples should be regulated by reason, by justice, by law, by negotiation—not by force, nor by violence, not by war, not by fear, nor by deceit.

Thus it must be. Allow us to congratulate you for having had the wisdom to open this hall to the younger peoples, to those states which have recently attained independence and national freedom. This presence is the proof of the universality and magnanimity which inspire the principles of this institution. . . .

An international authority is necessary

Your charter goes further than this, and our message advances with it. You exist and operate to unite the nations, to bind states together. Let us use this formula: to bring the ones together with the others. You are an association. You are a bridge between peoples. You are a network of relations between states. We would almost say that your chief characteristic is a reflection, as it were, in the temporal field, of what our Catholic Church aspires to be in the spiritual field: unique and universal. In the ideological construction of mankind, there is on the natural level nothing superior to this. Your vocation is to make brothers not only of some, but of all peoples. A difficult undertaking, indeed; but this is your most noble undertaking. Is there anyone who does not see the necessity of coming thus progressively to the establishment of a world authority, able to act effectively on the juridical and political levels?

Once more we reiterate our good wish: Advance always! We will go further, and say: Strive to bring back among you any who have separated themselves, and study the right method of uniting to your pact of brotherhood, in honor and loyalty, those who do not yet share in it. Act so that those still outside will desire and merit the confidence of all; and then be generous in granting such confidence. You have the good fortune and the honor of sitting in this assembly of peaceful community; hear us as we say: Ensure that the reciprocal trust which here unites you, and enables you to do good and great things, may never be undermined or betrayed. . . .

No more war, never again war!

And now our message reaches its highest point, which is, at first, a negative point. You are expecting us to utter this sentence, and we are well aware of its gravity and solemnity: not the ones against the others, never again, never more! It was principally for this purpose that the organization of the United Nations arose: against war, in favor of peace! Listen to the lucid words of the great departed John Kennedy, who proclaimed, four years ago: 'Mankind must put an end to war, or war will put an end to mankind.' Many words are not needed to proclaim this loftiest aim of your institution. It suffices to remember that the blood of millions of men, that numberless and unheard of sufferings, useless slaughter and frightful ruin, are the sanction of the pact which unites you, with an oath which must change the future history of the world: No more war, war never again! Peace, it is peace which must guide the destinies of peoples and of all mankind. . . .

Peace, as you know, is not built up only by means of politics, by the balance of forces and of interests. It is constructed with the mind, with ideas, with works of peace. You labor in this great construction. But you are still at the beginnings. Will the world ever succeed in changing that selfish and bellicose mentality which, up to now, has been interwoven in so much of its history? It is hard to foresee; but it is easy to affirm that it is toward that new history, a peaceful, truly human history, as promised by God to men of good will, that we must resolutely march.

The roads thereto are already well marked out for you; and the first is that of disarmament. If you wish to be brothers, let the arms fall from your hands. One cannot love while holding offensive arms. Those armaments, especially those terrible arms which modern science has given you, long before they produce victims and ruins, nourish bad feelings, create nightmares, distrust, and somber resolutions; they demand enormous expenditures; they obstruct projects of union and useful collaboration; they falsify the psychology of peoples.

As long as man remains that weak, changeable and even wicked being that he often shows himself to be, defensive arms will, unfortunately, be necessary. You, however, in your courage and valiance, are studying the ways of guaranteeing the security of international life, without recourse to arms. This is a most noble aim, this the peoples expect of you, this must be obtained! Let unanimous trust in this institution grow, let its authority increase; and this aim, we believe, will be secured. Gratitude will be expressed to you by all peoples, relieved as they will then be from the crushing expenses of armaments, and freed from the nightmare of an ever imminent war.

We rejoice in the knowledge that many of you have considered favorably our invitation, addressed to all states in the cause of peace from Bombay, last December, to divert to the benefit of the developing countries at least a part of the savings which could be realized by reducing armaments. We here renew that invitation, trusting in your sentiments of humanity and generosity.

Speaking of humanity and generosity, we become aware that we are echoing another principle which is structural to the United Nations, which is its positive and affirmative high point; namely, that you work here not only to avert conflicts between states, but also to make them capable of working the ones for the others. You are not satisfied with facilitating mere coexistence between nations; you take a much greater step forward, one deserving of our praise and our support—you organize the brotherly collaboration of peoples. In this way a system of solidarity is set up, and its lofty civilized aims win the orderly and unanimous support of all the family of peoples for the common good and for the good of each individual. This aspect of the organization of the United Nations is the most beautiful; it is its most truly human feature; it is the ideal of which mankind dreams on its pilgrimage through time; it is the world's greatest hope.

It is, we presume to say, the reflection of the loving and transcendent design of God for the progress of the human family on earth—a reflection in which we see the heavenly message of the gospel become earthly. Indeed, it seems to us that here we hear the echo of the voice of our predecessors, particularly Pope John XXIII, whose message of *Pacem in Terris* was so honorably and significantly received among you. You proclaim here the fundamental rights and duties of man, his dignity, his freedom—and above all his religious freedom. We feel that you thus interpret the highest sphere of human wisdom and, we might add, its sacred character. For you deal here above all with human life; and the life of man is sacred; no one may dare violate it. Respect for life, even with regard to the great problem of birth, must find here in your assembly its highest affirmation and its most reasoned defense. You must strive to multiply bread so that it suffices for the tables of mankind, and not rather favor an artificial control of birth, which would be irrational, in order to diminish the number of guests at the banquet of life.

It does not suffice, however, to feed the hungry; it is necessary also to assure to each man a life conformed to this dignity. This too you strive to perform. We may consider this the fulfillment before our very eyes, and by your efforts, of that prophetic announcement so applicable to your institution: 'They will melt down their swords into plough-shares, their spears into pruning-hooks' (Isa. 2: 4). Are you not using the prodigious energies of the earth and the magnificent inventions of science, no longer as instruments of death but as tools of life?

We intend to redirect the development of our charitable institutions to combat world hunger and fulfill world needs. It is thus, and in no other way, that peace can be built up.

One more word, gentlemen, our final word: This edifice which you are constructing does not rest upon merely material and earthly foundations, for thus it would be a house built upon sand; above all, it is based on our own consciences. The hour has struck for our 'conversion', for personal transformation, for interior renewal. We must get used to thinking of man in a new way; and in a new way also of man's life in common—with a new manner, too, of conceiving the paths of history and the destiny of the world, according to the words of Saint Paul: 'You must be clothed in the new self, which is created in God's image, justified and sanctified through the truth' (Eph. 4: 23). The hour has come for a pause, a moment of recollection, of reflection, almost of prayer. A moment to think anew of our common origin, our history, our common destiny. Today as never before, in our era so marked by human progress, there is need for an appeal to the moral conscience of man.

For the danger comes, not from progress, nor from science—indeed, if properly utilized, these could rather resolve many of the grave problems which assail mankind. No, the real danger comes from man himself, wielding ever more powerful arms, which can be employed equally well for destruction or for the loftiest conquests.

In a word, then, the edifice of modern civilization must be built upon spiritual principles which alone can not only support it, but even illuminate and animate it. To do this, such indispensable principles of superior wisdom cannot but be founded, as you are aware we believe, upon faith in God. That unknown God of whom St. Paul spoke to the Athenians in the Areopagus? Unknown by them, although without realizing it they sought him and he was close to them, as happens also to many men of our times. To us, in any case, and to all those who accept the ineffable revelation which Christ has given us of him, he is the living God, the Father of all men.

233

Council Speeches
I. A New Spirit

Drawing: A Roman angel

The Vernacular in the Liturgy and the Rights of Bishops' Conferences

PATRIARCH MAXIMOS IV SAIGH of Antioch
on October 23, 1962

Although the schema on the sacred liturgy concerns only the Roman rites, I would like, as an interested observer of the progress of the Latin Church, to contribute to the discussion the testimony of an Eastern patriarch. For the sake of brevity, I would like to limit myself to the problem of the language of the liturgy.

I would like first to say that the schema as a whole strikes me as extraordinary. Apart from a few necessary corrections, which will surely be proposed by interested bishops, this schema does honor to the liturgical commission and to the liturgical movement to which it owes its existence.

Five intelligible words better than ten thousand unintelligible ones

Yet it seems to me that the principle stated in the beginning, 'The use of the Latin language is to be retained in the Western liturgy', has been formulated too apodictically. The almost absolute value which is attributed to the Latin language for liturgy, instruction and administration in the Latin Church is, from the viewpoint of the Eastern Church, something entirely abnormal. Christ himself, after all, did use the language of his contemporaries. He probably used the language all his hearers understood—Aramaic—when he offered the first eucharistic sacrifice. The apostles and disciples did the same. It would never have occurred to them that the celebrants in a Christian assembly would read the passages from sacred scripture, sing the psalms, preach a sermon, or break the bread while using a language different from that of the congregation. St. Paul says explicitly: If I pray in a tongue, my spirit prays but my mind is unfruitful. What am I to do? I will pray with the spirit and I will pray with the mind also. I will sing with the spirit and I will sing with the mind also. Otherwise, if you bless with the spirit, how can anyone in the position of an outsider say 'Amen' to your thanksgiving when he does not know what you are saying? For you may give thanks well enough, but the other man is not edified. . . . In church I would rather speak five words with my mind in order to instruct others, than ten thousand words in a tongue' (1 Cor. 14:14—19). All arguments in favor of Latin as an irreplaceable language—a liturgical but dead language—must give way before this clear, unequivocal and precise consideration of the apostle. By the way, the Roman Church itself, at least until the middle of the third century, used to employ the Greek language in its liturgy, because this was the language spoken by the faithful at the time. And if at that time the Church began to give up the Greek language in favor of Latin, it was precisely because Latin had meantime become the vernacular language of the faithful. What is to keep the Church from applying the same principle today?

Latin dead but the Church alive

In the East, after the use of the Aramaic and Greek languages during the first generations, the Coptic language was introduced in rural areas in Egypt. Later, from the fifth century on, the same thing happened with Georgic, Ethiopian, Arabic, Gothic and Slavic languages.

In the Church of the West, it was not until the middle ages that Latin was considered the one universal language of Roman civilization. And this was in opposition to the languages of the barbarians who dominated Europe. Thus the Church of the West made Latin its official and sacred language. For the East, however, liturgical language never constituted a problem. Actually any language is liturgical. For the psalmist says, 'Praise the Lord, all you peoples.' And therefore God must be praised, the gospel preached, and the sacrifice offered in all languages, whatever they may be. Anyway, we in the East cannot understand how the faithful can be brought together to pray in a language they do not understand. The Latin language is dead; the Church, however, lives, and the language which mediates grace and the Holy Spirit must also be alive, because language is for men and not for angels. No language can be untouchable.

Two suggestions

We all realize that the vernacular must be introduced into the Latin rite step by step and with prudent circumspection. But I would like the rigor of the principle stated at the beginning somewhat attenuated. Instead of saying that 'The use of the Latin language is to be maintained in the Western liturgy', it could perhaps be said that 'The Latin language is the original and official language of the Roman rite.'

My second suggestion would be to have the regional conferences of bishops decide on their own authority whether and to what extent it would be useful to introduce vernacular into the liturgy. The text of the schema only gives the bishops' conferences the right to make proposals to the Holy See about this. But the making of a proposal does not require a bishops' conference. Any of the faithful could do that. The bishops' conferences must have more than the mere right to make proposals. They must have powers to make decisions, provided the Holy See approves. I suggest, therefore, this formulation: 'It is the right of the individual regional bishops' conferences to determine the extent and manner of the introduction of the vernacular into the liturgy, with the approval of the Holy See.'

Note: The first suggestion was not accepted. The old formulation was retained. The second suggestion was, however, incorporated into the Constitution on the Sacred Liturgy.

The Church's Mission in the World Belongs to the Church's Essence

LAUREAN CARDINAL RUGAMBWA, bishop of Bukoba (East Africa) on October 1, 1963

Venerable Fathers: It is after consulting with many bishops of Africa and Madagascar that I speak to you. There are many reasons why we are pleased with the schema on the Church. As far as we are concerned, however, the main reason is that, in keeping with the design of God, it proposes a broad view of the Church; and it presents fairly, distinctly, and better than ever before, the doctrine on the Church in its inner structure as well as in its relationship with the outside world in accordance with sacred scripture and genuine tradition. Preceding speakers have already stressed some points we enthusiastically agree with. We are prepared to subscribe to the schema but we would like to add three additional points:

1. The essential mission of the Church, which is identical with the mission of the incarnate Word and above all involves evangelization of the world, is not presented clearly enough in the mystery of the Church.
2. The present age urgently demands that we work out a truly ecclesiastical concept of mission, deeply rooted in the mystery of the Church.
3. The nature and vocation of the People of God must be brought into clearer relief, so that the Church's mission to save the whole world is more profoundly and clearly understood.

The evangelization of the world as an essential of the Church

1. Our first suggestion is that the missionary function of the Church should be emphasized in a better way. The prepared draft suffers in this respect from a very significant weakness. The schema claims 'to explain the universal mission of the Church in a more contemporary fashion', but the decisive element of this mission, evangelization, is almost completely neglected. If there is no reference to the evangelization of the world, the mystery of the Church will not be understood. That is why it must be clearly stated that the Church is sent into the world by virtue of the same mission the Father gave the Son, so that the work of Christ may be continued through the centuries. The whole matter becomes even more dubious if we glance at the formulations which are actually used. It seems to us that these formulations present the Church, in a purely static way, as a kind of 'fixed asset'. The Church of God here on earth is, however, no mere 'fixed asset', but 'a Church in process of becoming'. An inner dynamism animates the Church and, by virtue of this, it struggles not only for eschatological perfection in God but also for the missionary growth of the People of God.

All countries are mission territories

2. This brings us to the missionary aspect which also has been insufficiently worked out. Let us bear in mind, Venerable Fathers, that whenever we speak of the missionary function of the Church, we not only refer to the so-called foreign missions, but to the entire Church.

Evangelization is in principle coextensive with the fundamental mission of the Church. Today the Church is represented in almost every region of the earth. It is present there. Although the circumstances may be different in various places, there are groups of people in every country of the world who are outside the Church. They do not yet know Christ as the savior or they have forgotten him. So every country is a mission country. It is this sense of mission that the text should mention; and what is said should be said to the entire Church. The spirit of mission is needed everywhere. The Church must be missionary everywhere.

A special chapter on the People of God

3. A third request. To give a better idea of the nature of the Church and to more clearly illuminate its essential mission, we think it is necessary to speak more profoundly about the People of God and about the mystery of the covenant between God and man. Therefore we must ask the council to introduce a new second chapter in the schema, a chapter dealing with the People of God, as the coordinating commission has already proposed.

Note: The three requests of the cardinal were complied with.

A Correct Understanding of Papal Infallibility

JOSEPH DESCUFFI, archbishop of Smyrna (Turkey), on December 4, 1962

Venerable Fathers: I would like to recommend that the question of the infallibility of the Church's magisterium and of the pope, because of its great significance for reunification, be treated in a special paragraph, entitled 'The Teaching Office of the Church'. In this paragraph there should be a clear and unequivocal explanation of the privilege of infallibility and especially of what seems to me an ambiguous statement of the First Vatican Council: 'The definitions of the bishops of Rome are infallible *of themselves* ... and not from *the consent of the Church*.'

Papal infallibility at the First Vatican Council

I would like to preface my remarks with a few considerations explained by Bishop Gasser, the final 'relator' of the deputation on faith at the First Vatican Council: 'We do not exclude the cooperation of the Church because the infallibility of the bishop of Rome is not something which comes to him by inspiration or revelation but by divine assistance. From this it follows that the pope, because of his responsibility and the seriousness of the matter, must use appropriate means to properly explore and suitably express the truth. Such means include councils and even the advice of bishops, cardinals, theologians and so on. These means do, of course, differ at different times. We should devoutly assume that in the divine assistance given to Peter and his suc-cessors by Christ the Lord, there is also a promise to supply the means necessary and appropriate to assure that the pope's judgment is infallible' (Mansi 52:12—13).

The danger of misunderstanding papal infallibility

It seems to me that the First Vatican Council was correct in declaring that the definitions of the bishop of Rome are irreformable (1) 'of themselves' and (2) 'not from the consent of the Church'. But the declaration seems unclear, especially because the first and second points are juxtaposed. This juxtaposition can give rise to the following false interpretations: (1) the pope is infallible by himself even though the universal Church is opposed to him, or even without the Church; (2) the infallible Church can stand opposed to an infallible pope. Such a situation is, of course, quite unthinkable. The two infallibilities, that of the pope and that of the Church, though they differ in origin and in the subject in which they inhere, cannot be pitted against one another, but must be joined together in one and the same infallibility. The one infallibility inheres in the pope and has its origin in a special promise made to Peter who responded to Christ, in the name of all the apostles, as head of the apostolic college. The other infallibility belongs to the Church in its work of defining and proposing. This infallibility must always be in agreement with the pope or in concurrence with him.

Complementary understandings

Therefore: (1) 'of themselves' means that a special infallibility comes from Christ to the pope as head of the Church; it does not come 'from the consent of the Church'. Nor does it come from some special gifts of the pope, such as his knowledge or holiness, as some, in opposition to the Church, would like to think and teach. (2) 'Not from the consent of the Church' means that the Church's infallibility is not created by the pope but that it is corroborated by him; he is united to the Church as its head. But the consent of the Church may in no sense be considered non-existent or irrelevant; nor may it be passed over in silence. We have already said that infallibility does not consist in some kind of divine inspiration or revelation. It consists in a special kind of divine assistance which exempts from error, but not from the task of investigating the truth—through study, consultation, and other means which differ with the times. So when the bishop of Rome speaks *ex cathedra* (in other words, as supreme shepherd and teacher of the universal Church), and when he strengthens his brethren, he cannot do so without making inquiries about the consciousness of the Church, without consulting the Church either in councils or in regional synods or through other suitable means as has always been done up to now. The pope alone does not constitute the Church. But where the pope is, there the Church is, in agreement with him. These two members are as inseparable as head and body; and they are united in one identical infallibility. Moreover, when the pastor and ruler of the universal or ecumenical church most profoundly desires that unity and love rule in all parts of the Church throughout the world, he will surely be happy to use the unique means—the consultation of the universal Church. In other words, he will work with the college of bishops in a way indicated by divine providence.

Note: Although the archbishop emphasized this point again during the Council's second session (on October 10, 1963), the Council did not take it up. The reaction of certain fathers indicated that to do so would have led to an extremely bitter argument. The Council preferred, as in other cases, for example, on the question of the membership of the Church, to approach a solution by clearly stating the complementary truths (here it was the collegiality of the college of bishops), and letting intelligent theologians draw their own conclusions.

Eastern Church Synods and Bishops' Conferences

ELIE ZOGHBY, Melchite patriarchal vicar in Egypt, on November 15, 1963

Venerable Fathers: In a certain sense the Roman Church owes Orthodoxy a debt of gratitude: The Orthodox Church has been practicing since ancient times what the bishops' conferences are supposed to accomplish today. I want to summarize my thoughts on this subject under four points. Some of them may have ecumenical significance.

1. The relationship of the Roman Church to Eastern Orthodoxy grows out of ten centuries of union, during which Rome not only acknowledged their collegial and synodal form of government, but also lived collegially in common with the traditional or apostolic Churches of the East. In fact, even if we overlook the great ecumenical councils which brought together the episcopates of East and West under the unchallenged chairmanship of the bishop of Rome, we still have the fact that the Roman Church exchanged synodal letters with the traditional or apostolic churches of the East. These letters dealt with problems which affected the universal Church as well as the local churches. Today, when the Catholic Church is trying to become more accessible to the Orthodox East and is preparing for ecumenical dialogue, the only form of Church government which the Council can propose to the Churches of the East is synodal government—meaning government by genuine bishops' conferences having real power. To speak of conferences having a purely advisory function, would be to forestall from the start any possibility of dialogue.

2. Episcopal synods or conferences in Catholic Churches of the Eastern rite have been bled of all real power. This power had been handed over to the Roman Curia, especially the Congregation for the Eastern Churches. To be convinced of this, all we need do is consult the new code of Eastern canon law. What this congregation has actually done is assume the role of a pseudo-patriarchate. It is true that the six patriarchs of the East have been named associate members of the Congregation for the Eastern Church. But it already has about thirty members, all of them cardinals. This solution fails to achieve anything concrete and is neither an honorable nor an ecumenical solution. To take patriarchs who are by right the presiding officers of their synods, and to make them secondary and minority members of a Roman congregation given authority to deal with the affairs of their own patriarchates, is actually a condemnation of the synodal form of government. What should be set up in place of this congregation is a body whose members would be delegates of the episcopal synods or conferences of the Eastern rite churches.

3. Bishops, as pastors, are chiefly responsible for Catholic action and for the whole lay apostolate. Now the lay apostolate is no longer limited to the boundaries of definite parishes or dioceses. It is organized on a national or worldwide scale. Only the collective power of the episcopate will make it possible for bishops to continue their pastoral activities on a national or universal scale, through lay apostolic groups which should be under the control and the direction of the bishops.

4. In this hall we have heard the spectre of nationalism conjured up against collegiality and bishops' conferences with legislative powers. But we have now arrived at a moment in history when nationalism—at least if it is not a narrowly centralized nationalism—is no longer a danger to the universal common good, but is instead a way of enriching all human society. Actually, as young nations arise and gain their freedom, we see that international organizations are simultaneously accorded greater esteem than ever before. All nations participate on an equal basis in them. Should men of the Church be less open and magnanimous than statesmen?

Note: In regard to the patriarchs, the decree on Eastern Catholic Churches says 'that the rights and privileges which prevailed when East and West were united should again be restored'. The decree does not mention a reorganization of the Roman Congregation for the Eastern Church. But such a reorganization may be expected to follow.

Collegiality Means What it Implies

GASTON JACQUIER, auxiliary bishop of Algiers, in the name of 29 North African bishops, on October 14, 1963

The text of the schema on the Church illuminates the juristic aspect of collegiality.

Just as the Church contains both a visible and invisible element so, too, collegiality means essentially two things. The external element is unity in government. There can be no bishops' college, as several fathers have emphasized, without the authority of the successor of Peter. The inner element consists in unity through the same faith and the same love. Pius XI described this in his encyclical ECCLESIAM DEI (The Church of God), on November 12, 1923.

1. Unity in faith or in truth is what our Lord Jesus Christ requested from the Father on behalf of the apostles and their successors (John 17:17): 'Sanctify them in the truth.' Unity lives; it is profound; it engenders among the bishops, as Tertullian said, 'consanguinity of doctrine' which forms the basis of the apostolicity of the Church as founded by the apostles.

2. Christ also prayed that the apostles would have unity in love, 'that they may be one as we are one' (John 17:17). When he first sent them out as apostles, the Lord sent them in pairs. In this way he pointed to the fact that the Gospel, which is the revelation of divine love, can only be preached through the love of the preachers for one another. In his third letter John reprimands Diotrephes for wanting to put himself first, for refusing to welcome the apostle, for not even welcoming the brethren, and for stopping those who wanted to welcome them and expelling from the community (3 John:10). Ignatius of Antioch wrote to Polycarp: 'Cultivate unity. Nothing is better than this.' A wonderful example of this love is offered by St. Optatus of Milea, who wrote to the bishop Parmenias about the Donatist bishops: 'And because they do not want a common bishops' college in union with us, they obviously do not want to be our colleagues; nevertheless they are our brothers. . . .' Pius XI wrote to the Italian bishops, 'You are our brothers in the office of bishop within the apostolate' (June 29, 1931). The basis of this unity is faith, and love among bishops is their sharing in the priesthood of Christ. They are united to Christ more intimately than the faithful, more intimately than priests. The effective sign of this unity is the eucharist. Formerly the bishop read the names of other bishops while standing at the altar, just as bishops today mention the name of the Roman bishop and pray for the faithful of the Catholic confession, and especially for all the bishops.

The pastoral aspect of this collegiality consists in the mutual help which the bishops give one another in the exercise of their office, as others have already explained so very well. The Pope himself has expressed his will in this matter in several encyclicals. . . . However, the soul of this mutual assistance is love: The bishops, scattered throughout the world, thus become brothers with one another and with the successor of Peter. Without love the apostolic college means and accomplishes nothing. Unity in love is primarily the responsibility of the bishops; it is an apostolic responsibility. Moreover, we all know what a strong witness the unity of members of the Church is to the attractiveness of the grace of Christ. But the unity of the Church's members is based on unity of the episcopate.

The schema speaks more than once about love among the bishops. This is true. But it is done in the manner of a sermon. It would be better if, after a simple statement, there were at least a brief addition to the effect that this unity in love, which is unity in truth, is the 'purpose', the main purpose of collegiality. It is a gift which Christ prayed for on our behalf and which the Holy Spirit imparted to us.

Note: This underlining of the collegial attitude as a spiritual reality is to be found in almost all speeches given by French bishops on this theme. The *peritus* P. Congar, O. P., also repeatedly insisted on this point. However correct this viewpoint may have been, and however much it corresponded to the spirit of the Council, it did confuse the conservative minority and awoke its suspicion.

Cooperation of Bishop and Priests in Pastoral Service

DENIS HURLEY, O.M.I., archbishop of Durban (South Africa), on October 9, 1963

Venerable Fathers: By the very nature of his ministry, the bishop is supposed to teach, sanctify and rule. But if we look at what actually happens in practice, what do we see? It is not the bishop but the priest who carries out practically all of the actual day-by-day ministry of teaching and sanctifying.

Priests have pastoral contact

And certainly to ninety-nine percent of his flock the bishop seems an unfamiliar, distant figure, unknown on the personal and human level. His task is to lay down the general lines of policy, to bring together and organize the affairs of the diocese, to coordinate the various new projects which are begun; but he very frequently has no direct hierarchical influence on his flock; he does practically everything in the diocese through its priests. For the priests are the hands and feet, the eyes and ears of the bishop; indeed, they are even his voice. And just as no one can act without using the organs of his body, so the bishop, in whatever he wants to initiate, in all that he may hope to do, depends fully and completely on his priests to put his ideas into effect. We all know how much it depends on the way a priest reads out his pastoral letters whether the bishop's words will resound like an archangel's trumpet, or drone on like the columns of a telephone directory.

The bishops function as priestly leader

From all this it is clear that the bishop fulfills his three-fold responsibility of teaching, sanctifying and ruling, above all by the leadership he gives to his priests. Since modern circumstances make it practically impossible for him to have direct contact with his flock, the overriding concern of the bishop should be to provide his priests with pastoral leadership. For he should direct his priests, give them organization, inspiration, encouragement and help. Should anyone object that such a matter belongs to the practical order and does not belong in a dogmatic constitution, my answer is that a dogmatic constitution should pay attention to facts. And the principal fact which bears on the ministry of bishops (especially their ministry of teaching and sanctifying) is that in our time these ministries are usually not carried out by bishops but by priests; from this it follows that the principal duty of the bishop is to provide leadership and stimulation.

Bishops' failings in priestly leadership

I admit that in all of this I speak as one less wise, since I know that I am unable to show the precise nature of this task of leadership. Nevertheless, it is clear to me that this is a matter of supreme importance. For I believe that if in recent decades the Church seems to have been slow in responding to the exhortations of the pope on the social apostolate, on the missions, the lay apostolate, and the catechetical and liturgical renewal, the main reason is that we bishops have fallen short in fulfilling our role of leadership. For we have not known how to pass on the message of the pope's encyclicals to our priests as a living teaching so that they would be able to communicate it in similar fashion to the People of God. It is a lamentable fact that the initiative for Catholic renewal has frequently come not from us, but from select groups of priests and laymen.

Of this, then, I am fully convinced: We should lay it down as a clear principle that the implementation of this ministry consists principally in providing forceful yet tactful pastoral leadership for priests who, in their turn, with the cooperation of religious and laity, will accomplish the task which we ourselves cannot.

The natural and obvious conclusion to be drawn from these important reflections is that the priestly order is of supreme importance in carrying out the ministry of the hierarchy. But I have no time to develop this point further.

Note: The Council tried, in the third chapter on the Constitution on the Church, and in its special decree on priestly life and ministry, to follow the archbishop's suggestion; but it was unable to fulfill his wish that concrete tasks of leadership would be pointed up there.

Charismatic Gifts in the Church

LEO CARDINAL SUENENS, archbishop of Mechelen and Brussels, on October 22, 1963

The schema on the Church briefly mentions the charismatic gifts of Christians. The remarks made about charisms are so few that one could get the impression that charisms are nothing more than a marginal and non-essential phenomenon in the life of the church. Now the vital importance of these charisms for building up the mystical body must be presented with greater clarity and consequently at greater length. What is to be completely avoided is that the hierarchical structure of the Church appears to be an administrative apparatus with no intimate connections with the charismatic gifts of the Holy Spirit, which occur everywhere throughout the church. The encyclical on the mystical Body speaks far more profoundly about this matter than does our schema.

Charisms for all Christians

The time of the Church, which is on pilgrimage through the centuries until the parousia of the Lord, is the time of the Holy Spirit. For it is through the Holy Spirit that the glorified Christ unifies the eschatological people of God, purifies them, fills them with life and leads them to all truth, and this in spite of the weaknesses and sins of this people. The Holy Spirit is thus the first fruits (Rom. 8:23), the first installment of

the Church (2 Cor. 1:22; 5:5), in this world. Therefore the Church is called the dwelling of God in the Spirit (Eph. 2:22).

It follows from this that the Holy Spirit is not given to pastors only but to each and every Christian. 'Do you not know that you are the temple of God, and that the Holy Spirit dwells within you?' says St. Paul to the Corinthians (1 Cor. 3:16). In baptism, the sacrament of faith, all Christians receive the Holy Spirit. All Christians, 'living stones', as they are called, are to be built into a 'spiritual dwelling' (*oikos pneumatikos*: 1 Pet. 2:5). Therefore the whole Church is essentially a truly 'pneumatic' or spiritual reality, built on the foundation not only of the Apostles, but—as Ephesus 2:20 says—also of prophets. In the Church of the New Testament God 'gave some to be apostles, some prophets, some pastors and teachers' (Eph. 4:11; 3:5).

The Holy Spirit shows himself in the Church in the great number and richness of his spiritual gifts, gifts which Scripture calls *pneumatika* (1 Cor. 12:1; 14:1) or charisms (Rom. 12:6, 1 Cor. 12:4, 9, 28, 30f; 1 Tim. 4:14, 2 Tim. 1:6; 1 Pet. 4:10). Certainly in the time of St. Paul even very extraordinary and marvelous charisms such as 'ecstatic utterance' or charisms of healings, were shown forth in the Church. But we should not think that the charisms of the Spirit consist exclusively or even principally in these more extraordinary and marvelous phenomena. St. Paul speaks, for example of the charism of wise speech and knowledge (1 Cor. 12:8), of the charism of faith (1 Cor. 12:9), of the charism of teaching (Rom. 12:7; 1 Cor. 12:28; 14:26), of stirring or comforting speech (Rom. 12:8), and ministry (Rom. 12:7), of the charism of distinguishing true spirits from false (1 Cor. 12:10), of the charism of helping others and guiding them (1 Cor. 12:28), and so on.

Thus to St. Paul the Church of the living Christ does not appear as some kind of administrative organization, but as a living web of gifts, of charisms, of ministries. The Spirit is given to every individual Christian, the Spirit who gives his gifts, his charisms to each and every one 'different as they are allotted to us by God's grace' (Rom. 12:6). 'In each of us the Spirit is manifested in one particular way, for some useful purpose' (1 Cor. 12:7), for example 'to build up the Church' (1 Cor. 14:12). Each and every Christian, whether lettered or unlettered, has his charism in his daily life, but—as St. Paul says—'All of these must aim at one thing; to build up the Church' (1 Cor. 14:26)....

Charisms in the Church today

What would our Church be without the charisms of teachers or theologians? And what would our Church be like without the charisms of prophets, that is, men speaking under the inspiration of the Holy Spirit, who speaking out insistently 'on all occasions, convenient and inconvenient' (2 Tim. 4:2), woke up the Church at times when she was asleep, to prevent the practice of the Gospel of Christ from being neglected? It was not in past ages alone, not only in the time of St. Thomas Aquinas or St. Francis of Assisi, that the Church was in need of the charisms of teachers and prophets and other ministries; she needs them today as well and needs them in her ordinary everyday life. So let us pass over the more outstanding charisms and come to the more commonplace charisms the schema alludes to. Do we not all know laymen and laywomen in each of our own dioceses who we might say are in a way called by the Lord and endowed with various charisms of the Spirit? Whether in catechetical work, in spreading the Gospel, in every area of Catholic activity, or in social and charitable works? Do we not know and see in our daily experience that the action of the Holy Spirit has not died out in the Church? . . .

Pastors and charisms

It is the duty of pastors, both those in charge of local and individual churches and those in charge of the universal Church, through a kind of spiritual instinct to discover the charisms of the Spirit in the Church, to foster them and to help them grow. It is the duty of pastors to listen carefully and with an open heart to laymen, and repeatedly to engage in a living dialogue with them. For each and every layman has been given his own gifts and charisms, and more often than not has greater experience than the clergy in daily life in the world.

Finally, it is the duty of pastors themselves to aim at the higher charisms (1 Cor. 12:31). It is clear that all the faithful, even those endowed with the greatest gifts, give reverence and obedience to their pastors. But it is also true from the other side that similar attention and reverence is due to those charisms and impulses of the Holy Spirit, who very frequently breathes through Christian laymen who have no position of authority. Consequently St. Paul warns all Christians, pastors included: 'Do not quench the Spirit, and do not despise prophetic utterances, but put them all to the test and then keep what is good' (1 Thess. 5:19—21). This complex of gifts, charisms and ministries can be brought into play and serve to build up the Church only through that freedom of the sons of God which, following St. Paul's example, all pastors must protect and foster.

Suggestions

The suggestions to be made on the level of doctrine are that the chapter on the people of God be improved in the following ways:

1. Along with the structure of ministry, the charismatic dimension of the Church should be developed in the whole chapter. 2. The importance of charisms in the people of God should be given positive emphasis by more extended and concrete treatment. 3. In particular the importance of prophets and teachers in the Church should be given attention. 4. The relation of pastors to charisms of the faithful should be described in more positive and constructive terms. 5. The teaching of St. Paul about the freedom of the sons of God in the Church should not be forgotten.

On the practical level, I suggest that—in order to manifest, in the Council itself and before all men, our faith in the charisms given by the Holy Spirit to all believing Christians: 1. The number and universality of lay auditors should be increased. 2. Women too should be invited as auditors; unless I am mistaken, they make up approximately half of the human race. 3. Finally, religious brothers and sisters should be invited, since they too belong to the People of God, have received the Holy Spirit, and serve the Church as a choice segment of the Lord's flock.

Note: The remarks of the cardinal—who was a Council moderator, and who was, among the members of the coordinating commission, the competent specialist in these matters—left their traces in chapter 2 ('The People of God') of the Constitution on the Church. There are also several allusions to this dimension of the Church in chapter 4 of the same Constitution and in the decree on the lay apostolate. But in the schema on the missions, this important dimension of the Church has been almost completely neglected in favor of an overemphasis on organization and training.

The Council Fathers' Use of the Double Standard

LUIGI CARLI, bishop of Segni (near Rome), on September 18, 1964

Venerable Fathers: As the 'relator' (reporter) of the proposed text [on the pastoral office of bishops] has prudently and wisely remarked, its doctrinal statements are in several instances taken from the schema on the Church—and with the express proviso that no value judgment may be passed on these statements until the schema on the Church has been approved by the fathers (and, I might add, until the Bishop of Rome has finally sanctioned it).

May no one think it a violation of fraternal love toward a dear colleague on the commission, and may no one think it my intention to depreciate the overall value of our schema, if I take the liberty of objecting to two points.

The supreme and universal authority of the bishops is a chimera

1. I wish to reiterate my objections to the dogmatic statements in the schema on the Church, objections already filed in writing with the Commission on Faith. These objections have to do with collegiality, with the source of episcopal power and the relationship between this power and papal primacy.

[I can understand and am ready to admit that the episcopate, in union with the bishop of Rome, is permanently endowed with a charism of infallibility, because the ordinary teaching office is always being exercised, because it always has a precisely defined object, namely the deposit of faith given us by Christ, and because the unity of the episcopate with bishop of Rome is always possible and provable. Yet I cannot understand why there should exist in the episcopate a permanent, supreme, and universal power of governance, even outside of councils or conciliar forms. The reason is that the existence of such power, which never can be exercised on its own, seems to me to be a pure chimera. Besides, the object of these powers is something completely instable and nebulous. Finally, and this seems to me most important, the unity of the episcopate with the bishop of Rome, which is the necessary prerequisite for that supreme universal governing power (as has been rightly said) is neither possible nor provable until the papal will (which like anybody's will can naturally not be anticipated) decides to determine something concrete in common with his brothers of the episcopate and in the interest of the Church universal.]

Besides, I cannot help drawing attention to the fact that our schema contains a dogmatic assertion *not* contained in the schema on the Church —that all bishops by divine right have a share in the Council in virtue of their ordination. This allegation, for which no proof is offered, appears to me irreconcilable with the history of titular bishops, and it contradicts a centuries-old tradition of the Church. It also seems to me scarcely believable that so many bishops before now have been cheated of such a divine right, belonging to them by ordination. I do not deny, however, that it would be definitely desirable were titular bishops, at least in this respect, put on an equal footing with superiors of religious orders.

First the individual, then the community

2. In the introduction, there was a premise designed to determine and justify the whole structure of the schema: Being a bishop means first and foremost a relation to the theological premise, derived from the theory of collegiality, in line with which a bishop by virtue of ordination becomes a member of the college, and via this college obtains his powers for the common welfare of the Church universal. And yet is this premise true? What proofs support it? It seems to me we should reverse it and say that just as there are first individuals and then a community, so too there are first bishops and only then a community of bishops. The first and as it were characteristic function of the bishops is in their governance of their own churches; and it is thus that they contribute to the common good of the Church universal. And so to be a bishop means first of all a relation to the bishop's own individual church and through this to other churches and to the Church universal. Because:

(a) The very ancient theology of individual churches, which from the time of St. Ignatius of Antioch to the present has been alive in the East, sees in the bishop one sent by Christ, who realizes and 'makes incarnate' the Catholic Church in one particular place. The view which sees a collegiality between Christ and the bishops was entirely unknown. It could not even have come into existence, because each bishop could only have relationship with his fellow bishops insofar as he himself represented one part of the Church. When titular bishops were introduced in the twelfth century, the idea of a bishop having a relationship 'to the universal Church', was so alien to the thinking of the Church that bishops were assigned, at least in title, a relationship to some one particular place. Even the pope becomes bishop of the Catholic Church only via his relationship to the local church of Rome.

(b) Nor do the most ancient liturgical formularies for the ordination of bishops know anything of the entrance of the ordained into a college— not to mention the idea that this is the first and basic consequence of ordination. Even if the turn of phrase of these formularies sometimes seem universalistic, it becomes clear from the context that only the local church is referred to.

Venerable Fathers, I am coming to my conclusion. Perhaps the thoughts alluded to here do not seem convincing to some of you. But one thing is certainly clear: The theory of collegiality and its consequences is not incontestable. Rather it teems with difficulties. Exegetical, historical, liturgical, juridical research is still needed. It says in the text, and we have only recently heard this again in the aula, that it is not the intention of the Council to define anything in regard to any disputed theological questions about divine revelation or the Blessed Virgin Mary. Why do we not apply the same standards here where such important matters are involved, where the episcopacy and even the structure of the Church is concerned? Do we not expose ourselves to the reproach that we have weighed with two different kinds of scales and measured with two different kinds of measurements? In the Mariological and biblical questions, our speech was circumspect, reserved, and painstakingly cautious, but where our own interests were concerned, it was verbose, voluble, and overwrought!

Part of the text was bracketed because the speaker feared the moderator might interrupt him for saying something irrelevant to the subject. This was not read in the aula, but was only filled in writing. [Note by Bishop Carli.]

Note: Of the numerous speeches made by Bishop Carli, the spokesman of the minority, this was unquestionably the best. It clearly points to the controversial features in the question of the bishops' college. This attitude led to the addition of the famous 'explanatory note' to the third chapter of the constitution on the Church. Actually the text on the bishops no longer says that the bishop by ordination has a right to participate in the Council; but it now says that the bishops are members of the college by ordination, and therefore the holy Synod decides that all bishops have a right to take part in the Council. We can interpret this as we will. But what Bishop Carli had to say against collegiality and against the 'premise' which decided and justified the decree and its structural division, gained neither approval from the fathers nor support from the Pope. The decree remains as it was, and Pope Paul signed it, together with the fathers of the Council.

At the beginning of the Council, Laurean Cardinal Rugambwa (53) was the only 'black' cardinal. In his home country, Tansania (on Lake Victoria), he is simply the Bishop of Bukoba and his diocese is in the control of the archbishop of Tabora, a town of 13,000 inhabitants. But Rugambwa's diocese counts 181,000 Catholics, and the archdiocese of Tabora only 41,000. A real landslip took place in Bukoba a few years ago: many thousand people asked to be baptized. Not only amongst the blacks in Africa did Rugambwa's unpretentious, deeplyconvinced manner make a great impression. At the Council too, the audience each time listened to his words in great quietness. At the last session he was given a black colleague in the dignity of cardinal in the very youthful person of the White Father, Paolo Zoungrana (Overvolta).

Elie Zoghbi, Melchite patriarchal vicar of Egypt. This great orator, a native of Egypt, spoke eleven times at the Council. His chief interest was in questions of Church structure. He not only defended the Eastern Church practices against Western centralism, but even urgently asked that the West imitate these practices. In the third session he made a profoundly theological contribution on the missions as an epiphany for non-Christian nations, beautifully relating the creative word of God to his incarnate Word. When Patriarch Maximos IV accepted the cardinate he was vigorously opposed by Zoghbi. His proposal during the fourth session for a possible dispensation from marital vows created a huge sensation and plunged Zoghbi into a conflict with Cardinal Journet. Patriarch Maximos turned in a superior performance as mediator in this dispute.

Maximos Saigh IV, the 88-year old Cardinal Patriarch of the Melchite Church of Antioch, was one of the most notable speakers at the Council. This was not only because he was the only Council father not to speak in Latin—he spoke in French, to make his point that Latin cannot be considered *the* language of the Church; he also won attention by the really important speeches he made at decisive turning points. For example, he spoke in the first session on the vernacular liturgy; in the second session, on the council of bishops and the synodal structure of the Church as a whole; in the third session, on the development of morality, on contemporary problems of marriage and war; in the fourth session, on atheism and the indulgence question. He maintained throughout a broad international outlook, pointed toward the future. The picture shows him conversing with the soft-spoken Cardinal and Coptic Rite Patriarch, Stephen Sidarouss, age 62. Both were appointed cardinals by Pope Paul VI on February 22, 1965. They are both also members of the pontifical commission for the reform of canon law.

II. Dialogue within the Church and with non-Catholics

The Ecumenical Dialogue and the Council's Response

EMILE JOSEF DE SMEDT, bishop of Bruges (Belgium), on November 19, 1962

I am speaking in the name of the Secretariat for Christian Unity. Many fathers, in their examination of the schema 'On the Sources of Revelation', have shown a genuine ecumenical concern. Without exception, all honestly and positively desire that the schema serve unity. However, some find that the schema corresponds to the requirements of sound ecumenism; others deny this. In order to be better able to judge, it might be desirable to hear from the secretariat what precisely gives an ecumenical character to a presentation. For this is why our secretariat was set up by the Pope—to serve the bishops in examining the schemata from the viewpoint of their ecumenicity.

The problem is this: *what is required in the teaching and style of the schema, to make it a genuine contribution to the achievement of a better dialogue between Catholics and non-Catholics?*

Answer: All Christians in common recognize Jesus Christ. What the Lord himself has given us constitutes the content of faith and is our salvation. All of us, Catholics and non-Catholics, approach this unique source. Disunity begins when we ask how we approach Jesus Christ. We are separated brethren. We have been divided now for several centuries. We know that our disunity contradicts the will of Christ. When will our division finally come to an end? For several centuries we Catholics have believed that a clear presentation of our doctrine was sufficient. Non-Catholics believed the same thing. Both parties presented their doctrine in their own terminology, from their own point of view. And what Catholics said was not correctly understood by non-Catholics, and vice versa. But the method of 'clear presentation of truth' brought us not a single step closer to reunification. On the contrary, bias, suspicions, quarrels and polemical controversy increased on both sides.

We have seen a new method develop in the last decades. It is called ecumenical dialogue. What does this consist in?

What is characteristic of this method is that efforts are made not only in regard to truth, but also in regard to the manner and method of presenting truth so that it can be correctly understood by the others. The Christians of various confessions help one another so that each can understand those teachings of the other which he does not accept. Ecumenical dialogue therefore does not mean a deliberation or a negotiation about reunification; dialogue is not the same thing as a council of reunion, nor is it an attempt at conversion. It means for both sides testifying to one's own beliefs in a clear, objective, understandable and psychologically suitable way.

It is Pope John's wish that this new method be applied in this council of ours. Our conciliary declarations can be called ecumenical and can be of great value for ecumenica dialogue if they use really adequate means to give better insight to non-Catholics into the manner and way in which the Catholic Church sees and lives the mystery of Christ.

Ecumenical presentation by no means easy

How? All manner of indifferentism must be excluded. An ecumenical presentation must faithfully render all Catholic teaching on a particular subject, without omission. For how could non-Catholics learn from us what Catholicism teaches, if we present our doctrine in a doctored, distorted, unclear fashion? It has been said in this aula that an ecumenical way of speaking is irreconcilable with complete presentation of doctrine. Whoever holds this view has not understood what ecumenical dialogue means. The purpose of such dialogue is not mutual deception.

If presentation is to be precisely understood by non-Catholics, these conditions have to be fulfilled:

1. We must be familiar with the present-day teachings of the Orthodox and the Protestants; in other words, we must have faithfully studied their faith, their liturgical life, their theology.
2. We must know what they think of our doctrine and on what points they interpret it correctly and on what points incorrectly.
3. We must be aware of what non-Catholics think is deficient in Catholic doctrine or what is insufficiently stressed. (For example, the teaching on the word of God, on the priesthood of the faithful, on religious liberty.)
4. We must examine whether there are, in our manner of presentation, forms or formulations which non-Catholics find hard to understand. Our customary scholastic manner of speaking presents great difficulties to non-Catholics and frequently results in errors and preconceptions. The same thing applies to such abstract and purely conceptual ways of speaking as are unintelligible to Eastern Christians. For them a biblical and patristic manner of speaking would prevent many difficulties, misunderstandings and mistaken preconceptions.
5. The terminology employed (words, images, qualifications) must be well chosen; consideration must be given to the reaction likely to follow in the minds and feelings of non-Catholics.
6. Judgments must be balanced and seen in the context in which non-Catholics will see them.
7. We must so formulate our proofs (quotations, statements of principle), thought-structure and textual arrangements that these are clear to non-Catholics.
8. All sterile polemic must be avoided.
9. Error should be clearly refuted, but in such a way that those who hold erroneous opinions do not feel personally offended.

The theological commission's refusal to cooperate

All this, venerable Fathers, goes to show that a text, by the mere fact that it presents truth is by no means as yet an ecumenical text. The preparation of a genuinely ecumenical text is an extremely difficult and delicate enterprise. The Pope has appointed experts, bishops and theologians with ecumenical experience, to the Secretariat for Christian Unity. The Pope has commissioned these experts to assist other preparatory commissions, and especially the theological commission, so that the preparation and editing of the schemata be really ecumenical. Our secretariat has offered its help to the theological commission, but, for reasons I should not pass judgment upon, the commission refused this help. We suggested the establishment of a mixed subcommission, but the theological commission replied, 'No, we do not want that.'
This is how it came about that the theological commission took it upon itself to cope with the difficult task of giving our schemata an ecumenical character. And the result? We have heard the judgment of many fathers on the ecumenical spirit of the present schema. They denied that it was ecumenical. These were fathers who live among Protestants or in the East. Other fathers who live in predominantly Catholic countries thought differently. For them the schema did not lack in ecumenical spirit. Forgive me, but I would in all humility like to ask these fathers to ask themselves whether they have sufficiently considered the real nature and consequences of the new method called 'ecumenical dialogue'.

Be this as it may, we who are commissioned by the Pope to see to it that the dialogue with our non-Catholic brethren proceeds successfully at this council beg all of you venerable Fathers to listen to what the Secretariat for Christian Unity has to say about the present schema. The schema suffers greatly from lack of ecumenicity. There is in it nothing for the dialogue with non-Catholics; rather it represents a step backward. It is no help; it is a hindrance; yes, it is injurious. Venerable Fathers, consider this: a new method has been found, with the help of which a fruitful dialogue is possible. The fruits of this method are already seen in this aula, in the presence of the observers. The hour is providential. But the hour is also serious. If the schemas done by the theological commission are not rewritten, then we will be answerable for the fact that Vatican Council II brought to naught a great, an immeasurable hope. A hope, I say, of all those who—under the leadership of Pope John XXIII—have waited with prayers and fasting in the hope that now at last serious and noteworthy steps may be taken toward a unity and brotherhood of all those for whom Christ our Lord has prayed 'that they all may be one'.

Note: Three days later the Pope established the mixed commission which Bishop De Smedt had suggested and which the theological commission had previously refused to accept. This commission was to revise the schema on divine revelation. This work did not make suitable progress until, through additional elections to the commission ordered by Paul VI at the end of the second session, the theological commission was given a different composition.

Ecumenism and Salvation History

ANDREA PANGRAZIO, archbishop of Gorizia (Italy),
on November 25, 1963

In order to improve on the schema, which seems to me on the whole satisfactory, I would like to make three remarks in connection with (1) the description of the Catholic Church in the schema; (2) its description of non-Catholic communities, and (3) the description of the Catholic Church in comparison with other ecclesiastical communities.

The mystery of the Church's history

1. The description of the Catholic Church is too static and abstract, and the dynamic and concretely historical aspects of the Church are neglected; yet these seem to be extremely important for the ecumenical dialogue. In my opinion, the mystery of the Church's history does not get enough attention. In the history of the People of God in the Old Testament the Church can and should contemplate the mystery of her own history mirrored in a type, as Paul says to the Corinthians: 'All these things that happened to them were symbolic, and were recorded for our benefit as a warning. For upon us the fulfillment of the ages has come' (1 Cor. 10:11). Just as God in his unsearchable justice punished his people of the Old Covenant in their history for their infidelity, and raised them up again in his almighty power, as he saved them and exalted them when they repented and begged for divine mercy, so he does the same thing now for his people gathered together in the Church of the New Covenant. In the history of the Church, through the work of the Holy Spirit and the cooperation or resistance of men, events often follow one another in a completely unsuspected and unexpected way, so that no theological system can foresee or understand them. For example, which of the great thirteenth-century theologians would have conceived the possibility of that great Western schism which tore the Church into shreds in the sixteenth century, or of the distortions and abuses which defaced the Church in the period before the Reformation? On the other hand, who at the time of the Reformation could have foretold that remarkable strengthening of the Church which God through his grace brought about after the Council of Trent? It seems to me that such reflections on the mysterious character of the Church's history are of supreme importance for Catholic ecumenism. For just as the people of God in the Old Covenant, knowing by revelation the merciful purpose of God, always could and should have hoped that God, even by unsuspected deeds, would bring good out of the history of this people weighted down with calamity, so in similar fashion the people of the New Covenant can and should nourish the hope that in his gracious mercy and in a way as yet unknown to us, God will lead his Church along paths which none of us can foresee or predict.

In my humble opinion, this aspect of the divine dynamism which pulses in the history of the Church should be more clearly emphasized. Through this dynamic force God can produce events, developments and changes, not only in separated communities but also in the Catholic Church, which our generation and our Council as well simply cannot foresee. By such deeds God can make possible that desired union of separate Christianities which today still seems impossible. This will be possible, however, only if all Christians will be obedient to the inspirations of divine grace.

Christ as 'center' of ecumenism

2. My second remark touches on the description of non-Catholic communities. It is a good thing to list all those elements of the Church which by God's grace have been preserved in these communities and continue to produce saving effects. But to express my honest opinion, it seems to me that this catalogue is too 'quantitative', if I may use the expression. It seems that these elements have simply been piled together. I believe that a bond is needed to unite these separate elements. We should point to the center, to which all these elements are related, and without which they cannot be explained. This bond and center is Christ himself, whom all Christians acknowledge as Lord of the Church, whom the Christians of all communities unquestionably want to serve faithfully, and who graciously accomplishes wonderful things even in separated communities by his active presence through the Holy Spirit, not by any merit of men but by his gracious mercy alone. I believe that our schema would be more useful for ecumenical dialogue if the text would express this explicitly.

A hierarchy within revelation

3. To arrive at a fair estimate of both the unity which now exists among Christians and the diversity which still remains, it seems very important to me to pay close attention to the hierarchical order of revealed truths which express the mystery of Christ and those elements which make up the Church. Although all the truths revealed by divine faith are to be believed with the same divine faith, and all those elements which make up the Church must be kept with equal fidelity, not all of them are of equal importance. Some truths are on the level of our final goal, such as the mystery of the Trinity, the Incarnation and Redemption, God's love and mercy toward sinful humanity, eternal life in the perfect kingdom of God, and others.

Other truths are on the level of means toward salvation, such as that there are seven sacraments, truths concerning the hierarchical structure of the Church, the apostolic succession, and others. These truths concern the means given by Christ to the Church for her pilgrim journey here on earth; when this journey comes to an end, so also will these means. Now doctrinal differences among Christians have less to do with these primary truths on the level of our final goal, and deal mostly with truths on the level of means, which are certainly subordinate to those other primary truths.

But we can say that the unity of Christians consists in a common faith and belief in those truths which concern our final goal. If we explicitly make these distinctions in conformity with the hierarchy of truths and elements, I think the existing unity among all Christians will be seen more clearly, and it will become evident that all Christians are already a family united in the primary truths of the Christian religion.

Note: This speech received great attention from the observers. Some thought it the most penetrating contribution on the ecumenical issue at the entire council. Accordingly, the third part was in substance incorporated into the decree on ecumenism.

Genuine Ecumenism Means no Oversimplification

PAUL GOUYON, coadjutor archbishop of Rennes (France), on November 27, 1963

... I would like to offer what I have to say as a sign of respect for those beloved observers who attend our discussions every day in such a friendly and discreet way. To give to our work all the ecumenical value which men expect from it, I ask that as far as possible, nothing be left out, nothing be confused, nothing be oversimplified, in our schema.

Nothing should be forgotten

1. We should not forget anything which deserves to be remembered. The schema is obviously directed to all those large communities in which men today gather together, which acknowledge Christ as Lord and Savior. But we look in vain for any clear allusion to the great Anglican community, which in its origins is certainly quite distinct and different from the communities of the Reformation. I would very much like to see explicit mention of this community.

Besides, the word 'community' suggests a meaning which belongs almost exclusively to sociology or the non-religious world. Would it not be possible for us to find another term in sacred scripture or in tradition which would be more in conformity with the religious character of these communities? I would suggest the word 'communion' *(koinonia)* which, furthermore, is fully in accord with Church tradition.

Nothing should be confused

2. Nothing should be confused, but instead those things which are different should be clearly distinguished from one another. It is rather unusual that the Orthodox Churches should be dealt with along with the communities of which we have just spoken. It would satisfy me better if there were different and separate chapters for the Orthodox Churches, for the Anglican communion and for the communions which grew out of the Reformation. It would be good to take account of the distinct personality of each community.

Where the text approved at New Delhi by the World Council of Churches is cited, I would like to take this opportunity to show our respect for that extraordinary ecumenical organization and to express our joy at the remarkable work it is carrying on, unquestionably guided by the inspiration of the Holy Spirit. However, I should like to point out that such a text should not be presented as if it were a formal creed, since in the minds of its authors it is nothing more than a 'basis of union' for those Churches and communities which belong to the World Council of Churches. ...

No oversimplification

3. Nothing essential should be oversimplified. Our text says that the denominations which have grown out of the Reformation, in their desire to emphasize the transcendence of God, have come to deny the essential mediation of the Church. By saying that, we attribute to them an opinion which they do not hold. There are also other opinions attributed to them which they do not hold. Even the famous sayings 'SOLI DEO GLORIA, SOLA SCRIPTURA, SOLA FIDE' ('To God alone be glory, by scripture alone, by faith alone') do not exhaustively express what they think. The causes of the Reformation cannot be explained in terms of doctrine alone; there are other causes as well, which have nothing to do with theology.

It is very good to remember that the goal set up by the Secretariat for Unity excludes everything which would imply that a separation exists between us and other Christians on the deepest level. We should rejoice that the spirit of love is replacing attempts at apologetics which, while not altogether useless, were also the source of fruitless quarrels. Truth itself demands that we at least carefully mention what we do not have in common so that we may experience compunction for our division and may desire and seriously strive to fulfill the last prayer of Christ Our Lord 'That they may be one'. This could be the theme of the practical directory for ecumenism promised by the secretariat. ...

Note: The archbishop's desire that the Anglican community should be given special mention was fulfilled. Paragraph 13 of the decree says explicitly that the Anglicans have a 'special place'. The third chapter has two sections, of which the first deals with the problem of dialogue with Eastern churches and the second is titled 'The Separated Churches and Ecclesial Communities in the West'. Note that the term 'community' was retained, probably due to the difficulty of translating *communio* into modern languages. The third chapter expressly recognizes the legitimacy of the archbishop's concern for distinctly separate treatment of the different denominations. But this is not the intention of the chapter. It only aims to mention the topics which are important for dialogue. The quotation from New Delhi was omitted. The warning against oversimplification was heeded in the revised text.

Ecumenical Mission Projects

JEROME RAKOTOMALADA, archbishop of Tanarive (Madagascar), on November 7, 1964

I am speaking for all the bishops of Africa and Madagascar. Ecumenism is of great importance everywhere but especially in our mission territory. Historically speaking, we can say that this movement began, by the help of the Holy Spirit, in mission countries. The division among

Christians is a great scandal for pagans and non-Christians. In Western areas, memories of past events, such as seditions, religious wars and persecutions, still linger. These in some way explain the division, but they do not justify it.

Why, I ask, do some preachers of the gospel still nurture these memories today? The time has come for ecumenism to be a fraternal actuality. It should not be something merely proclaimed here at the Vatican Council or at the World Council of Churches; it should also be a fact of life in our own far-away mission countries. This demands the approval and cooperation of all heads of the various Christian churches. We were filled with joy when the Pope, on the day of the canonization of the martyrs of Uganda (October 18, 1964), commended heroic non-Catholic witnesses to Christ, who offered the highest sacrifice possible to man. We may add that during the last century, when the evangelization of our island Madagascar began, many Anglicans shed their blood for Christ. How many non-Catholics in Russia and China have through their martyrdom lived genuine ecumenism! This is the seed of unity. Blood, prayers, fasting, and lives of unshakable faith will all lead gradually not only to ecumenism, but to actual unity.

Practical suggestions

More must be said about ecumenism in our schema on the Church's missionary activity, and it should be said in the spirit of the decree on ecumenism so brilliantly worked out by the Secretariat for Christian Unity and now accepted almost unanimously by the Council.

Besides, a 'Unitas' center should be established within every bishops' conference for the promotion of ecumenical enterprises, both those under way and those yet to be undertaken.

Many and various attempts need to be made to foster cooperation with the separated brethren. And this not only in the interest of humaneness or politeness but of Christian witness. I am thinking of common collaboration in technological and cultural affairs, and also in spiritual matters whenever there is no danger of confusion, as for example in the publishing of sacred books, charitable and social undertakings, and in public actions for the sake of the common good. We must seize the initiative in a Christian spirit, which will always prove itself to be a spirit of genuine service.

Christians should strive for an increasingly effective and fraternal cooperation in the question of examining and adapting folk customs—for example, in the rites for the sacrament of marriage, in the abrogation of detrimental customs (such as tribal feuds, polygamy or that terrible evil, divorce). And why don't theologians and pastors confer more often on methods to combat that plague which might be summarized as the politicization of problems? Problems of family life would also provide a vast area for cooperation. After careful deliberation, a two-fold action should be initiated: one on the missions and one in a center attached to the Congregation for the Propagation of the Faith. An ecumenical ministry for the mission churches should be instituted in both centers; the one in Rome should be in permanent contact with the Secretariat for Christian Unity, and the other in the mission countries should be a center for information and action for ecumenical work.

The harvest is ripe; hope is increasing; I mean the theological hope given us by God, which sees with incontrovertible certainty that unity is coming, although numerous difficulties must still be overcome. May God grant us this, and soon!

Note: Some passages of this speech were incorporated almost verbatim into the schema on the Missions, especially the passage on the common Christian witness in technical and cultural questions, but also the recommendations made about common texts of the bible. The 'twofold action' suggested at the end has in the meantime been put into practice by the pan-African bishops' conference.

Painful Points in the Ecumenical Dialogue

JOSEPH CARDINAL FRINGS, archbishop of Cologne, on November 29, 1963

At the council we are going to school to the Holy Spirit. We all have to learn. After having heard so many things here, we must necessarily be convinced that the ecumenical movement is a work of the Holy Spirit. Certainly this movement also entails dangers. But where in the world and when in the history of the Church was there so great a movement without its attendant dangers? In Germany three neuralgic points play a part in this matter. I would like to deal with them here briefly:

1. It must be clearly said that we do not have to wait for the Church of Jesus Christ as something to come. His church, founded by the Lord, built upon Peter, is present in the Catholic Church. It is this Church that must constantly renew itself and which will be perfect only at the end of time.

2. What Pius XI and Pius XII said about the establishment and maintenance of denominational and parochial schools, must remain in force. We are not moved to this by desire for domination over children and young people, but by the good intention of offering a spiritual center of power and direction for all teaching and study—Christ and the Church. The same right should be accorded other churches and ecclesial communities. So it is not intolerance but the love of Christ which urges us.

3. Mixed marriages should be avoided. The Catholic partner in a mixed marriage remain seriously obliged to bring up all the children in the Catholic faith. If the non-Catholic Christian is prevented in conscience from consenting to this, no pressure should be brought to bear on him.

But the Church should in future declare valid also those mixed marriages not concluded in the juridical form approved by the Church. Moreover all canonical penalties heretofore incurred by the Catholic partner should be eliminated.

Note: The instruction issued by the Congregation for Faith did not incorporate the simple and clear suggestion on the form of marriage.

But the cardinal's second request has been partly fulfilled. (The text of Cardinal Frings' address was originally written down by a listener in the Council hall.)

Mixed Marriage and Catholic Education of Children

JOHN HEENAN, archbishop of Westminster, on November 20, 1964

I am speaking in the name of the entire hierarchy of England and Wales as well as numerous bishops from other countries.

This text on marriage deserves the same comment we recently heard in this aula in regard to other texts. It is good, even superior; but it is much too short. The subject deserves much more detailed treatment. Marriage is a sacrament; this gives it much dignity. In a certain sense, marriage is the center of all Christian social life. St. Paul said to the Ephesians, 'This is a great mystery—I mean with reference to Christ and the Church' (Eph. 5 : 32). By the beginning of the next session a truly dignified and beautiful schema could be worked out, which would present in detail the theological, biblical, and above all the pastoral aspects of marriage. Some of the points now made in Schema 13 [on the Church in the contemporary world] would much better fit in here. But I may have said enough on this in my talk on Schema 13.

Words which should be written in gold

I am very happy with the statements which speaks of a better prepara- tion for marriage and the more rapid handling of matrimonial litigation. There are words in this schema which I would like to see written in gold: 'Pastors should treat non-Catholics with love, when a couple appears who want to enter into a mixed marriage. The pastor should take time to point out the very real difficulties which result from a mixed marriage, not only for the couple but also for their children.' There are two reasons these words should be written in gold letters. First, because for a young couple who want to marry, this first encounter with a priest is of great importance. If the priest, as the schema demands, is obliging, understanding, and full of love, the couple will see that the Church really is a mother. The good will of the non-Catholic partner, who may here have his first encounter with a priest, can easily be strengthened or destroyed, depending on how the conversation is handled. My second reason for praise is that the schema says frankly that mixed marriages necessarily entail many serious problems. True, we do live in an ecumenical time, but these problems and difficulties are not less real for that. One could even say that they have become more numerous. From the way in which some ecumenists express themselves, ordinary people could even get the impression that basically there is no difference between Jews and Greeks, between Catholics and Protestants. After the wedding, however, it does not take the couple long to discover that there still remain many differences. The schema is well- advised in saying that young people must be reminded that they should not be guided by blind instinct when choosing their partners.

Mixed marriage ceremonies should not look like funerals

I wholeheartedly agree with the suggestions for mixed marriage ceremonies. Until now, mixed marriages were performed in many places with such lack of ceremonial solemnity and so joylessly that they looked much more like funerals than weddings. There was no blessing of the ring, no candles, no flowers, no organ music, and so on. It was not uncommon for the bride to break into tears. If the Church gives a dispensation, she should do so amicably and generously but not with coolness and reserve. A wedding must be beautiful and radiant, even in a mixed marriage. The Church should prove herself a true mother, not only for Catholics but for non-Catholics as well.

Religious upbringing of children

The crucial problem for mixed marriage is, as all know, the religious upbringing of children. It is not always the faith or pious zeal of one of the partners that causes the difficulty; all too often it is the family tradition or the prejudice of one or other party.

The non-practicing non-Catholic

Before examining the suggestions made by our schema, we must face the problems of mixed marriages with entire objectivity. The vast majority of mixed marriages, at least in England, are entered upon by Catholics and Protestants who are Catholic or Protestants only in name. In general, the non-Catholic party does not practice his religion at all. I worked for twenty years as a pastor in the parishes of London's East End, so I am speaking from experience. Very rarely did I encounter in mixed marriages a non-Catholic party who was an active member of a religious community. Therefore the promise to bring up the children in the Catholic religion only rarely caused difficulties. I am therefore of the opinion that it is better to retain the promise of Catholic upbringing of children as a general rule.

The practicing non-Catholic

But when a mixed marriage is entered into by a Catholic and a Protestant whom we will here call a 'practicing' Protestant, special regulations could be provided for in a new schema.

In this last case, the problem can become very real, but otherwise it is not difficult to gain the consent of the non-Catholic for the Catholic upbringing of children. The reason for this is probably the religious indifference which is very common in our part of the world. What I have said here of England is true, I imagine, of Australia, New Zealand, the United States and Canada, at least in its English-speaking part. Experience shows that even Protestants who go to Church are fre- quently—I do not say always—prepared to have their children brought

(Continued on page 255)

Emil De Smedt (57), bishop of Bruges, was the spokesman for the Secretariat for Christian Unity in the Council hall. In this capacity he proved himself an animated speaker, even in the first session when explaining the meaning of the word 'ecumenical'. Later, in the second, third and fourth sessions, he acted as the '*relator*' (reporter) of the text on religious liberty both before and after the debate. He did not hesitate to give the Council fathers a glimpse behind the scenes at the delaying maneuvers and other multiple machinations that threatened the declaration, overshadowed more than any other by all kinds of rumors. In this respect he was anything but gentle with the theological commission, the secretary of state and Cardinal Ottaviani.

Paul Gouyon (55), archbishop of Rennes. French bishops did not distinguish themselves by important speeches at this Council. There were a few exceptions, such as Cardinal Liénart (Lille), Emile Blanchet, rector of the Institut Catholique in Paris, Auxiliary Bishop Alfred Ancel (Lyon), Bishop Huyghe of Arras, and others, who had eager listeners each time they spoke. Most certainly Paul Gouyon should be counted among this number. He surprised the Council, as early as the second session, with his clear and well-argued proof that episcopal collegiality reached back to the first centuries. He thought the schema on the Church in the contemporary world weak in tone. He demanded a 'harsh and powerful language' because that was 'the language of the prophets and Christ', one that would 'get across' to men today. He himself had a rare gift for such language.

The Minority

Many things written and said about the minority are of no help in understanding the Council. The so-called minority was not a kind of parliamentary party to which its members owed allegiance. Therefore, there was no party line or party discipline. In the final analysis, every bishop was alone with his own conscience; only this could govern his decisions. Of course all the bishops shared a common Catholic faith, and none of them even thought of bringing things to the point of schism or a division within the Church. Nevertheless, there were commonly held opinions; consequently, more or less cohesive groups formed. We could, perhaps, speak of a small circle which always belonged to the 'minority'. It included: Cardinal Ruffini (78), archbishop of Palermo; Archbishop Dino Staffa (60) of the Roman Curia; the Irish Cardinal Browne (79), former general of the Dominicans and member of the Roman Curia; Marcel Lefebvre (61), of France, general of the Holy Ghost Fathers; Bishop Carli (52) of Segni; and de Proença Sigaud (57), archbishop of Damantina (Brazil).

The list itself shows that the minority was not based on membership in the Roman Curia, nor on nationality or age. It was a matter of a certain direction of thinking. Around this core which called itself 'Coetus Internationalis Patrum' (International Group of Fathers)—with its own press service (ROC), its own 'Roman Encounters' organized through lay people—rallied various Council fathers, depending upon what issue was up for debate. Sometimes there were many fathers, sometimes few; and sometimes almost half the bishops were included. But most of the time there were about 300. The direction of the Council seemed 'dangerous' to them. They zealously fought for tradition, and their unflagging efforts gave witness to the fact that something was really changing at the Council.

Left above: No Council father spoke as frequently as Cardinal Ernesto Ruffini. He proved himself to be a good exegete, always careful to make certain that no text was cited inaccurately. In this sense, he saw eye to eye with Cardinal Bea. Still, he showed little sympathy on many points for the concerns of the Secretariat for Christian Unity. Ecumenism meant one thing to him: conversion to the Catholic faith. Religious liberty meant nothing to him but 'tolerance of error'; and lay people were only the long arm of the hierarchy.

Left below: Paul Yu Pin, archbishop of Nanking, now lives in Taipei, Formosa, as rector of the university there. He was an energetic proponent of the restoration of the diaconate, and even of married deacons. He emphatically demanded a new and explicit condemnation of communism. He tirelessly reiterated his view that in a few generations the Chinese would be the leading nation in the world. He reproached the Council for its shortsightedness on this point.

Right: Bishop Luigi Carli of Segni, Italy, was considered by many Italians to be one of the great theologians of the Council. He fought passionately against episcopal collegiality; religious liberty, to him, seemed to promise only a spirit of revolution in the seminaries. His greatest notoriety, however, resulted from his war against the declaration on the Jews, which he carried forward with flags flying, not only in his Council speeches but also in pastoral letters and magazine articles.

The importance of the Archbishop of Vienna, Franz Cardinal König, increased from year to year. He stayed in the background during the first and second sessions but he distinguished himself during the third session with speeches on religious liberty, on the Jews and on non-Christian religions. During the same session, when the schema on Eastern Catholic Churches was being debated, he surprised even the Eastern bishops with his strong support of genuine independence for them. 'Even the Latin sector of the Church is made up of local churches,' he said in his demand for a genuinely ecumenical attitude toward non-Catholic Eastern Churches. On April 7, 1965, he was appointed president of the secretariat for non-believers, and in the debate on atheism he played a decisive role. Through his various speeches about the press outside the Council hall, he gave status and strong encouragement to the journalists at the Council.

up in the Catholic religion. Let us not forget that the upbringing of children in the Catholic religion in no way violates the conscience of a non-Catholic. None of the other Christian Churches claims to be the only true Church. But perhaps someone will say in this fourth session that such a claim constitutes a dangerous triumphalism which should be condemned.

If the non-Catholic party, for reasons of conscience, is unable to promise that the children should be brought up in the Catholic religion, no pressure must be brought to bear on him. It is sufficient that the non-Catholic does not raise any objections against the promise made by the Catholic party.

The schema is, however, not entirely clear on this point. It is my guess that it wants to say that the non-Catholic, without making a promise, should agree to respect the promise made by the Catholic partner to bring the children up in the Catholic religion. But the way the text reads, it could also mean that the non-Catholic, although agreeing to the promise, could lack the intention of permitting the promise to be kept. On this point the text needs more precision.

The expression 'to the best of my ability'

I also suggest that the expression, 'to the best of my ability', be stricken. According to the schema the Catholic is required to make an honest promise, binding in conscience, that all children will be baptized and brought up in the Catholic religion. This is what the text says. So I cannot see why the phrase 'to the best of my ability' is added. Certainly nobody is obliged to the impossible; but these words could also be interpreted in a different sense. They could mean that the Catholic partner is not bound by his or her promise whenever the promise becomes difficult to keep. Therefore these words should be stricken from the text. Because otherwise the Church would be saying, as it were: 'You don't have to fight for your children. If peace cannot be maintained another way, then let them leave their faith.' If the Church were to say that, she would be promulgating a rather strange doctrine. Venerable Fathers, the Vatican Council was convoked by the good Pope John to renew the Catholic Church, not to destroy her.

A blessing in the non-Catholic Church

Finally, I want to remark that if our text is really to be ecumenical, it should also say something about the way in which a mixed marriage ceremony is to be celebrated if the non-Catholic party is an active member of another religious community. I find—and I am speaking here only for myself—no objection to the couple, if they so desire, going together, after the wedding ceremony in the Catholic Church, to the Church of the non-Catholic party, to pray there and to receive a blessing.

Note: On his return from the Council, where he had been an observer, the Anglican bishop of Ripon, England, Dr. John R. H. Moorman, criticized a statement by Archbishop Heenan as offensive to Anglicans. Naturally, Moorman said, there are many indifferent people in all parts of the Christian Church. It is also true that the number of them in the Anglican Church is much greater than elsewhere, because those who have no confessional affiliation generally have their children baptized in the Anglican Church. It was contrary to the truth, however, to imply that the Anglican Church, not to mention the free Churches, was more or less sick unto death. Thus Moorman. Cardinal Spellman, in a statement made in the name of 100 bishops and read by Auxiliary Bishop John M. Fearns of New York, took even sharper issue with Heenan's speech. Cardinal Ritter, archbishop of St. Louis, took a very positive stand in favor of giving far-reaching powers to the bishops.

The instruction issued by the Congregation for the Faith in early 1966 took a position approximately half-way between the positions of Heenan and Spellman. It seems certain that this instruction would never have gained a majority vote at the Council; and for that reason it can only be considered a 'first step' on the way to achieving the wishes of the majority. (The translation of Cardinal Heenan's address was made from a German version.)

The Declaration on the Jews is the Result of the Church's Self-awareness

GIACOMO CARDINAL LERCARO, archbishop of Bologna (Italy), on September 28, 1964

Other speakers have explained, better than I can, the immediate reasons for the present declaration on the Jews. Why a declaration on the Jews precisely at this time?

I only want to discuss one point—the ultimate and most profound reason why our Council must inevitably make such a declaration at this specific time, in this historical hour of the Church of Christ. This most profound reason, as others have already emphasized, actually has nothing to do with politics in the immediate and concrete sense of the term. Moreover, this reason is extra-political in a broader sense: it has nothing to do with the historical events of the last war which have deeply moved every right-thinking man. Nor is it a consideration of morality and humanitarianism that leads the Catholic Church to issue this declaration precisely at this hour.

Rather, it is a series of essentially interior impulses which, without any outside influence, are coming to maturity in the innermost, supernatural heart of the life and awareness of the Church of Christ in this particular era of history.

It is today that the Church is making this declaration because the Church . . . in this Council is now becoming aware of some of the supernatural aspects of the Church's essential mystery and its own life. This is why the declaration on the Jews may be called a ripe fruit and a necessary complement to the Constitution on the Church and the Constitution on the Sacred Liturgy.

If anyone should find it strange that the Church is only now beginning to discuss the Jews in this manner, after so many centuries, he could be answered in many ways. We could point, for example, to the norms of both the old and newer canon law which protects the freedom of conscience of the sons of Israel. But the principal answer will have to be that the Church today must complement these norms, because now, for the first time, it has dedicated a special text (the Church constitution) to the religious mysteries which abound in the Church, and another text to the most precious values by which it lives its daily life—the word of God and the Eucharist (the liturgy constitution). The Church has not done this solely to defend its divine origin, its properties or its own powers.

The fact is, in my opinion, that there is a basic motive which justifies the declaration on the Jews and necessarily involves clear, concrete consequences of an objective kind. I am speaking especially in reference to two important characteristics needed in the declaration and which the present text should bring into clearer relief. I mean by this a more powerful dynamism similar to that found in the Dogmatic Constitution on the Church, where the Church speaks of its mystery. Secondly, I mean that a religious, not a merely human respect should be shown in view of the special vocation of the Covenant People, not only in the past, but in the present and the future.

Constitution on the Liturgy and the Jewish People

Since my time is limited, I would like to say something about the relationship between the present declaration and the Constitution on the Sacred Liturgy.

When the declaration speaks of the 'heritage common to Christians and Jews', it appears to refer primarily to the 'beginnings of faith and of election'—meaning the Church's past inheritance from the Jewish people, and ending with the Virgin Mary, Christ and the apostles. Certainly all these should be mentioned and perhaps even more specifically. For example, Rom. 9:4—5 should be cited in its entirety, not only in abridged form. But that is not enough. The people of the Covenant, in the eyes of the Catholic Church, do not possess dignity and supernatural value merely because of their past history or in light of the Church's beginnings. Their value is also in their present significance in what is the most essential, highest, most religious, most divine and most permanent in the daily life of the Christian Church—i. e., precisely what the Constitution on the Sacred Liturgy wants to make ever more real and effective in the Church of our time. We are involved here with the most important of all the activities of the Church and source of its power, that is, its daily life, nourished by the word of God in the liturgy of the word, and its life as lamb of God in the daily liturgy of sacrifice. But it is precisely these two supreme values, these two actions, which constitute the one and only, and really the most perfect, action of the Church on earth. Both come to the Church as a heritage from Israel. This heritage is evident not only in scripture, which is obvious, but also in a special sense, in the eucharist, whose antetype was the paschal lamb and the manna, and which Christ himself deliberately accomplished within the framework of the paschal Haggadah of the Jews. Still more: the Word of God in the eucharist—the lamb of God—mysteriously achieves, even in the present, an effective community between the liturgical community—in which we find the Church of Christ in its supreme moment—and the holy Kahal of the sons of Israel. Even in the present time the word and the blood feed a deeper interchange *(commercium)* of spirit and life in which every day, precisely at the climax of the mass, we justly speak of Abraham as 'our patriarch', as the father of *our* race: and of 'the sacrifice of our patriarch Abraham . . .'

Four practical consequences

1. If this 'interchange' is not yet fully revealed for the Jews, it is still true that today it already constitutes an objective bond of a special kind and intensity between us and them. The draft seems to be inadequate in what it says concerning our attitude and our dialogue with the Jews. I feel that this should be complemented by an explicitly stated desire for biblical dialogue with the Jews, and by grateful recognition of a function which the Jews, as the bearers of a certain biblical and paschal witness, could exercise even in the present order of salvation. This at least applies to those Jews who are faithful to the tradition of their fathers and zealously guard the religious meaning of scripture. This witness, even if still veiled *(sub velamine,* 2 Cor. 3:15), could also be very valuable for us Christians in deepening our spirituality, which must become increasingly more biblical and paschal.

2. It should also be added that the hatred and persecutions against the Jews (the term, *vexatio*, plague, is too weak in view of what the history of past centuries tells us on this point) must be repudiated and condemned not only 'as must any injustice inflicted on humanity', but 'far more because of the special fact of divine election'.

The reverence and respect which the Church of Christ must show to all men of all nations and all religions, would suffer no diminution if the Council were to express its special respect for the Jewish people specifically and solely as a religious community. This would in no way mean a depreciation of the Arabic peoples and the Islamic faith in which, even in a different fashion, the Catholic Church recognizes a descent from Abraham and a bond with biblical revelation. They are a brother people to the chosen people. Islam has a faith which, despite everything, remains a faith in the unique and living God. I have recently had living personal experience of this, when I was received with the greatest cordiality at Haram-El-Qalhil at the venerated tomb of the patriarch.

3. Furthermore, from the same motives so intimately connected with the renewed and deepened biblical and paschal awareness of the Church, the hope of the Church in regard to the future destiny of the Jewish people should be expressed much more considerately than it is in our text. The 'unification' *(adunatio)*, which the schema mentions, between the Jewish people and the Church, could be misinterpreted in a material and superficial way as if it implied a disrespectful proselytism which does not correspond to the intentions of the Church and is most certainly not in keeping with the direction of our Council. So it would be better if, instead of speaking of 'unification', we were to content ourselves with saying, as St. Paul did, that the sons of Israel will forever remain beloved and marked by the love of God (cf. Rom. 11:28). For 'God has

not rejected his people, whom he foreknew' (Rom. 11:2), and 'The gifts and the call of God are irrevocable' (Rom. 11:29), even if their fullness is not yet revealed (Rom. 11:12). This love of God's, which has no regrets, will manifest itself towards them [the Jews] in the future as in the past, and it will reveal itself in ways whose religious secrecy we must respect. For truly they are concealed in an abyss of the wisdom and knowledge of God, and therefore cannot be reached by methods of propaganda and persuasion or even of historical development such as apply to the rest of mankind.

4. One last concluding reflection. We must always speak with deepest reverence of the Jews, in view of the unfathomable designs of God and the fulfillment of the scriptures in Christ. So it seems inadequate to say, as the schema does, that the death of Jesus, which resulted from the agitation of the chief people of the Jews, must not be imputed to the Jews of today. Rather it should be said that one cannot and must not speak of an accursed and deicide people. Certainly those who rejected Jesus and crucified him committed a horrible sin. But fundamentally they were only the representatives of the entire twisted and sinful race of man. In truth, not only they but also 'all we like sheep have gone astray; we have turned everyone to his own way; and the Lord has laid on him the iniquity of us all' (Is. 53:6). It should finally be remembered that this truth is not one taught for the first time today; it has always been taught by the Catholic Church. If the Jews, who did not know what they were doing when they crucified the author of life (cf. Acts 3:15)—if they sinned, then the Christians sinned even more and crucified again the only begotten son of God, when, knowing what they were doing, they blasphemed his name and violated his law of holiness and love. This was the teaching of the catechism of the Council of Trent, a doctrine which our Council must also teach, not weakening it but strengthening it!

Note: These four conclusions are reflected in the Council text. But the ideas in the main section of the speech were apparently too unfamiliar to the members of the commission.

Responsibility of Christians for Atheists' View of God

FRANJO CARDINAL SEPER, archbishop of Zagreb (Yugoslavia), on September 24, 1965

We must certainly not be silent [in the Church and the contemporary world] on the issue of atheism. Not merely because atheism is one of the most difficult problems of the Church today but especially because in the contemporary world there are people and movements which consider atheism a prerequisite for a true humanism and a requirement for the progress of the world and society. We want to take a Christian position in our schema with regard to the problem of our world. The question about atheism, then, belongs to the very basis of our schema as the necessary justification of what we want to say.

We speak to all men of good will

It is necessary that we clarify the viewpoint and approach from which we want to proceed in speaking of atheism. The character and context of our schema call for a complete presentation of the problem of atheism. What the draft contains is insufficient and unsuitable.
We must ask ourselves to whom we are speaking, why we are speaking and what is our objective. We are speaking not only to Catholics but to all men of good will; not only to philosophers and influential leaders but to everybody in general. We must speak in such a way that not only faithful Christians but also atheists will pay attention to us.
Our approach to this problem must be positive. We must find the reasons why atheism has become such a widespread phenomenon today. Let us not forget that at present there are already many people who have, so to speak, inherited atheism without having made a personal decision in favor of it. Atheism today is frequently presented to people as the normal and natural consequence of greater progress in science and culture. This is important in judging the progress of atheism, especially since there are members of religious orders and preachers who enthusiastically, and without differentiation, denounce the modern world and sing hymns to 'what used to be'.
The purpose of this schema, in the context of all its statements, is not a simple condemnation of atheism; nor is it primarily a proof of the existence of God. To be more precise, we have no intention in this schema of converting atheists. We want to state the way in which Christians understand contemporary atheism and how they explain the existence of atheists. We want to explain clearly why belief in God does not obstruct effort and self-involvement in human progress and the cause of better living conditions, nor hinder the dignity of the human person. Rather faith urgently requires all these things.

Christian responsibility

So we must much more openly and honorably admit that a share in the responsibility for modern atheism falls on those Christians who all too stubbornly defend and still go on defending an unchanging social structure while falsely invoking the name of God. Certainly this reproach cannot be visited upon the Church as such, in an unqualified and unrestricted way. But there is no denying that even among the People of God there can be found those who gave religion this one-sided kind of interpretation and thus—even when in good faith—abused it. Let us declare in unmistakable terms that stubborn conservatism and immobilism, which some still continue to attribute to the Catholic Church, is irreconcilable with the true spirit of the Gospel!

The false and true God

We must also explicitly state that the atheists' concept of God is insufficient and dehydrated and thus out of harmony with the truth. The true God is not a God who wants to distract men from the struggle for justice and from active love toward all men, promising nothing but eternal justice and bliss. Instead the true God is the God who orders and demands that we make every possible effort to make justice and love real in this world, and in this world first of all! Heavenly justice must be seen as a kind of an analogy to the justice which man seeks to achieve on this earth.

The true God whom Jesus taught and proclaimed reveals himself to men not only through the order of nature but also through his people and individual members of his people, who give witness to him through life and action on behalf of their brothers in this world. The true God calls all men; and he helps them to give testimony to the truth, to live the truth, to love and to make the entire world, through their spirit of cooperation, an even greater witness to the revelation of God.

Anonymous Christian values

So a genuine and honest faith can be no obstacle to progress. It is rather a stimulus and a help. Moreover, we Christians must believe that it is God who is the unique and real foundation for man's upward growth in dignity, and for true humanism. There can be true values whose divine origin is not always immediately recognizable but which, nevertheless, constitute anonymous affirmation of God's will and of eternal law. These remarks on atheism belong within the context of the schema.

Note: The Cardinal later became a member of the commission whose task was to revise the text on atheism. The revision in general corresponds to the considerations presented here, but without achieving the same sweep of expression and depth of thought.

The Roots of Atheism and Ways of Overcoming It

FRANZISKUS CARDINAL KÖNIG, archbishop of Vienna, on September 27, 1965

I am speaking on atheism. I agree with the criticism of Cardinal Seper presented during the last general congregation. The schema's presentation of this problem is inadequate and the reason is that various kinds of atheism are not differentiated. Militant atheism, which is the only form treated in paragraph 19, represents only one aspect of the question. The next is also unsatisfactory because it says nothing about the means of overcoming atheism; it also says nothing of the attitude to be taken by the Church in the face of these facts which, as the schema very correctly says, are among the 'most difficult of the contemporary era'. Mere 'bemoaning' of atheism is not enough.

I therefore suggest expansion of the text to include the following four points: (1) the various forms of atheism and its inner nature; (2) the roots of this phenomenon; (3) the methods of overcoming atheism; (4) the Church's attitude.

On point 1 : Theological exploration must first take into consideration the fact that atheism is a worldwide phenomenon; and second, the axiom about the '*anima naturaliter christiana*' (the soul's natural Christianity). How can these two things be mutually reconciled?

On point 2 : The roots of atheism appear to lie exclusively in the Western world. We do not find it in India or elsewhere in Asia, nor in Africa.

Catholic and non-Catholic Christian experts describe the fundamental development of atheism in approximately the following terms: Christian unity broke down in the sixteenth century. In the seventeeth and eighteenth centuries illuminism and deism destroyed the supernatural and divine-human order, meaning the incarnation. In the nineteenth century people tried to ban God himself from the world. Perhaps this development might be said to have started earlier with the division between Eastern and Western Christianity. All this shows the culpability of Christians.

The roots of atheism can be found in the false idea of God possessed by many Christians. God and the world are either seen to be so much in confrontation that, according to Hegel's idea, human liberty and full humanity are completely restricted and suffocated; or God is conceived of as an intermediate principle, in other words, merely as the primary cause, called upon for help only if the evolutionary process requires such a primary cause as an explanation of progress. God is seen merely as a consolation for human beings; and the next step from this position is the so-called 'opiate of the people'. The roots of atheism also come from a false concept of man with all the consequences of such a concept.

On point 3 : What is needed is unceasing cooperation in the interests of Christian unity. Inasmuch as this unity is still lacking, efforts must be in those areas where differences of doctrine are not touched upon. The

Church must fearlessly and vigorously, without respect of persons, defend social justice and initiate necessary changes to this end. The arguments of atheism and our answers must be presented in detail and communicated at all levels of Catholic education and in the formation of lay people.

Since ignorance constitutes such a great danger, ecclesiastical superiors, priests and missionaries should have a comprehensive knowledge of atheism. Its origin, its arguments, its methods must be familiar to them. For this purpose, analyses and books should be prepared by experts.

On point 4: We want to condemn no one. We must pass just judgment without passion or prejudice when our office so requires, but we seek a certain community and a peaceful coexistence with all men of good will. On the other hand, the Council should not neglect to say—on the contrary it should distinctly emphasize—that it is not permissible to coerce the faithful of any Christian denomination or of any religion into atheism; freedom of conscience is given to every man as an inalienable right. We should demand that atheistic governments publish documents, now in preparation at the Council, on true freedom as grounded in natural law.

In areas under Communist domination, the following procedure seems advisable: Christians should give testimony to the living God and honest cooperation with the economic progress of the homeland. They should give proof, not only in words but also in deeds, that religious life does not paralyze but instead is capable of inspiring greater energies than atheism does. But above all, the brotherly love of Christians should excel that of all others.

Because the historical development of atheism began, so to speak, with the denial of the incarnate God whose work of incarnation continues in the Church, and since the Mother of God was chosen to be the instrument of incarnation, she will come to our help in overcoming atheism. These are the reasons why the schema fails to deal with the question of atheism. If it is agreeable to the fathers of the Council and the standing mixed commission, it would be my pleasure to prepare a suitable text together with experts.

Note: The Council approved the suggestion, and a commission from the secretariat for dialogue with unbelievers under Cardinal König was directed to prepare the text which is now part of the Pastoral Constitution on the Church in the Contemporary World.

III. Signs of the Times

The Church's Debt to the Modern World

PAUL SCHMITT, bishop of Metz (Germany), on October 1, 1965

I should like to make a few remarks concerning the preface of the second part of the schema on the Church in the contemporary world.

The schema points up the need for the Church to see the contemporary world as it really is. The schema is also very fine in showing how the Church could help this world by aiding man in his vocation and in calling him to Christian grace.

We would like, however, to hear a little bit more in regard to another aspect of the dialogue between the Church and the world. How does the Church in the present world find various positive opportunities for greater self-knowledge, for better expression of its message, and for fulfillment of its mission? Any contribution to the improvement of the human condition in this world also serves in its way in the plan of God for the improvement of the Church, and challenges the Church to self-renewal. This holds true for family life, culture, economic and social life, and even for national as well as international politics.

I would like first to give a few examples. Then I would like to propose some theological reflections on what the Church receives from the contemporary world.

Factual examples

The contemporary world wholeheartedly fosters man's dignity as a responsible person, which is what he is and should be. Doesn't this make the Church, on its part, indebted to the world—so that the Church in turn ought to give greater attention to human liberty and show due moral respect even in religious matters?

The contemporary world emphasizes the reality of socialization very clearly. Doesn't the Church in turn owe the world a greater appreciation of community and collegiality in its own life?

In the social area the contemporary world strives for an intensification of social justice and an extension of human leisure. Doesn't the Church in turn owe the world a more adequate sense of justice and also love?

The contemporary world is becoming increasingly aware of the mutual dependence and the necessity of dialogue between peoples and civilizations. Doesn't the Church in turn owe the world a deeper and better understanding of its own catholicity?

The contemporary world sees more and more clearly the horror of war. Doesn't the Church in turn owe the world today a development of doctrine that goes beyond traditional statements, as the encyclical PACEM IN TERRIS illustrated so vividly?

The contemporary world struggles for a clear distinction between the political and religious orders. Doesn't the Church in turn owe the world today a clearer manifestation and a purer proclamation of its evangelical transcendence?

The contemporary world is filled with a spirit of scientific research and discovery. Doesn't the Church in turn most urgently owe the world today an exploration of its own revealed doctrine?

Drawing: Coliseum

261

The contemporary world searches for the ultimate meaning of human existence. Doesn't the Church in turn owe the world today a certain effort to make a pure proclamation of man's divine calling to the Father, through Jesus Christ and in the Holy Spirit?

Theological reflections

These facts among many others make the Council responsible for acknowledging its debt to the modern world honestly, modestly and gratefully. Perhaps the following guidelines will help to clarify this aspect of the Church's dialogue with the world.

The Church should not present divine salvation to modern man merely as a doctor who wants to cure a patient. The Church should gratefully acknowledge that the world cooperates in the mystery of salvation in the ways already mentioned.

The Church should be grateful for everything achieved by the world in the struggle to improve the human condition. Nothing in this struggle is alien to the aims of Christian grace.

The Church should accept all the prompting of the contemporary world on behalf of freedom, the dignity of man, scientific and historical truth; the Church should accept these for the sake of its own life and definite mission even if such promptings force us to moral self-examination.

The Church should realize that its own future is already involved in the progress of the modern world and in the rightful demands of these times.

The Church should firmly and actively respond to what has been said in the Constitution on the Church—that the grace of God is active in the plans of men, tending to the realization of the ultimate intentions of the creator, even if such plans operate outside the visible kingdom of the Church.

It would not be enough for the Church to consider the contemporary world as a purely peripheral region or as merely an advantageous field for its activities. The Church must learn to understand that the plans of men are part of the active vocation to the kingdom of God and are integrated with Christ's work of salvation.

In conclusion, it is very desirable that this aspect of the dialogue between Church and world be more clearly worked out in the preface to the second part of the schema. The God of Christian salvation is the selfsame God as the God of creation and the Lord of human history.

Note: The pastoral constitution tried to comply with the bishop's request, not so much in the recommended preface as in the fourth chapter of the first part; but the theological underpinning is still meager.

On Evangelical and Subhuman Poverty

RAUL CARDINAL SILVA HENRIQUEZ, archbishop of Santiago (Chile), on October 27, 1964

The draft on the Church in the contemporary world speaks in chapter 3 of fraternal community in the spirit of poverty. On behalf of Caritas International, I would like to propose a practical suggestion in regard to this statement. What is at issue here is the exercise of Christian poverty common to all brethren of every denomination, which would bring us solidarity on the issue of wealth, in order that we might in some sense share in the poverty of Christ and alleviate the poverty of man by giving from our abundance to the poor.

Two kinds of poverty

For a correct understanding of this we must distinguish between two kinds of poverty familiar to us from history—poverty resultant from grace, or evangelical poverty, and poverty consequent upon sin, or subhuman poverty. Both mean lack of wealth, but both strive for possessions. Possessions mean human fulfillment. The perfection of God consists in being, that of man in having. God is, man has.

The two kinds of poverty are entirely different even if one is mistaken for the other. Evangelical poverty springs from free choice; it is the sign of human perfection precisely because here man strives for the possession of eschatological values, while avoiding the danger of remaining tied to earthly wealth. Evangelical poverty is not simply a virtue; it is rather a Christian way of life in which all virtues, illuminated by Christian hope, find application. It is a dynamic movement which pervades history, using all things while actually possessing nothing earthly. It is a sign of freedom, a sign of dominion. It comes from the kingdom of the spirit, and spiritualizes man.

Subhuman poverty, on the other hand, is a consequence of a condition of servitude and of human imperfection. It is a sign of the failure in brotherhood and of shortsightedness. It suppresses the full freedom of the person and impoverishes the human heart. Such poverty can never be a thing of virtue. It is a social evil which must be torn up by the roots because it 'materializes' man.

It was said of evangelical poverty, 'Blessed are the poor, for theirs is the kingdom of heaven.' But under the spell of subhuman poverty virtue becomes impossible. Evangelical poverty should flourish upon the earth; subhuman poverty should be destroyed.

A practical and ecumenical suggestion

Now it seems to me that all those who profess to live evangelical poverty should do something practical, communal, organized, something very concrete, to diminish subhuman poverty. The earth has riches enough for everyone, but only the poor in spirit can know how a community of spirit and of love can make these riches serve the welfare of man.

The exercise of evangelical poverty today requires that man not only separate himself from riches but also that he use these riches for the good of the poor. This means that all Christians are together called to work in solidarity to make their evangelical poverty effective for the service of their needy brethren. They should always keep in mind:

(a) The enormous amount of subhuman poverty which still actually exists in our century (this was already mentioned in this hall by Cardinal Landàzuri Ricketts, for example).

(b) The special opportunities of Christians who, in large part, belong to the wealthy nations.

(c) The positive value of organized effort which has immensely increased in our time.

(d) The ecumenical movement which joins Christians together in ever-closer relationships.

I therefore venture to suggest that the Council consider organizing an international union to study the opportunities all have for testifying to their solidarity with needy peoples, and to coordinate and further such opportunities. There are three aspects to this suggestion:

(1) The help given should not be a temporary and extraordinary effort, but rather a permanent assistance to the needy classes and nations. It should be clearly said that the help in this regard must aim as far as possible to eliminate the causes of social evils in order to free the poor from their misery.

(2) Even if this organization is at first Catholic, it must become truly interconfessional; all Christians who strive to follow Christ in his poverty should be represented in it.

(3) In order to better achieve this purpose an annual general collection should be made, as Professor Oscar Cullmann, here as an observer, has often suggested. Such a general collection could constitute a genuine 'sacramental', a holy and sanctifying sign, a witness to international unity, to evangelical poverty, and to the desire for true unity in Christ.

Note: The proposed secretariat was established.

Marriage as Community of Life and Love

PAUL CARDINAL LÉGER, archbishop of Montreal, on September 29, 1965

I would like to make two points on the first chapter, where the problem of marriage is treated. I would first like to present my views on the teaching of the schema; then I would like to say something about the arrangement and presentation of the material.

On the teaching of the schema

The revised text improves upon the previous version in affirming the significance and legitimacy of conjugal love. Yet I feel that even the revised text will be of little help to the faithful of our time, and I fear that it will disappoint their just expectations. Since a correct explanation of the nature of marriage is of very great importance to the daily life of the faithful, I may be permitted to show in a little more detail why the text is still unsatisfactory.

I am sure that the faithful will be happy that the schema in several places commends and praises conjugal love. They will feel, however, that the most important formulations in which the schema describes the nature of marriage seem to be somewhat out of harmony with those passages which praise and commend it. They might even have the impression that these statements deface the true countenance and beauty of marriage. Take, for example, the definition of marriage as 'an institution ordered to the procreation and education of offspring'. In my opinion this statement is incomplete and ambiguous, and the schema itself admits this when it corrects itself a little later on and says that marriage is 'not merely an institution for procreation'.

Certainly these formulations could be considered correct in the way they define marriage from the point of view of the human 'species' (as the philosophers call it).

For from the viewpoint of the human species, marriage has no other meaning; marriage is the way in which the human race is maintained and propagated. But since marriage binds persons to one another, its meaning must be described primarily from the viewpoint of the *person*, without ignoring thereby the meaning marriage has for the species.

The formulations mentioned do not correctly define marriage from the viewpoint of the human person. Therefore they must be changed. In the first place, these formulations are incomplete. For the human person, marriage is not primarily an institution for the procreation of children, but also—and this is primary—a community of life and of love. In the second place the formulations are ambiguous. It might seem as though conjugal community and conjugal love were mere means for procreation, or as though they had no meaning at all except as means for procreation. This would certainly be false and would have devastating effects on the dignity of the human personality.

I therefore suggest that in defining the nature of marriage, the relationship of conjugal love and conjugal community to offspring be described as follows:

(1) It should be said clearly and openly that marriage is an intimate community of life and of love.

(2) The profound significance which the procreation of offspring has for conjugal community and conjugal life should be presented in an illuminating manner. Thus the married couple should understand the child is the crown of love with which they love one another. Finally it should be said that it is the will of God that the couple beget children and thus become his collaborators. This comes from the words of scripture and the whole structure of married love and conjugal community. Thus the married couple should understand that their love is not simply for themselves but rather is a part of God's plan and his creative providence.

On the division and style of the schema

There are still other reasons why the text of the schema will disappoint the faithful. These refer more to the form than the content of the schema. But this does not make them less important.

(1) The doctrine of the schema is presented in such an unorganic way that it is very difficult to discover its real intention. In its vital statements the same thoughts are reiterated two or three times, without ever coming to a conclusion. Often there is no logic in the way the thought develops. Too often ideas are merely juxtaposed or are linked together rather artificially. If we want to avoid the impression that the text is really a kind of diplomatic compromise between divergent theological schools, and if we really want to enlighten the faithful, then the presentation must be better and more clearly structured.

(2) The schema is too preachy and therefore often becomes moralizing in its tone. And it seems to me that the frequent switching from pure description or simple statement to passages of admonition represents a stylistic fault.

In conclusion: the Council should speak clearly to the world and to the Christian people about marriage. Despite the very great and very special difficulties the Council has met with in this topic, it cannot publish a text the intentions of which are not understood even by the bishops. I may therefore be permitted to file with the appropriate commission concrete written suggestions which could be of assistance in improving this text.

Note: The commission revised the passages most objected to, in line with the cardinal's suggestion. His criticisms of structure and style were, however, not heeded, since the editors lacked the intellectual capacity necessary for such a task.

Cultural Reform in the Spirit of Evangelical Poverty

GIACOMO CARDINAL LERCARO, archbishop of Bologna, on November 4, 1964

Paragraph 22 of the draft is in many ways a model for the entire schema. It touches on a very important issue in which a synthesis becomes clearer and, in a sense, more evident: it shows how the Church and world are distinct from one another and yet closely linked together.

The problem

In the draft a very deep and difficult problem is continually clarified: Why and in what sense is divine revelation needed for the progress of human knowledge so that human knowledge (in all its depth and compass) may become ever more human? Then, too, why and in what sense is human progress (even in secular knowledge) a contribution to the integral presentation and development of revealed truth?

The commission should be praised for its efforts in presenting the schema and its additions. Yet the text is not entirely satisfactory because it stops short precisely where it should begin. We read in the schema that culture has the highest importance for the Church of today; the Church derives the greatest benefits from culture. Therefore it takes an open and trustful attitude toward scientific, technological and artistic progress, and so forth. This seems insufficient! And it is not enough to add that the Church is vitally interested in the proper progress of culture—in maintaining a harmonious balance between different orders without conflict with what is called 'spiritualistic humanism' or with a legitimate cultural pluralism. These are all platitudes which mean very little and do nothing to advance a genuine meeting of Church and culture. When I say culture, I mean not the culture of a bygone age, but of the present and the future. For this to be a real encounter that will endure and grow, certain crucial changes in the entire educational system, which is an innermost concern of the Church, must be sought and evaluated. Such changes are obviously needed in the special circumstances of culture today.

The Church in poverty

(1) First and foremost, the Church must recognize its cultural poverty, and realizing this, must strive for even greater poverty. I am not speaking here of material poverty, but of a specific consequence of evangelical poverty in regard to the Church's education. As with the yielding of customs and inherited values, here too in the field of education the Church guards certain treasures of a bygone era, which although glorious are not entirely in keeping with the spirit of our time. There are, for example, scholastic, philosophical and theological systems, academic and educational principles, curricula which are still in use at our universities, methods of research. The Church must have the courage when necessary to renounce these inherited treasures or place little trust in them; it should not boast of them; and it should rely

on them only sparingly. For these treasures do not always place the light of the evangelical message on the candlestick, but tend to hide it under a bushel. They often set up obstacles to the enlargement of the Church by way of new cultural achievements, and through the treasures of old cultures which come to flourish outside the borders of Christendom.

These treasures could limit the universality of the Church's dialogue, could separate more than unite, could exclude people rather than convince and attract them.

I certainly do not wish only a theological and merely negative poverty. The distinction between evangelical and subhuman poverty holds even in reference to education. I do not look for subhuman but rather evangelical poverty; not narrow-mindedness and ignorance, but rather sobriety and purposefulness, flexibility and chastity of mind and humility, as well as generosity and initiative. I mean initiative to try out new methods which cannot be done without risk. This is the true and richest supernatural wisdom. It also makes for a very sensitive grasp of actuality and genuine historical realism.

Finally we do not want to renounce our cultural heritage simply for the sake of renunciation. We want a renunciation through which new treasures are won and greater sharpness of intellect and firmer diligence achieved, at least as far as purely human judgment can determine.

The Church has always maintained that it does not identify itself or its doctrine with any system, with a specific philosophy or theology. Up to the present, however, this distinction has been recognized formally rather than in fact.

The time has now come for the Church to separate itself and its essential message increasingly more *in fact* from a certain cultural instrumentality whose eternity and omnicompetency all too many men of the Church still seriously maintain out of a spirit of possession and self-sufficiency. In order to open to a genuine dialogue with present-day culture, the Church must in a spirit of evangelical poverty make its education increasingly more flexible; it must turn increasingly to the super-essential treasures of sacred scripture and of biblical thought and speech. The Church must not fear that this will make it less understood by men or will disappoint them. The people, when we really see them close up, expect nothing less from the Church. Thus the culture of the Church will in the final analysis cease to seem to be a rationalism or a scientism of secular origin; instead it will seem to be a highly effective religious force able to leaven any culture, today or tomorrow.

The schema really demands reforms

(2) From what has been said hitherto, it follows immediately that a new course must be chosen for the Church's education and that the Church must introduce a new pedagogy in the training of its own seminarians and its scientific research.

This touches on the innermost core of our schema. How can we hope for a continuing dialogue directed toward the future if the spokesmen of the Church, priests and lay people continue to be educated according to a completely obsolete curriculum? If today the scientific language in which they are required to think is, for all its past glory, simply dead; if it is no longer a universal language, no longer suited to express modern ideas which predominate today throughout the world?

And so it follows from the innermost core of the schema, from the issues it sets out to treat, that reforms are necessary (I will return to these later), reforms which no one will ever believe that we are taking seriously, or that we really welcome the need and true achievements of the culture of our era.

Bishops as theologians

(3) The issues of this age demand the restoration of an old tradition of bishops as teachers. This should again gradually become the custom. For Christian culture was in large part the work and the product of great bishops who excelled in the fact that they were simultaneously pastors and teachers. Even after the glorious institutions of the middle ages or modern times, it was and is true that ecclesiastical formation did not receive its truest and proper form from institutions above; it received at least as much from the teaching of the bishops, bishops who could be called theologians. I understand the term theologian in its original and truest meaning as one who has more than a mere school-book knowledge of God. We must restore the episcopate to its full meaning (as far at least as this depends on us and not directly on God, especially where the choosing of bishop is concerned). We must return to the idea of the perfect bishop, who should be a man of the spirit, or better a man who speaks with God, and who derives from this the essential direction of his government and his teaching office, a man truly capable of interpreting the circumstances and the significance of an age.

Lay people as theologians

(4) Finally we must explain a requirement which is really a presupposition for the entire schema. This of course goes beyond the limits of this paragraph 22. It is a requirement to return to old customs in regard to another central issue: we must encourage lay people to tackle scientific work on theological problems in a really adequate way.

Among the most important prerequisites for a fruitful exchange between Church and culture, this one is listed by our schema—that many lay scholars should wholeheartedly dedicate themselves to scientific research. But the schema only speaks of secular learning, thinks only of secular learning, and refers only to this. Why should this not apply also to dogmatic theology and theological sciences?

I have just spoken of the bishops as theologians. The lay person as theologian would complement the bishop as theologian. The Church needs plenty of lay theologians who are trained according to the rules of strict science in theology. This was the case before Christian education became a monopoly of the clergy, and this is still the case today in the Orthodox Church and in a few Reformation Churches.

Finally—and only in this aspect should we look for something entirely new in the Church's education—it is not enough for us to open up to lay people a road of lesser significance, admitting them to second-class theological schools. Nor is it enough if we permit only a few choice people to enroll at the theological schools for the clergy. We should rather open up the royal road of special institutes, where they would work more or less scientifically in theological disciplines; these should be staffed by lay people in the way that seems good to them, under the supervision of the hierarchy.

Then will theological schools and seminary education really find new ways. Then will the Church's institutes of education experience a thoroughgoing renewal; their pedagogy will gain a greater dynamic force; their cultural instrumentality will experience, so to speak, a new dawn. And all of them, priests and lay people, will be trained to such a way that they will understand the world. Even those sons of the Church—who, as the schema desires, are active on the frontiers of human scientific endeavor—they too will be helped to inspire the culture of this age in a Christian direction. Then all educated people—in a 'psychological' fashion and spontaneously—will find the way to theology which is the wisdom of God.

Note: Amazingly, the revision of the text shows no response to this speech.

The Church and Contemporary Culture: the Central Problem

LÉON ARTHUR ELCHINGER, coadjutor bishop of Strasbourg (France), on October 1, 1965

I would like to address a few considerations—first negative, then constructive—to the second chapter on the proper development of culture. I will submit concrete suggestions to the Council's secretariat. Here I only want to point to the deeper foundations.

The problem with which this chapter is concerned is the attitude which the Church should take toward the technological civilization of the modern world.

In the text presented to us all too many questions are broached. The result is an abundance of platitudes and pious admonitions. The presentation is not high-level. The very serious questions which press in today upon the conscience of the Church are flattened out. The concept of culture is here far too narrowly conceived. Culture comprises all that indicates how people in a particular locale and in a particular time express themselves. But this includes not only religious forms, intellectual and artistic life, but also works of technology, the attitude toward work, and the use of leisure time.

If the Council is to gain the world's attention, this chapter must be fully restructured.

The real pastoral problem which the hierarchy is faced with here seems to me this: The Church feels alarmed at the fact that opportunities for influencing men of today are diminishing, and that the readiness of man to accept its message is declining. Therefore the question concerns the Church's 'presence'. What is the Church to do to come in contact with the world, where people for the most part no longer seem to need the Church because they feel autonomous and independent of the Church and in some cases have even constructed in opposition to the Church a humanism of their own, an anthropology and even an ethic, and beyond this a secular messianism? How can the Church, despite this, maintain contact with world and fill it with the Christian spirit?

The Church should seek contact with the cultures of the whole world. It can attain this through dialogue and cooperation, provided this is done in the spirit of serving and not domination.

The Church should see to it that genuine Christians are enabled to take an active part in cooperating to shape the new visage of the world: where study programs are being worked out, where the problems of living accommodations, work, leisure are dealt with. These Christians must be well aware of the ambivalence of human progress, so that they are able to discern genuinely human values, and they must take a courageous stand for a genuine hierarchy of values. But this presupposes an open-minded and educated clergy, capable of advising lay people and giving support to their efforts.

Furthermore the Church should institute various forms of interchange and cooperation so as to enable scholars in various areas of specialization to compare their research with authentic Christian tradition. Only thus will the gap between knowledge and faith be bridged.

Finally, the Church must provide theologians who can discover and express whatever in the gospel and biblical culture appeals to contemporary man, and who are also able to include in their own work whatever is positive in modern philosophies, and in the problems resulting from the development of science. These theologians would have to be sensitive to the factors in the modern world that need and 'await' the gospel message. Such people are 'the stepping stones' to the kingdom of God, who in the world of today prepare the way in the spirit of the gospel and in eschatological hope.

What is new in the Church's situation is not that it is faced with new culture but that it is no longer capable of maintaining its claim to leadership.

The causes of this condition

Demographic causes: The population increase is greatest in countries and continents which have not accepted Christianity or where it constitutes only a tiny minority. So cultural strivings for the most part are not based on Christian values.

Historical causes: Even in countries whose traditions are Christian, there is in many people a certain distrust of the Church. The Church is reproached in cultural matters as narrow-minded, domineering, lacking in respect and love. And the reasons for this lie in the history of the last five centuries. In addition the Church has itself become encapsulated in a particular culture, fixed in a particular philosophy. This has made the Church incapable of understanding the thought and language of people whose intellectual background is different. *(Continued on page 271)*

The Spaniard, Pedro Arrupé, was elected general of the Jesuit order at the Jesuit General Congregation held between the third and fourth sessions of the Council. Here was a man who, for thirty-five years, had been active in the missions in Asia and especially in Japan. With its 36,000 members, the Society is one of the largest religious orders in the Catholic Church. Arrupé spoke twice at the Council, basing his talks on his experience with atheism and with the missions. Because of his call for 'analysis' and 'planning', both talks created something of a sensation. This was due partly to misunderstanding and partly to the missionary perspective of the talks. What may have shocked Western minds, used to precise distinctions, was his broad 'global' approach.

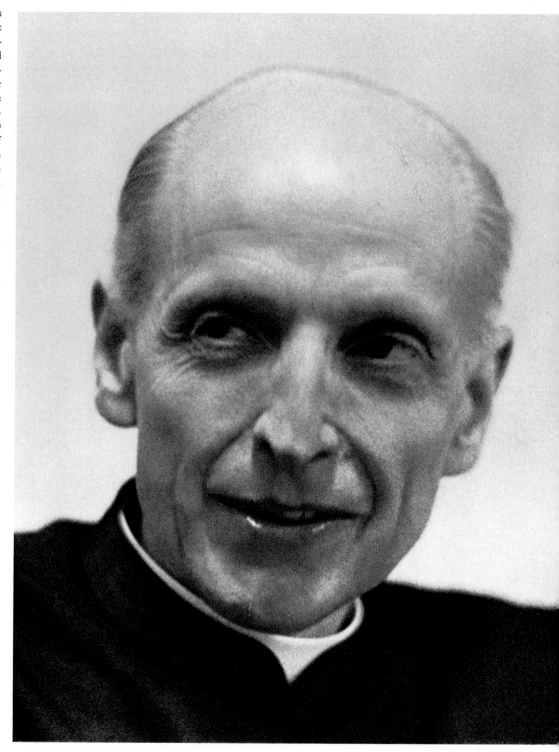

Bishop Franjo Seper of Zagreb, the successor to Cardinal Stepinac, who died a martyr during internment in Yugoslavia, was observed carefully ever since the beginning of the first and second sessions. Among East European bishops, who had been cut off from Western theological development for decades and consequently had been completely preoccupied with preserving the Catholic heritage in their countries, he was a rare exception. He was enthusiastically in favor of introducing the diaconate; and he showed great understanding on the ecumenical issue. At the Council he was truly deep and comprehensive in his analysis of atheism. But even before this, Pope Paul had named him a cardinal.

Cardinal John Heenan, archbishop of Westminster, is an excellent illustration of how superficial it is to make distinction between 'conservative' and 'progressive' bishops. A member of the Secretariat for Christian Unity, John Heenan made very positive contributions on the Jewish question; in connection with this he made a sharp attack on Cardinal Ottaviani's theological commission. The same thing was true on the question of religious liberty. Yet he was fully as sharp in his polished attacks on progressive theologians when the so-called 'question of the pill' came up in connection with birth control; and he made clear his reservations on the issue of mixed marriages. English Catholic lay people find his attitude distinctly 'reactionary'. In general, the Council did him greater justice.

Cardinal Paul Silva Henriquez of Santiago, Chile, was unquestionably one of the great figures in the Council. As early as the first-session debate on the liturgy, he demanded a cutting back of Roman centralism; the majority responded with applause. Even with the troublesome problem of the relationship between the Church and the world, he showed himself one of the few capable of coping with its theological complexities. He can also be considered one of the great proponents of the land reform so desperately needed in South America. It is hardly an exaggeration to say that without the Cardinal's work Chile would have by now succumbed to Communism. He doesn't condemn Communism but he seeks to overcome it through creative initiative.

Cardinal Paul Léger, archbishop of Montreal and a Sulpician, was rated a '*converso*' by the Italians. This is what they called the bishops whose viewpoints were changed during the course of the Council sessions; they were 'converted'. Paul Léger was by no means a 'progressive' when he came to Rome. Yet he had a clear and devout mind and quickly perceived what Pope John had in view. He took a vigorous stand in favor of renewal, and by 1964—he spoke almost as often as Cardinal Ruffini during the third session—he had become perhaps the leading figure of the entire Council. His speeches centered on two issues: first, on the Church in the contemporary world; here, especially on the topics of marriage and war, he excelled all others in depth and power. A second favorite topic of his was priestly life and seminary training. Léger was in advance of the Council and was often concerned with the fact that the great mass of people frequently could not understand him.

IV. The Church on the Move

A Decent Respect for the Opinions of Mankind

RICHARD CARDINAL CUSHING, archbishop of Boston, September 23, 1964

The declaration on religious liberty in general is acceptable. In saying this I speak not only in my own name but also in the name of almost all the bishops of the United States.

'At long last'

It is most gratifying to us that at long last a full and free discussion on this subject will take place in this council hall. For in our time this is a practical question of great importance, both for the life of the Church and for the social and civil life. It is also a doctrinal question. For the doctrine of the Church on religious liberty in modern civil society has not yet been declared clearly and unambiguously.

This clear declaration is owed to the whole world—both Catholic and non-Catholic—which is indeed awaiting it. Therefore, in making this declaration, this ecumenical council will manifest, if I may quote words famous in our American history, 'a decent respect for the opinions of mankind'.

As the relator he said, the text of the declaration as it stands needs amendment here and there. But it is earnestly hoped that the amendments be such that the declaration be stronger in the meaning it already expresses and not weaker. For the substance of the doctrine as we have it here is true and solid. And it is aptly appropriate for our times. Therefore the declaration must remain intact as to its essential meaning.

One thing is of the greatest importance. In this declaration the Church must show herself to the entire modern world as the champion of civil liberty, of human liberty and of civil liberty, specifically in the matter of religion.

On the one hand this whole question of religious liberty is somewhat complicated. On the other hand, it seems to me, the question is simple. The whole matter can be reduced to two propositions.

First: Throughout her history the Catholic Church has ever insisted upon her own freedom in civil society and before the public powers. She has fought for the freedom of the pope, of the bishop to teach and govern the people of God. She has fought for the freedom of this same people of God, who have the right to live in civil society according to the dictates of Christian conscience without interference. The first proposition, therefore, is contained in the traditional formula *'libertas Ecclesiae'* (freedom of the Church).

The second proposition is this: That same freedom in civil society which the Church has ever insisted upon for herself and her members, she now in this our age also champions for other churches and their members, indeed for every human person.

Let me present some reasons, briefly, for this statement. They are taken from the encyclical letter PACEM IN TERRIS of Pope John XXIII, of most blessed memory.

For Pope John said in his encyclical that every well ordered society is grounded in truth, in justice, in love, in liberty. Now in the first place, equal and universal religious liberty is demanded by that fundamental truth according to which all men, in so far as they are human persons, are of equal dignity; equally endowed with the same human rights, among which Pope John specified the right to religious liberty.

Secondly, religious liberty is demanded by justice. For justice requires that all citizens equally enjoy the same civil rights which in our age are acknowledged as necessary for due civil dignity. And among these rights the first is the right to religious liberty.

Thirdly, religious liberty is demanded by love. For nothing is more violently destructive of unity and civic concord than coercion or discrimination, either legal or illegal, because of religious reasons.

Fourthly, religious liberty is demanded by the very principle of civil liberty. For as Lord Acton said, speaking in the tradition of Christian civilization: 'Freedom is the highest political end.' Now, as the political end, civil liberty is also the means necessary to attain the higher ends of the human person. And this is the mind of Pope John. In particular, religious freedom—or the immunity from all coercion in religious affairs—is a necessary means by which man, in a manner which is human and willed by God, can seek God, can find Him, can serve Him. There are other arguments for the validity of the human and civil right to religious liberty in society, and these are stated in this declaration, which as I say 'in general is acceptable'. And so I praise and approve this declaration.

Note: Although some fathers made desperate attempts to modify crucial statements in the declaration, they did not succeed. Though it was added to a great deal as a result of amendments, the declaration remained substantially intact, as even its opponents admit.

Suppression of Liberty and Confession of Guilt

JOSEF CARDINAL BERAN, archbishop of Prague (Czechoslovakia), on September 20, 1965

The declaration of religious liberty, which also has an application wherever true freedom of conscience is concerned, is of great theological as well as practical importance.

Sacred scripture states openly, 'Whatever does not proceed from faith is sin' (Rom. 14: 23b). This means, in the context of the letter to the Romans, that whatever is not done with an upright conscience is sinful. Whoever therefore coerces anyone through physical or moral force to act against his conscience, seduces him to sin against God. To us, too, Venerable Fathers, the admonition of St. James is directed: 'So speak and so act as people who are to be judged by the law of liberty' (James 2: 12).

These principles are confirmed by experience. And here I humbly venture to add my own personal testimony.

The testimony of personal experience

From the moment freedom of conscience was radically restricted in my homeland, I witnessed the grave temptation this state of affairs meant for many people. In my flock, even among priests, I observed not only serious difficulties of faith but also strong temptations to lie, to be hypocritical, and to other moral vices which easily corrupt a people deprived of real liberty of conscience.

Where such a thing is deliberately done to the damage of the true religion, everyone of the faithful sees what a grave scandal unfreedom is. But experience also teaches that such actions directed against freedom of conscience are detrimental even if they intend the advantage of the true faith, or pretend to intend such advantage. Always and everywhere, suppression of freedom of conscience produces widespread hypocrisy. And perhaps we can say that a hypocrisy which pretends faith does more damage to the Church than a hypocrisy which seeks to conceal faith. This is today much more frequent.

The burning of John Hus

So the Catholic Church in my country seems today to be making a painful atonement for the sins and errors committed in its name in the past against freedom of conscience. Such as for example the burning at the stake of the priest, John Hus; or the external coercion with which a great part of the Czech people were forced in the seventeenth century to return to the Catholic religion, in line with the principle, *cujus regio, ejus religio:* whoever the region belongs to determines its religion. The secular authorities, even if they wanted to serve the Catholic Church, or pretended to, by doing this actually left the heart of the people secretly wounded. This trauma was an obstacle to religious progress, and supplied cheap grist for the mills of the agitators, both the enemies of the Church in the past and those of today.

Thus history exhorts us to declare at this Council in unmistakable words the principle of freedom of religion and of conscience, without any opportunistic limitations or restrictions. If we do this, and do it in a spirit of atonement for past sins, the moral authority of our Church will grow again to the advantage of the nations. Even those who today suppress freedom of conscience will feel shame today before all men of good will. If they see themselves exposed to the modern world, this could be the beginning of a healthy disillusionment. This Council will gain a new moral force and will intervene on behalf of the persecuted brethren.

Proposal

I therefore entreat you, Venerable Brothers, not to diminish the force of this declaration in any way, and I also suggest that we add at the end of the declaration these or similar words: 'The Catholic Church implores all governments of this world to give actual validity to the principle of freedom of conscience for all citizens, even for those who believe in God; and that they terminate any suppression of religious liberty. All priests and lay people who after so many years are still in prison on

(Continued on page 279)

Richard Cardinal Cushing, arch-bishop of Boston, was not always present at the Council. He made a special trip to Rome only on behalf of the Jewish question and the declaration on religious liberty. Many people supposed that the reason for this was his distaste for Latin. He actually offered Pope Paul VI a simul-taneous translation system—an offer which did not work out. He himself gave another reason for his absence: 'Every time I leave, my charities suffer', he said. He estimated the loss at $20,000 a day. Religious liberty and the Jews therefore cost him, accord-ing to the computation of Abbé Laurentin (*Figaro*, Oct. 5, 1964), $400,000.

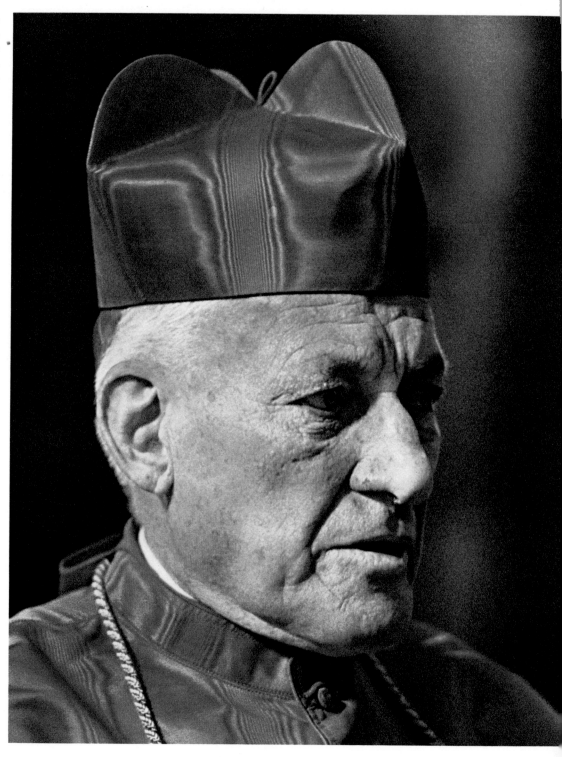

Arthur Elchinger, coadjutor of Strasbourg, was one of the most inspiring Council speakers. He hit the target every time, and he was a man who knew no compromise. The French bishops were not always happy with their courageous and candid 'colleague', because they preferred a policy of prudent reserve at the Council. But this troubled the bishop very little. He also spoke to lay people and observers, perhaps more frequently than to the bishops. Since 'dialogue' was the motto of the Council, didn't he have the responsibility of showing what dialogue was like in practice—unless everything was supposed to remain in the realm of abstraction and declamation? (*A Challenge to the Church* was the title Bishop Elchinger gave to a book he had written in collaboration with Pastor Marc Boegner in 1964. This was his constant plea to the bishops—and it did not fall on deaf ears.)

Cardinal Joseph Beran, archbishop of Prague, was unable to participate in the first three Council sessions because he had been virtually confined since the Communist takeover of Czechoslovakia. In 1952 John XXIII wrote him a letter; it had no address since his residence had been kept secret. Beran was eventually 'released' but he was unable to resume his activities as bishop. Much negotiation was necessary before he was authorized to leave the country. He has, in fact, been replaced in Prague by Msgr. Tomasek who acts as 'apostolic administrator', thus providing at least the necessary minimum of pastoral organization. Beran, made a cardinal by Paul VI, now lives in Rome. His valiant, ecumenical intervention on behalf of religious freedom aroused considerable attention.

various pretexts because of their religious principles should be set free without delay. The bishops and priests who are prevented in such great numbers from carrying out their duties should be permitted to return to their flocks. Where unjust laws put the Church at the mercy of hostile authorities and their arbitrariness, inner freedom and autonomy and unobstructed contact with the Holy See should be restored to the Church. The practice of obstructing young people on the way to the priesthood or religious life should be stopped. The religious orders should be permitted to resume community life. Finally, real freedom should be granted to all the faithful, so that they become able to proclaim revealed truth in a positive way and bring up their children in faith. In this way, a true work of peace, needed by our time more than anything else, would be achieved.'

Note: This version was made from a German translation supplied by Cardinal Beran himself. The confession of guilt was incorporated into the declaration on religious liberty (in section 12), in the words: 'In the life of the People of God as it has made its pilgrim way through the vicissitudes of human history, there have at times appeared ways of acting which were less in accord with the spirit of the gospel and even in contradiction to it. Nonetheless, the doctrine of the Church that no one is to be coerced into faith has always stood firm.'

A Cautious Spaniard on Religious Liberty

JOSE CARDINAL BUENO Y MONREAL, archbishop of Seville, on September 23, 1964

I think the doctrine of this schema is correct. But the text needs more precise formulation so as not to be misunderstood, because some of the statements, if misinterpreted, might no longer be universally true.

The ecumenical viewpoint is too narrow

1. Nobody denies the declaration's significance. But this significance is not expressed in the text, but rather is even weakened.
Religious liberty is the first and basic prerequisite for the Church to be able to carry out the mission given it by Christ, to preach the gospel to all creatures.
This prerequisite is unfortunately not found today in some nations. It is also a postulate of human dignity which should be proclaimed and protected by the Church and all courageous men.
It is therefore not a question of establishing peaceful contacts between Christians and of cultivating ecumenical dialogue; the problem is much broader and deeper.
The text's introductory statements imply that the purpose was to establish a connection with the preceding chapters on ecumenism. All the text seems to be aiming at its improved fraternal relations, as though the problem was to settle a domestic quarrel which may exist within Catholic nations. This, however, diminishes the text's significance.

What we need is a solemn declaration in which the Church will address itself to all nations, demanding religious liberty for all, be it because all men are called to share in Christ's divinity, or because human dignity demands it.

2. It is my impression that two ambiguities permeate the entire declaration.
(a) The text mixes Christian doctrine and politics. The text draws conclusions which are valid in the political sphere, inasmuch as an effective protection of the Church's liberty and a peaceful coexistence among people would be impossible without them. But that does not mean these conclusions have general validity in the sphere of doctrine. The Catholic Church alone has been given by Christ the mission to teach all nations and incorporate them into Christ, and in and of itself this is the only way to arrive at our ultimate goal. Objectively, then, no other religious doctrine has a right to be preached and propagated, because that would run counter to the commission given us by Christ. Nonetheless, it remains true that for other reasons—i. e., because of the requirements of the circumstances—in most cases other religions also must be granted freedom to propagate their doctrine publicly. The distinction should always be made clear, so that nobody may think that in Catholic teaching all religions lead to God and therefore have equal rights.
(b) The text confuses the individual and social spheres. We all agree that from the beginning it has been considered unjust to force anyone to accept religion, or to harm him for religious reasons. He who seeks God in another way, due to an honestly mistaken conscience, must undoubtedly enjoy the freedom to do so, in the individual or private sphere, as long as this does not involve any social repercussions. But if what he does, in his sincere but erroneous conscience, involves other peoples, then these others are by no means obligated to tolerate the consequences of his error if this is scandalous or dangerous to them. This is particularly true when the errors not only involve the presentation of a doctrine, but also involve practical standards of morality, perhaps in conflict with the normal and universally approved behavior of the others.
Any freedom, not only religious freedom, is subject to restriction on the social level, because this is necessary for peaceful coexistence so that all may live freely. The right of propagating a religion may be exercised among those who willingly choose to listen, but not among those who do not want or are not supposed to listen, or who are not capable of free choice—for example, children, against their parents' will.
Public propaganda that reaches all, whether they want it or not, through today's mass media, and that makes its impression on free choice through strong stimulation and psychological pressure, could violate the consciences of Catholics who do not want to listen to such doctrines because they constitute a danger to true faith.
Therefore we cannot deduce from a general principle the universal right of every religious community to propagate publicly its teaching.
It is a matter of political prudence for the public authorities—in their effort to protect the rights and liberties of all citizens, to assure a

peaceful coexistence—to grant to the various religious communities, in view of various social circumstances—either within a nation or on an international scale—a larger or smaller scope for freedom. Public authorities should of course strive that in the area of conscience and intimately personal objectives—which only indirectly and rather accidentally fall under public jurisdiction inasmuch as there must be a peaceful balance between the rights and freedoms of citizens—all enjoy the widest possible freedom.

3. The text says: 'Proselytism happens when inappropriate and immoral means are used.' Here should be added: 'Or when propaganda is addressed to human beings over which such propaganda does not have the power of disposal, such as children against the will of their parents or guardians.' Because rights and freedom must be assured here, too.

Note: This penetrating speech, which definitely accepts the principle of religious liberty, yet sees fit to call for restrictions in the text because of the consequences of liberty, did much to bring about a better formulation. The amended text avoided the first mixing (of doctrine and politics) but the second mixing (individual and social spheres) remained necessary; indeed it argued legitimately, inasmuch as religious liberty is in itself essential to the common good in the nations of our time. The scope of this is something which Spain has to learn.

Tradition and Its Correction in Sacred Scripture

ALBERT CARDINAL MEYER, archbishop of Chicago, on October 5, 1964

I agree with the entire second chapter, especially paragraph 8, which says that tradition is something living, dynamic and all-encompassing. This means that it does not consist only of dogmatic propositions, but also of the worship and practice of the Universal Church.

I am also pleased to see that it shows that tradition does not grow simply through the definitions of the magisterium but also 'through considerations by the faithful, and through a very interior experience in spiritual matters'.

I also applaud the allusion to the Blessed Virgin Mary, who is emulated by the Church in that the Church ponders in her heart the events and words of tradition.

Nevertheless, this section smacks a little of triumphalism. For it shows the life and worship of the Church under only one positive aspect. But since in this paragraph tradition is extended beyond the infallible magisterium, tradition is also subject to the limits and shortcomings of the pilgrim Church, which is a Church of sinners, which therefore sees the divine through a glass darkly (1 Cor. 13:12).

The history of the Church offers abundant examples of such shortcomings. For instance, the theological doctrine of the resurrection of Christ remained obscure for a long time; beginning with the eighteenth century, an evil moralism predominated; there was an exaggerated

casuistry; for centuries a non-liturgical piety predominated, which moreover frequently became sentimental during the last century; the sacred scriptures were neglected. And so on.

This is why a few words should be added to this paragraph, saying something about overcoming and correcting these shortcomings. I suggest the insertion of the following sentence: 'Yet this living tradition does not grow in all times and places. And since the Church, as long as she is a pilgrim, can err and actually does err in considering divine things, she carries within herself the eternal norm of sacred scripture; comparing herself with this norm, she constantly corrects and perfects herself.'

This short insertion, which is well harmonized with what precedes and follows, could bring paragraph 8 into balance, I hope, and give it the necessary complementation.

Note: The suggestion was not incorporated into the final text of the Constitution, since it would have predetermined the moot question whether all revealed truth is contained in sacred scripture alone. The Council did not want to settle this question. (This translation of the late Cardinal Meyer's address was made from a German version.)

Freedom for Scriptural Research

CHRISTOPHER BUTLER, O.S.B., abbot of Downside (England), on October 6, 1964

The paragraph of the present schema which deals with the historical character of the gospels is a restrained and generally satisfactory statement. Everyone knows that anxieties have been felt in this field from two sides. Some fear that we are in process of losing the necessary historical foundation of our faith. Others want our scholars to have all rightful liberty in pursuing their task which is of such great service to the Church.

I wish to say something more about this liberty. The question of the historical value of the gospels can be looked at from two angles. From the point of view of faith, there is no doubt that the gospels, along with the other books of the Bible, are inspired—with all the consequences deriving from that dogma. It is however certain that the notion of 'literary types' is applicable to the gospels as it is to the other inspired books. Who would question that many difficulties in the Old Testament have been solved by the application of this notion, without detriment to the faith? And by means of it apparent contradictions between the Bible and other ascertained truths, of natural science or history, have been removed. Neither faith nor defined doctrine precludes the same process from application to the gospels.

The historicity of the gospels can also be looked at from the point of view of an *approach* to faith—what is called the point of view of 'apologetics'. From this point of view it is neither useful nor permissible to appeal to dogmas (e. g., inspiration), since apologetics cannot argue from dogmas of faith. From this angle it would be quite deplorable if we let it appear that a Catholic scholar is not free in the pursuit of his scientific task.

Our paragraph states that the evangelists *always* wrote in such a way as to impart to us 'not inventions sprung from the creative faculty of the primitive Christian community, but true and genuine information about Jesus.' I suggest that the thought here might be better expressed. Neither faith nor, still less, scholarship can assure us that the evangelists never used a 'literary type' which current speech today would describe as 'invention'. Many instances of this occur in the Old Testament historical books, and there is no *a priori* reason why what happened in the Old Testament should not have happened in the New Testament. So I suggest that before the word 'inventions' we should insert the word 'mere', and before the word 'creative' should be placed the word 'simply'. I also propose that before the words 'about Jesus' should be inserted 'according to their chosen literary type'.

In general, in the course of this almost miraculous Council, we have done much to drive out that spirit of fear and excessive anxiety by which at times our labors were hindered.

Today I say: Let us not be afraid of scholarly and historical truth. Let us not be afraid that one truth may tell against another truth. Let us not be afraid that our scholars may be lacking in loyalty to the Church and to traditional doctrine.

One of two things is true: *Either* there is a worldwide conspiracy of scholars to undermine the bases of Christian faith (and a man who can believe that can believe anything); *or* the aim of our scholars is to reach the full, objective and real truth of the gospel tradition. In this task they play a dual role: they are loyal Catholics; and they are at the same time scientific scholars whose first presupposition is honesty of investigation. Doubtless some will turn liberty into license—but we must risk this for the sake of a greater good. Doubtless mistakes are made and will be made in this field—but it is one where trial and error are the road to truth. What we want is not the childish comfort which comes of averting our gaze from the truth, but a truly critical scholarship which will enable us to enter into 'dialogue' with non-Catholic scholars.

Note: The Council has assured the wide freedom for scripture scholars that Abbot Butler wanted. The objectionable passages in the schema on revelation were to be changed in various ways. Butler should be quite satisfied with the final text, even though it lacks the desired clarity.

Disappointment in the Schema on Priestly Life and Ministry

JULIUS CARDINAL DÖPFNER, archbishop of Munich, on October 15, 1965

The new text on the schema on priestly life and ministry is much improved over the draft of last November. This is the result of the many amendments suggested to the commission. I am particularly pleased that the idea of priesthood is not seen in the schema under the aspect of cult—i. e., as limited to offering of mass and administration of sacraments—as it was seen for centuries, but is extended to encompass the triple office of Christ and considers the essence of priestly holiness to be the honest and proper discharge of this triple office. Yet the schema still suffers, in my opinion, from many and serious defects. I mean first its manner of expression and structure; and second its description of the modern priest's problems and the means for overcoming these. . . .

Today's priests would not stand for it

All too frequently the schema still suggests a pious treatise. In view of the modern mind, the style should be more sober and theologically more accurate.

Today's priests would not stand being called 'the precious spiritual crown of the bishop', even if this beautiful thought comes from St. Ignatius of Antioch. Nor would they accept the text's adducing of religious motives for everything, even the most minute and commonplace features of priestly life—when, for example, on fraternal and amicable recreation, it is added, '. . . remembering the words with which the Lord himself mercifully invited the tired apostles, "Come apart a little, and rest awhile".' Nor will today's priests accept graciously things that have been said *ad nauseam* a thousand times before. But this is what the schema frequently does.

As to theological phraseology, there are many things in the schema which could be said in a pious book for the edification of souls but have no place in a document of a Council. How, for example, could priests share with the faithful 'the faith, grace and fullness which they have in the Lord'? I have always thought it was for Christ alone, through the Spirit, to communicate supernatural life. How can we seriously say that priests ought to imitate 'Our Lord Jesus whom the Father has sanctified and sent into the world, the incarnate Word of God, who chose to become like his brethren in all things save sin'? This sounds as though the priest becomes through ordination some kind of superman. But exaggerations such as this in reference to the relation between priests and lay people are found in several passages!

Structure of the material: The first paragraph deals with the nature of the priesthood and the condition of priests. This should be divided into two separate paragraphs. The third section of the seventh paragraph, which deals with the common life of priests, does not belong in the discussion of ministry but of priestly life. It should therefore be transferred to the second part of the schema.

The second part (on the life of priests) leaves much to be desired. There is nothing on the priests' personal situation. But many expect something on this—and rightly so. Nothing can be found on the attitude of the priests toward the world and earthly values, except for a few remarks on the right use of earthly goods in paragraph 17—and what is said there is very one-sided. What is further disappointing is that there is a special paragraph explicitly dealing with the evangelical counsels in the life of the priest. So that the way of holiness proper to secular priests will come into focus in a way contradistinguished from that of people in religious orders, I would suggest that we deal in separate paragraphs, first with celibacy as a gift that must be respected, second with the right use of secular things and with poverty, and a third with the spirit of humility and obedience.

A basically changed pastoral situation

We all know that the difficulties of priests are much more numerous in the contemporary world. These difficulties have primarily to do with the personal and pastoral situation of the priests.

Due to far-reaching sociological changes and the disappearance of many forms and orders prevailing until now, priests today live in a kind of diaspora, and thus suffer much more than formerly from loneliness and isolation. The pastoral situation has in the last decades fundamentally changed and deteriorated. Therefore many priests, especially older priests, no longer feel up to their tasks. And many new things have to be learned in theology, anthropology, and many other theoretical and practical fields of knowledge. The result is that many priests despair of success and become depressed. It is not even rare for them to encounter doubts of faith.

The schema, especially the second part, gives insufficient attention to these and other problems of priestly existence today. Too little is said about the new pastoral situation, and what is said is scattered over various passages; no adequate and honest information is given about the pastoral difficulties of priests.

The problem of celibacy must be honestly treated

For example, an open statement on celibacy is in place. Celibacy is on one hand a gift 'given to *some* by the Father' (paragraph 42 of the Constitution on the Church, with regard to Mt. 19: 11); on the other hand its observance is required of all priests in the Western church. The schema's answer to this difficulty is entirely inadequate and has nothing to do with the real problem. To the objection that complete continence is impossible, the response given is the saying of the Lord (Lk. 18: 27): 'What is impossible to men is possible to God.'

But this citation does not fit here and is not addressed in this context to celibates; it has to do rather with the wealthy, and the danger their wealth is to their eternal salvation. This schema should therefore say that the Church is aware of this problem, but that the Church is justified in the hope that the gift of celibacy will be given to a sufficient number of candidates for the priesthood, if only God is asked for it humbly, and the candidate for priesthood does everything in his power. Finally,

nothing is said in the schema on pastoral care for pastors who bear the brunt of the arduous work for the souls of men.

I conclude that in its style, theological expression, and structure of the subject matter, the schema seems to me in need of amendment. Moreover, since the schema has been expanded anyway, it should treat in more detail of priestly ministry and life in our time, so that it could become the Magna Carta of the Second Vatican Council.

Note: Although the commission made valiant efforts to comply with the wishes of the cardinal and other speakers' proposals for amendment, which made for an essential improvement of the text, the result can hardly be called a 'Magna Carta'.

Married Part-time Priests and Pastoral Needs

PEDRO KOOP, bishop of Lins (Brazil), on October 15, 1965

I want to say immediately what I am driving at here. In order to save the Church in Latin America, a married clergy should as soon as possible be introduced in our region. This clergy should be recruited from the best among married men with the existing law of celibacy left fully in force.

Statistically documented facts show that the Catholic Church is in constant decline in the world in general, but especially in Latin America due to population growth and the attacks mounted by atheists, religious sects, and the great non-Catholic religions. During the last 250 years the Church has decreased from 30 to 20 per cent of the increased population of the world. If this continues, then the Church will be reduced within the next 200 years to exactly ten per cent.

In Latin America the Church loses one million souls every year, in Brazil one thousand each day. On other continents, for example in Africa, the Church is unable to attract the millions which other religions absorb, maybe permanently.

The increasing shortage of priests

The main reason lies in the shortage of priests and of vocations to celibate priesthood. The shortage becomes daily more discouraging if we consider the rising population. Thirty-three per cent of the total number of Catholics live in Latin America, but only six per cent of the priests. Thirty-five years from now, in the year 2,000, Latin America will number six hundred million souls. This will constitute 50 per cent of the Catholic Church, and require 120,000 priests to make one pastor available for every 5,000 souls, not to mention the huge area over which they will be spread.

The newly restored diaconate will somewhat alleviate the problems but will not eliminate them by any means. For pastoral reasons in the true sense of the word, i. e., in order to save the faith of so many people, to administer the sacraments of penance and the eucharist, to serve them in their last hour with the sacrament of anointing, to celebrate the

Albert Cardinal Meyer, archbishop of Chicago, was considered the most open-minded United States cardinal at the first three sessions. He was one of the ten (later twelve) Council presidents. As an outstanding scripture scholar, he was able to make vital contributions to the schema on Revelation and to the first part of the schema on the Church and the modern world. Here he elaborated on the cosmic position of Christ and the way work is reevaluated in light of it. He died on April 7, 1965, in the period between the third and fourth sessions. Cardinal Shehan of Baltimore replaced him as Council president. Shehan gave a brilliant talk on the progress of the doctrinal development on the question of religious liberty in papal documents.

Christopher Butler, abbot of Downside, England, and head of the English Benedictines, was described by John Todd, a leading English layman, as 'the only figure among the older men in the Church . . . able to bring English Catholics together'. At any rate, Todd was correct in saying that it was only at the Council that Butler 'was recognized and honored for his importance'. He spoke difficult Latin in a low voice, but each time he did speak, the bishops cupped their hands to their ears so as not to lose a word. 'The most important result of the Council will be,' the Abbot wrote, 'that we learn to treat one another as adults.'

Who would have expected to find in a South African bishop a first-class expert on the relationship between Society, Church and State, and in addition a judicious interpreter of the writings of Teilhard de Chardin? And yet Archbishop Denis Hurley of Durban was both. His effort to get both these topics treated with more depth had little success. He nevertheless did succeed in getting some small amendments made in the chapter on lay people in the schema on the Church. But his work on the commission on seminaries was crowned with real success. Unless we are mistaken, this will have far-reaching consequences during the post-conciliar period.

liturgy of the word and especially the eucharistic sacrifice, we urgently need priests. Only the eucharistic sacrifice, as the meal of community, is a suitable means to gather together the people of God, to educate them, nourish and strengthen them. These congregations must not be too large; they must be like spiritual cells in the wilderness and in the crowded large cities. If the people are left to themselves, they perish spiritually due to lack of priests and fall prey to sects and superstition.

It is therefore required, in fact urgently required today, that we increase the number of priests 'a hundredfold'. Even more will be needed later for the Church to approach people in their places of living, especially since the insufficient number of church buildings makes it impossible for them to find Christ and the Church.

There now live in Brazil 80 million people; 60 million of them are not reached by the Church, usually due to lack of priests, although these people properly belong to the Church.

God's commandment

May the fathers of the Council reflect on this: the Church is divinely commanded to proclaim the gospel and to sanctify men. The people of God have a strict right to hear the gospel and to receive spiritual life through the sacraments. This is a God-given right, which no human right can supersede. The Church is obliged in law to respect it.

Venerable fathers and zealous pastors: Since a divine commandment to preserve and propagate faith commands us, I suggest that this Council create the possibility of ordaining as priests qualified laymen who have been married for a minimum of five years. After a not too extended training period, they should act in their leisure time as assistant or auxiliary priests. They should exercice their priestly office simply and honestly as pastors at least of smaller congregations.

This proposal is not an unheard-of innovation. For this has existed in Eastern churches from the earliest times. And these Eastern married priests are very deserving and truly apostolic men!

The priests recruited from the ranks of the married should remain married, should retain their family life and their economic and social status, which will undoubtedly give their service a great attraction and dynamism. They will be quite dependent on the bishop in their work in that they will give their free time to serve at least smaller congregations in assigned places. So nothing will be changed. Only a new pastoral instrument would be added, which might be able to remedy our distressing religious situation—today and tomorrow.

Let the bishops have no illusions. The destiny of the Latin American Church is in great danger. The decision must be made. We either increase the number of priests—celibate or married—or we face the destruction of the Church in Latin America.

I therefore propose that we insert in our text the following section: 'The number of celibate priests in wide areas of the Church must be considered highly inadequate. And since the demographical indications are that it will still further decrease in comparison to the population growth, this holy Synod decrees, for the good of so great a number of souls whose salvation is entrusted by God to her care, that the competent regional bishops' conferences are empowered to decide whether and where mature men who have been married for a minimum of five years will be ordained priests for the good of souls, following the norms which the apostle Paul laid down in his letters to Titus and Timothy.'

Note: On the advice of Cardinal Lercaro, this intervention was not delivered as a speech but filed only in writing. The text of the schema was not changed—but the problem still exists.

Final Address
of Paul VI
on December 7, 1965

Today we conclude the Second Vatican Council. The presence of so many of you clearly demonstrates that we bring it to a close while it is still full of health and ambition. The well-ordered pattern of this assembly is proof of it; the planned conclusion of the Council's work confirms it; the harmony of opinion and decision proclaims it. If quite a few questions raised during the course of the Council itself still await appropriate answers, this only shows that its labors are concluded not in weariness but in the vitality this universal synod has awakened. With God's help, this vitality will resolve such questions generously and completely when the Council ends.

This Council gives to history an image of the Catholic Church as this hall symbolizes it: filled with pastors professing the same faith, animated by the same love, united in the same communion of prayer, discipline and activity—and this is truly marvelous—all desiring nothing else than to offer themselves like Christ, our teacher and Lord, for the life of the Church and the salvation of the world. This Council gives posterity more than an image of the Church. It also gives the heritage of teaching and commandments, entrusted to her by Christ. For centuries mankind has appropriated this heritage, translating it into flesh and blood, and expressing it through their way of life. Now the Council has illuminated many of its parts, has reworked and rearranged the whole. This heritage lives on because of the power of divine truth and grace in it. Therefore, it can fill with life anyone who receives it and makes it a part of his own existence.

Was the Council religious?

What did this Council mean? What has it accomplished? These, perhaps, are the questions we should answer here. But this would take too much time and attention. Besides, this solemn hour is not the time to sum up such important things. We should like to devote this precious moment to one single thought which both humbles us and lifts us to the summit of our hopes. We should like to ask ourselves: What is the religious value of this Council? By 'religious' we mean our relationship to the living God. This is central to the Church. It is the source of all her faith, hope and love, of all that she is and does.

Can we say that we have glorified God, that we have sought to know and love him, that we have made progress in our effort to contemplate him, in our effort to honor him, in our ability to proclaim him to men who look to us as their pastors and teachers in the ways of God?

We sincerely think so. Because it was this thought, more than any other, that guided the Council. The words of the opening address of our venerated predecessor, John XXIII, who without doubt was the originator of this great Council, still resound in the basilica of St. Peter. He said: 'The greatest concern of the ecumenical Council is this: that the sacred deposit of Christian doctrine should be guarded and taught more effectively.... The Lord has said: "Seek first the kingdom of God and his justice." The word "first" expresses the direction in which our thoughts and energies must move.'

The times we live in

The purpose now is matched by the deed. To appreciate it properly, we must remember the time in which it was realized: a time which, everyone admits, is more interested in the conquest of the world than the kingdom of God; a time in which forgetfulness of God has become the rule—as though scientific progress demanded this; a time in which the human person, more clearly aware now of himself and his freedom, strives to be totally free, unbound by any supernatural law; a time in which secularism seems the inevitable result of modern thought appearing to be the highest wisdom available for the ordering of social life; a time, moreover, in which man's mind has been pleased to represent the absurd and the utterly hopeless; a time, finally, which is characterized by upheavals and a hitherto unknown decline even in the great world religions.

It was at such a time that our Council was held, to the honor of the Father, in the name of Christ and with the help of the Holy Spirit who 'searches all things', and who is now quickening the Church, 'making us understand God's gifts to us' and giving her a renewed vision

of the life of men both profound and all-embracing. This Council has given, as they say, a new prominence to the theocentric and theological concept of man and the universe. She has done this almost in defiance of the charge of anachronism and irrelevance. She has done this through claims which the world may at first judge to be foolish, but which, we hope, will be recognized as truly human, wise and salutary—the claim that there is a God. Certainly there is a God. He really exists. He lives. He is a person. He is concerned and he is infinitely good—not only good in himself, but also immeasurably good to us. He is our Creator, our truth, our happiness. When we fasten our minds and hearts on God in contemplation, we do the noblest and the most perfect thing we can. Even today this can and must be the finest and worthiest act of any man.

Was the Council self-complacent?

It will be said that the Council devoted itself less to divine truths than to discussion of the Church—her nature and make-up, her ecumenical vocation, her apostolic and missionary activity. This centuries-old religious community which is the Church has tried to study herself, to know herself better, to define herself better and thus to clarify her true spirit and directives. All this is true. But this self-examination has not been an end in itself; it has not been merely a display of worldly wisdom and culture. The Church is assembled here in deep spiritual awareness, not to produce a learned treatise on religious psychology, nor an account of her own experiences, nor even to devote herself to reaffirming her rights and explaining her laws. Rather, it was to find—living in herself, and by the power of the Holy Spirit—the word of Christ. And it was to probe more deeply into the mystery, the plan of God and his presence in her. She wanted to rekindle the fire of faith which nourishes the mysterious power of her strength and wisdom, and that fire of love which impels her to sing without ceasing the praise of God. 'Whoever loves, sings', says St. Augustine.

The Council documents—especially those on divine revelation, the liturgy, the Church, priests, religious and lay people—leave wide open to view this central religious perspective; they also show how clear and fresh and rich is the spiritual stream which wells up in the heart of the Church through living contact with the living God, and which flows from her bosom into the dry wastes of our world.

The challenge of the modern world

We cannot overlook one important aspect of the Council's religious meaning: The Council has been deeply committed to the study of the modern world. Never before perhaps has the Church so felt the need to know, to approach, to understand, to penetrate, to serve and evangelize the society in which she lives; and to come to grips with it, in a sense to run after it in its rapid and continuous change. This attitude is a response to the alienation of the Church and her separation from culture in recent centuries—in the last century and especially in our own. Yet this essentially missionary attitude found in the Council is part of the Church's mission at all times and it has been powerfully and ceaselessly at work here. So much so that some have been inclined to suspect that an easygoing and excessive responsiveness to the outside world, to passing events, cultural fashions, and pluralistic ideas may have influenced the members of this synod to a 'relativism' in their teaching at the expense of the fidelity due to tradition—and to the detriment of the Council's own religious goals. We, however, do not believe this charge against the Council can be justified, when we see its genuine and deeper purposes and its authentic achievements.

We much prefer to point out that love has been the principal religious feature of this Council. Now no one can complain that such a basic orientation implies a lack of religion or infidelity to the gospel. We recall that Christ himself taught us that love for our brothers is the distinctive mark of his disciples, as we hear in the words of the apostle: 'Religion pure and undefiled before God the Father is this: To give aid to orphans and widows in their tribulation and keep oneself unspotted from this world' (James 1:27). And again: 'How can he who does not love his brother, whom he sees, love God, whom he does not see?' (I John 4:20).

The diversity of man

Yes, the Church in Council has been concerned, not only with herself and her relationship with God, but also with man—man as he really is today; living man as he actually lives; man concerned only with his own success—who makes himself the sole center of his every interest, who even dares to claim that he is the beginning, the season of all reality. All aspects of man, all the countless masks he wears, have in a sense been openly displayed before the Council fathers. They also are mere men; yet they all are pastors and brothers with hearts full of love and concern. They have seen tragic man disconsolately acting out his fate; the superman of yesterday and today—so frail and unreal, so selfish and savage; then the man who is unhappy with himself as he laughs and cries; flexible man ready to join any party; man for whom only scientific reality has value—man as he is, a creature who thinks, loves, works, and is always waiting for something; the 'growing son', the young fruit tree of the Bible—sacred because of his childhood innocence, the mystery of his poverty, the honesty of his suffering; individualistic man and socially adjusted man; man who everlastingly lives on past glories and dreams of future better times—man the sinner and man the saint. . . .

Then appeared laic and profane humanism, in threatening might, to challenge (in a certain sense) the Council to hand-to-hand combat. The religion of the God who became man confronted the religion (for religion it is) of the man who makes himself God. And what happened? Was there a clash, a battle, a condemnation? There could have been, but there was none. The old story of the Samaritan has been the model of the Council's spirituality. A feeling of boundless sympathy has permeated it. The Council has been absorbed in the discovery of human needs—and these needs grow greater as the claims of this son of earth increase. But we ask all who call themselves modern humanists, yet deny the transcendent value of the highest realities, to give the Council credit at least for one thing—recognize our new humanism: we too, and we more than any others, are friends of mankind.

The Council's message to mankind

And what aspect of humanity has this senate studied in the light of God? It has studied man's two faces—his misery and his greatness; the deep misery from which he suffers as from a long incurable disease, and the enduring good in him, full of hidden beauty and invincible nobility. We must realize that this Council, subject to human judgment, stressed man's goodness far more than his evil. Its attitude was emphatically and consciously optimistic. The Council was filled with sympathy and admiration for the modern world. Errors were indeed condemned, for love no less than truth demanded this; but to human beings the Council offered only exhortation, respect and love. Instead of depressing diagnoses, it offered encouraging remedies; instead of dire forebodings, it offered a message of encouragement to the contemporary world. The Council not only respected but honored the world's values, candidly and vigorously praising its endeavors.

So, for example, the countless different vernacular languages of today were adopted for the liturgical expression of man's communication with God and God's communication with man. The fundamental calling of man as man was recognized—his calling to full possession of his rights, the achievement of his destiny; his supreme aspirations to life, to personal dignity, to genuine liberty, to culture, to the renewal of the social order, to justice and peace were purified and promoted; and to all men the Council addressed a pastoral and missionary invitation to see the light of the gospel . . . .

A dialogue with man

We must note one thing here—that the Church's teaching authority, though not wishing to issue extraordinary dogmatic pronouncements, has throughly made known its authoritative teaching on many questions that weigh upon man's conscience and activity today. It entered, so to speak, into a dialogue with him. While preserving its own power and authority, it spoke with the pleasant and friendly voice of pastoral love. It wanted to be heard and understood by every-

As early as the first session, Archbishop Pessôa Helder Câmara (Brazil) outlined plans for the Council's closing ceremony. He had in mind a worldwide festival of love, involving a mutual confession of past shortcomings by the pope and representatives of other churches—the pope and the Jews, the pope and non-Christian religions, the pope and representatives of the secular world. Each part of the celebration was to end with an embrace. Well, it was not done this way. But representatives of the various secular occupations—political leaders, scholars, artists, workers, women, the sick, the young—actually did appear. To each group a message was read as a sign that the Church feels itself united with all mankind.

(Continued on page 295)

290

one; it did not concentrate merely on intellectual understanding but also tried to express itself in a contemporary conversational style—the language of everyday actual experience and the language of the heart. . . .

The service of man

We want to call your attention to yet another point: All this rich teaching is channeled in one direction, the service of men—men of every condition, in every weakness and need. The Church has, so to speak, declared herself the servant of humanity—and this precisely at a time when her teaching and pastoral roles have, through the splendor of the Council, assumed greater beauty and vigor. Service has been the keynote. It might be said that this and everything else we might say about the human value of the Council, means that the attention of the Church in Council has been diverted toward culture's preoccupation with humanity. Not diverted, but directed! Anyone who has seen the Council's overriding concern for human and temporal values cannot deny that the pastoral spirit gave the Council its program. He must grant, too, that this concern was never separated from a deeply religious concern. This was due to love—the sole inspiration of the Council (and where love is, God is!) and to the Council's continued and express efforts to link human and temporal values with those that are specifically spiritual, religious and eternal. Its concern was with man and with the world, but it pointed toward the kingdom of God.

The modern mind, accustomed to assess everything pragmatically, will readily admit the great value and importance of the Council, if only because it was solely concerned with human needs. So no one should ever say that a religion like the Catholic religion is useless. For, after all, when the Church was at its peak of self-awareness and effectiveness—in the Council—it declared itself entirely on the side of man and at his service. Thus the Catholic religion and human life reaffirm their alliance—their convergence on one single human reality: the Catholic religion exists for mankind. It is in a certain sense the life of mankind. Why? Because it gives an extremely precise and sublime interpretation of humanity. (Is not man of himself a riddle to himself?) It gives this interpretation due to its knowledge of God: To know man as he really is, in all his fullness, we must know God. . . .

The Catholic religion is man's life because it shows the limits of life's nature and destiny. It gives life its real meaning. It defines the supreme law of life and infuses it with that mysterious power through which, we may say, it becomes divine.

Christian humanism

Consequently, if we remember, venerable brothers and sons present here, how in every man's face we can and must recognize the face of Christ, the Son of man—especially when tears and sorrows make it plain to see. And we can and must recognize in the face of Christ the face of our heavenly Father; 'He who sees me', Jesus said, 'sees also the Father' (John 14:9). Thus our humanism becomes Christianity and our Christianity becomes centered on God. So much so that we may also say: To know God we must know man.

Isn't it the task of this Council, then, which has turned principally to man, to show the modern world the way to freedom and consolation through which it can rise step by step? In the final analysis, could we not say that this is a simple, new and solemn teaching—to love man in order to love God? To love man, not as a means, but as the first step toward the final, transcendent goal which is the beginning and basis of every love. In its ultimate religious meaning this Council can be summed up as a strong and friendly invitation to contemporary mankind to rediscover in fraternal love the 'God to turn away from whom is to fall, to turn to whom is to rise again, be born again, in whom to dwell is to live.'

This is our hope at the end of the Second Vatican Ecumenical Council, and at the beginning of the human and religious renewal which the Council has proposed to study and promote. This is our hope for you, brothers and fathers of the Council. This is our hope for the whole of mankind which we have learned here to love more and to serve better.

The 16 Documents and their Consequences

CONSTITUTION ON THE LITURGY

1962: October 22 to November 13: Debate.
    November 17 to December 7: First voting.
1963: October 8 to 30: Continuation of the first voting.
    November 18 to 22: Voting on the amendments *(modi)*.
    December 4: Final voting and promulgation.

Past: The liturgy of the Western Catholic Church, because of a dead Latin language totally incomprehensible to the people, was exclusively an affair of the clergy; it was, because of the petty rules that governed it, conducive to a magical kind of thinking; religious feeling was endangered through an overemphasis on pompous high masses, while private masses prevented a sense of community and led to onesidedness, to a neglect of preaching.

Future: The whole People of God joined in divine worship with everyone taking an active part; common prayer, singing, and common reception of the Body of Christ. Private masses deemphasized. An awakening of the sense of the 'living God', who still acts on us today through word and sacrament. Expanded scripture readings with a richer, more varied arrangement of passages, with services of the word of God even outside mass. Adjustment to national differences through introduction of the vernacular. Immediately understandable ritual; purifying and tightening of the liturgical structure with an emphasis on essentials. Concession of the chalice to lay people on special occasions. Concelebration of several priests made possible. Revision of the liturgy for the administration of the sacraments; rearrangement of the ecclesiastical year.

DOGMATIC CONSTITUTION ON DIVINE REVELATION

1962: November 14 to 21: Debate (on original schema, 'The Sources of Revelation').
1964: November 30 to October 6: Debate on the reworked schema 'On Divine Revelation'.
1965: September 20 to 22: First voting.
    October 29: Voting on amendments.
    November 18: Solemn final voting and promulgation.

Past: Catechisms generally taught that not all revealed truth was contained in Holy Scripture. A biblical theology was largely lacking. The Bible played a secondary role in the religious life of the faithful. Ecclesiastical authority narrowly restricted modern scriptural study. The biblical movement met with many difficulties.

Future: The view that all religious truth is found in the Bible is permitted by the Church. Scripture and tradition form a unity. Development within doctrine is possible. The Church's teaching authority is not above the Bible but must serve it. Genuine science is fully recognized in biblical research. Scripture study must be the soul of theology. Preaching and proclamation must be biblical in approach. The scriptures are inerrant only insofar as truths of salvation are concerned; this inerrancy does not extend to secular statements. All are to diligently study the Bible, and provision is made for translations and for cooperation in this with non-Catholics.

DECREE ON THE MEDIA OF SOCIAL COMMUNICATION

1962: November 23 to 27: Debate.
1963: November 14: First voting.
    November 25: Voting on amendments.
    December 4: Solemn final voting and promulgation.

Past: Modern mass media were often viewed with distrust in ecclesiastical circles. They were often judged in an almost purely negative way and exclusively from the standpoint of morality.

Future: The importance of press, film, radio and television for the evangelization of the world is officially recognized. Guidelines should be issued for their proper use. Evaluation of secular production should be raised to a higher level. The responsibility of lay people is emphasized; they will be more heavily counted upon in staffing the Church's media reviewing organizations.

DOGMATIC CONSTITUTION ON THE CHURCH

1962: December 1 to 7: Debate on the first schema.
1963: September 30 to October 30: Debate on four chapters of the revised schema.
1964: September 15 to 18: Debate on two new chapters: eschatology, Mary.
    September 16 to 30: Voting on chapters discussed in 1963.
    October 19 to 20: First voting on the eschatology chapter.
    October 29: First voting on the chapter on Mary.
    October 30 to November 18: Voting on the amendments to the whole schema.
    November 21: Solemn final voting and promulgation.

Past: Since the Reformation the Church had chiefly been viewed as a spiritual super-state: the Pope at its head, like an absolute monarch, then in graduated order bishops and priests. Ranged almost passively below them were the 'faithful'. Its legal and unchangeable aspect was obvious in the sharp opposition against all that was not the Church. Here triumphalism was mixed with clericalism.

Future: More emphasis placed on the Church as mystery and as People of God: the equality of all is stressed. Biblical images are used to highlight the various inner aspects of the Church, which is seen here as a Church 'on the move', and thus always in need of reform. The Church's boundaries extend far beyond the visible Catholic Church; this is clear in the recognition given to Christian Churches and ecclesiastical Church communities outside of her and even to non-Christians; even atheists can be saved. The Church's hierarchy is seen as service and not as domination; it must be seen as derived from the broader priesthood which belongs to all Christians, and not the reverse. Pope and bishops share a common collegial responsibility for the whole Church, though the overall government has been invested in a special way in the Pope. An individual bishop is given collegial responsibility by his very ordination as bishop. The permanent diaconate is revived; even married people may become deacons. The doctrine on Mary is included in the teaching on the Church; it is no longer something separated from the Church.

DECREE ON ECUMENISM

1963: November 18 to December 2: Debate.
1964: October 5 to 8: First voting.
    November 10 to 14: Voting on amendments.
    November 21: Solemn final voting and promulgation.

Past: The prevalent attitude toward other Christians was hostile and purely defensive; the object was to prove to them their deficiencies and errors. In contrast the Church tried to cover its own deficiencies. There was little concern to understand the others, and the common heritage was rarely mentioned. Other Christians were simply a danger to the Catholic faithful. Authorities regarded the developing ecumenical movement with reserve.

Future: There is an effort here to understand other Christians and make the Church's position understandable to them. Recognition is made of the Church's guilt for the division of the Church and the Church's present shortcomings. The common heritage is recognized, and the Church is supposed to live up to the Christian responsibility stemming from this heritage. The others are recognized as Churches and church communities; it is even admitted that the Church can learn something from them. What separates is not glossed over, but ways are sought to overcome divisions through common dialogue, with deepened knowledge of scripture. Common desire for unity should be awakened in all through common prayer and through avoiding all conflict and all competition.

DECREE ON EASTERN CATHOLIC CHURCHES

1964: October 15 to 20: Debate.
    October 21 to 22: First voting.
    November 20: Voting on amendments.
    November 21: Solemn final voting and promulgation.

Past: The Catholic Churches of the Eastern rite were considered primarily as relics of a bygone age. They were not recognized as genuine parts of the Church and attempts were constantly made to Latinize them in their law, liturgy and theological thinking. Thus they had become an obstacle rather than a bridge to reunification with the non-Catholic Eastern Churches.

Future: The existence of different parts of the Church all equal in standing—the Western, Latin Church is only one of many—is recognized and even encouraged. Therefore the rights and individual approaches proper to the Eastern Churches, even before the division, must be restored. They also have the right of naming bishops. Priestly ordination in the separated Orthodox Churches is recognized. Their faithful can, if they so desire, receive the sacraments in Catholic Churches, just as Catholic Christians may receive them in Orthodox churches when no Catholic priest is available. Marriages before an Orthodox priest are valid. Joint use of the same church is permitted.

DECREE ON THE PASTORAL OFFICE OF BISHOPS

1963: November 5 to 18: Debate 'On the Bishops and Governance of Dioceses'.
1964: September 18 to 23: Debate on passages taken from the schema 'On the Pastoral Office'.
    November 4 to 6: First voting.
1965: September 29 to October 6: Voting on amendments.
    October 28: Solemn final voting and promulgation.

Past: The bishops, with their powers increasingly whittled away, were in practice nothing but an executive organ of the Roman central administration. There were often no horizontal ties between country and country; the bishops' responsibility for the Church as a whole was scarcely realized.

Future: The bishops' collegial responsibility is expressed in the institution of a council of bishops (synod) together with the pope. Since these general synods are largely to consist of representatives elected by the conferences of bishops, such conferences should be established on national and supra-national levels, with fixed statutes, standing secretariats and the authority to make binding decisions in certain cases. They may rearrange dioceses, transfer bishops' sees to more suitable locations, and make contacts with other countries for supra-national pastoral problems. The Roman administration is increasingly to include diocesan bishops as well as lay people. Roman offices must reform their procedures. The power required for normal administration of dioceses is to be restored to bishops. The powers of nuncios must be strictly defined. The bishops of each diocese enjoy independent, immediate authority; they should adapt their boards of consultants to the times and set up pastoral councils made up of priests and lay people. Even parishes are to create pastoral councils.

DECLARATION ON NON-CHRISTIAN RELIGIONS

1963: November 18 to 21: General debate on the schema on ecumenism of which this text is still chapter 4 (on relationship to non-Christians and especially Jews).
1964: September 28 to 30: Debate on the declaration 'On the Jews and non-Christians', meant to be a second appendix to the decree on ecumenism.
    November 20: First voting on the now independent declaration.
1965: October 14 to 15: Voting on amendments.
    October 28: Solemn final voting and promulgation.

Past: Catholic missions formerly took an almost purely negative stand against the world religions. They were seen only from the viewpoint of conversion. The stand was even stronger in the case of the Moslems, who were considered militant enemies of the Church, and the Jews, who were considered an obdurate people. The Catholic attitude was permeated by an anti-Semitic strain without which there might have been no persecution of the Jews by the Nazis.

Future: The activity of God in all religions is recognized, notwithstanding the conviction that the Church was given the fullness of truth by and in Christ. All therefore deserve understanding and esteem.

Moreover, the Church is linked to the Moslems in as much as Moslems honor Jesus and the prophets. The Church must recognize its unique relationship with the Jews: they also possess the Old Testament as sacred scripture. The Jews were and are God's chosen people. The idea that all Jews are collectively guilty for the death of Christ is rejected. They must not be called an 'accursed people'. All anti-Semitism must be uprooted from preaching and education; common biblical studies are especially recommended.

DECLARATION ON RELIGIOUS LIBERTY

1963: November 18 to 21: General debate on this topic as chapter 5 of the schema on ecumenism.

1964: September 23 to 28: Debate on the 'declaration', now considered an appendix to the decree on ecumenism.

1965: September 15 to 22: Debate on the completely revised declaration.
October 26 to 27: First voting.
November 19: Voting on amendments.
December 7: Solemn final voting and promulgation.

Past: Religious liberty as a human right was considered a product of relativistic thinking and therefore unacceptable; only truth could have rights. Religious tolerance was permissible as a lesser evil, but as far as possible any propagation of error was to be suppressed. Wherever Catholics were in the minority, they worked for religious liberty; where they constituted a majority, they claimed liberty for the Catholic religion alone.

Future: Because of the dignity of the human person, every man has the right to free exercise of religion, private and public, individually and collectively. Therefore, nobody must be prevented by force from practising his religion or be discriminated against because of his religion. Political authority must not interfere in pastoral appointments, nor in free interchange between believers and their co-religionists and Church leaders abroad. It is the state's responsibility as well as that of society and Church, to protect religious liberty as a fundamental common good. Wherever a restriction upon religious liberty becomes necessary because of the rights of others or public safety, this restriction must be limited to the minimum. Wherever a particular religious community has for historical reasons a special position, this must not cause a restriction of the right of all others to religious liberty.

DECREE ON THE LAY APOSTOLATE

1964: October 7 to 13: Debate.

1965: September 23 to 27: First voting.
November 9 to 10: Voting on amendments.
November 18: Solemn final voting and promulgation.

Past: The clerical view was dominant, which meant that laymen were given a more passive role. They were to accept and obey. Lay people were the object, not the foundation of the Church. The Church often simply meant the clergy. Models of holiness proposed to lay people were often characterized by monastic traits. In ecclesiastical affairs the lay person was most often treated as a minor.

Future: The lay person is recognized as a fully responsible member of the People of God. He has a much larger share of self-determination in the modern world. He shares in the universal priesthood and in the gifts of the Holy Spirit—who works where He pleases. That is why the hierarchy is to regard the lay person with great trust, and his advice must be valued and sought. All are obliged to be witnesses in their own sphere; the lay person has a share in shaping the structures of the world in line with the Christian spirit. And finally, he has a direct apostolate of preaching the word of God, especially within the family. The various forms the organized apostolate may take are secondary. Nor must collaboration with other Christians and even non-Christians be neglected.

DECREE ON PRIESTLY FORMATION

1964: November 12 to 17: Debate on a 'guideline draft'.
November 17 to 18: First voting.

1965: October 11 to 13: Voting on amendments.
October 28: Solemn final voting and promulgation.

Past: It was not until some time after the Council of Trent that seminaries were established everywhere. Trent had not intended to make their establishment generally mandatory. In seminaries a life of monastic seclusion became customary. Such a life was little suited to personality development and to adult assumption of responsibility. Human virtues took second place to the exercise of obedience. The teaching was abstract and often polemically pointed.

Future: Great freedom is given to bishops' conferences in organizing seminaries. Seminaries must be adapted to practical needs. A biblical piety should be promoted; study of the Bible and biblical theology should be emphasized. Contrasting views should no longer be presented only in their negative aspect. There should be more contact between seminarians and people in the world. All seminarians should be encouraged to be open and aware of the problems of contemporary man. More opportunity must be provided for personality development and for amicable teamwork. And the seminarians must also get to know and respect non-scholastic ways of thought.

DECREE ON THE CONTEMPORARY RENEWAL OF RELIGIOUS LIFE

1964: November 10 to 12: Debate on a 'guideline draft'.
November 12 to 16: First voting.

1965: October 6 to 11: Voting on amendments.
October 28: Solemn final voting and promulgation.

Past: During the middle ages the religious orders were the agents of culture and civilization. Their ideal of holiness was formed by scripture on the one hand and by the needs of the age on the other; this ideal frequently marked the entire era. In the rapid development of modern times, many religious communities arose to provide for temporary special needs. Religious orders often lost contact with reality in the course of this modern development; they came to symbolize a bygone era, and thus their function of service within the Church at large came into question.

Future: The guidelines leave it to the individual orders to renovate themselves. They are encouraged to go to the sources—sacred scripture, the spirit of their founders, and the needs of the contemporary world. Therefore they are to discard all outmoded forms, and renovation is to be carried forward, not by the superiors of the orders alone but through the cooperation of all members. Class distinctions within religious orders are to be eliminated. Subjects are no longer to be kept in a kind of state of spiritual dependency. Orders which have no promise of productive work may not accept any new candidates.

DECREE ON THE MISSIONARY ACTIVITY OF THE CHURCH

1964: November 6 to 9: Debate on a brief schema.
1965: October 7 to 13: Debate on a longer, completely new draft.
      November 10 to 11: First voting.
      November 30: Voting on amendments.
      December 7: Solemn final voting and promulgation.

Past: By and large, the basis of missionary activity used to be the idea that pagans who were not baptized were doomed to eternal damnation. Missionary activity had a 'colonialist' cast. The way of life and thought of the new converts was Europeanized. There were often rivalries between Christian denominations; thus Christianity seemed unworthy of belief.

Future: Non-Christian religions now meet with great understanding. The special cultural values of other peoples are sincerely respected and the Church intends to root itself in these cultures. They can enrich the Church and help it to discover new perspectives in scripture. Fraternal relations should be established with other Churches; all should give a common witness to Christ in their everyday life. At the suggestion of the bishops' conference, a commission on missions made up of bishops and experts is to be formed which will exercise a decisive influence on the activities of the curial Congregation for the Propagation of Faith.

DECREE ON PRIESTLY LIFE AND MINISTRY

1964: October 13 to 15: Debate on 'guideline schema'.
1965: October 14 to 26: Debate on new schema.
      November 12 to 13: First voting.
      December 2: Voting on improvements.
      December 4: Solemn final voting and promulgation.

Past: The priest used to be a one-dimensional, sacral figure, seen only as a minister at the altar and administrator of the sacraments. The priestly ideal was strongly marked by a monastic type of asceticism. The priests were separated from the people; sociologically they constituted a kind of 'privileged state'; they were differentiated from the bishops by their comparative lack of personal responsibility.

Future: The emphasis now is on the priest as servant. The priest is to be fully a man, not separated from lay people but with them in his life and work. He is really a leader within his congregation. An appropriate kind of priestly piety should be developed, deriving from priestly service within the world. The bishop should listen to and work with his priests; he should form his own council of priests. The text especially commends married priests of the Eastern Churches.

DECLARATION ON CHRISTIAN EDUCATION

1964: November 17 to 19: Debate.
      November 19: First voting.
1965: October 13 to 14: Voting on amendments.
      October 28: Solemn final voting and promulgation.

Past: The introduction of general compulsory education caused difficulties in Christian schools. They were too few in number and unable to compete with public schools. And they were too much focused on preserving truth rather than on developing minds.

Future: The educational obligations of parents get primary emphasis; the state's right to cooperate in education is recognized. The right of the Catholic Church to maintain schools is emphasized. But it is also recommended that more be done to encourage individual student initiative. Catholic schools should accept non-Catholic students. Finally, more attention should be paid to Catholic students in non-Catholic schools.

PASTORAL CONSTITUTION ON THE CHURCH IN THE CONTEMPORARY WORLD

1964: October 20 to November 10: Debate on a first draft.
1965: September 21 to October 8: Debate on a newly revised draft.
      November 15 to 17: First voting.
      December 4 to 6: Voting on amendments.
      December 7: Solemn final voting and promulgation.

Past: Because of the autonomy of the exact sciences and the spirit and style of modern civilization, there had been a growing cleavage between Church and world. The Church tried partly to defend its former position of dominance, partly to recover it. This often put it in a posture of hostility toward the world, which no longer felt that the Church understood it, and which regarded the Church as outmoded.

Future: The Church recognizes on principle the progress of man and feels bound to gratitude for this. But it cannot overlook dangers and errors. Human achievements which made for a deepened receptivity to the gospel message, and therefore have an eschatological connotation, are valued by the Church as 'signs of the time'. The Church sees itself as in solidity with the world and as sent into the world for the service of humanity.

As to details, the Constitution speaks especially of the roots of present-day atheism, which leads the Church to self-criticism. On marriage, there is strong emphasis on conjugal love and the personal responsibility of the married couple. In the analysis of the present-day process of human socialization, there is a call for vigorous effort on behalf of the weak. In connection with the common progress of mankind toward an international community, modern war is unmasked as a criminal enterprise.